NEVER LOOK BACK

NEVER LOOK BACK

The Career and Concerns of John J. Burke

John B. Sheerin, C.S.P.

PAULIST PRESS
New York, N.Y./Paramus, N.J.

Libra-y of Congress
Catalog Card Number: 75-19689

ISBN: 0-8091-0200-5

Published by Paulist Press
Editorial Office: 1865 Broadway, N.Y., N.Y. 10023
Business Office: 400 Sette Drive, Paramus, N.J. 07652

Printed and bound in the
United States of America

contents

introduction   Who was John J. Burke?   9

chapter 1   A New Yorker goes to Washington   14

chapter 2   The articulate editor   25

chapter 3   The War Council   36

chapter 4   The beginning and sudden suppression
              of NCWC   56

chapter 5   The golden twenties   85

chapter 6   Peacemaker in Mexico   108

chapter 7   The signing of the Ruiz-Gil Agreement   133

chapter 8   Burke, Roosevelt and the fragile peace   155

chapter 9   The Depression and the New Deal   172

chapter 10   Birth control and immigration laws—black
              Catholics—red Russia—Hitler and
              anti-Semitism   191

chapter 11   Friends and associates   219

chapter 12   The summing up   241

              Notes   249

              Further Reading   253

Who
was
John J. Burke?

"We believe that the name of Monsignor Burke will be recorded in the history of the Catholic Church in the United States high among the very greatest leaders of Catholic Action —on the same level of creative influence where stand such figures as Cardinal Gibbons, Archbishop Hughes and Bishop England." Michael Williams, editor of *Commonweal*, wrote these words in a lengthy editorial in the November 12, 1936 issue of that magazine, shortly after Burke's death. From time to time, others have alluded to the biography of Burke that must some day be written but the anticipated volume has never materialized.

Archbishop John Murray of St. Paul paid tribute to Burke in words that piqued the curiosity of readers: "Of all his activities in behalf of Church and country, the most productive of good were in a sphere of diplomacy touching the interests of the countries of North and South America as well as Europe. It is not permitted to this generation to reveal what he has done as a humble servant of his Church and of his country in this field. The day, moreover, will come when some historian in the distant future will be justified in telling to another generation what may not now be told" (*Catholic Action*, December 15, 1936). A fifty-year ban had sealed the Burke materials in the archives of the National Catholic Welfare Conference, now known as the United States Catholic Conference, in Washington. (The canonical entity is called The National Conference of Catholic Bishops.) Precisely because the world has turned upside down in the forty years since his death, his story must now be told.

In May, 1973, the President of the Paulist Fathers, Thomas F. Stransky, asked me to do a biography of John Burke, the Paulist who guided the destinies of NCWC from 1919 until his death on October 30, 1936. With the gracious cooperation of Bishop James S. Rausch, general secretary of USCC, and with invaluable assistance from Monsignor George G. Higgins, USCC secretary of research, I began to explore the old NCWC files which proved to be a rich vein of Burke records. The Paulist archives in New York also contained some papers from his pre-NCWC days.

In his 1936 editorial tribute, Michael Williams described John J. Burke as a man of extraordinary originality, a pioneer and pathbreaker whose originality and personal force were not blunted or muffled by authoritarian forces. This is not altogether correct; his originality and initiative were inhibited in his early years as editor of *The Catholic World* by the repressive atmosphere generated by the papal condemnations of Americanism and Modernism. But in his later years his creativity as organizer and administrator flourished in the warm support and encouragement given him by the American bishops. It would be an exaggeration to call him a herald of Vatican II; he was much too busy with the problems of his own tumultuous era to gaze off into the future. But it can be said in all honesty that he anticipated the broad and fresh perspectives of Pope John's ecumenical council.

Who was John J. Burke? His major contribution was the National Catholic Welfare Conference, a national conference of American bishops designed to unify and coordinate Catholic activities. The value of a national episcopal conference was attested to by the Second Vatican Council which stated in the decree on *The Bishops' Pastoral Office*: "Therefore, this most sacred synod considers it supremely opportune everywhere that bishops belonging to the same nation or region form an association and meet together at fixed times" (V. 37). Vatican II looked on national episcopal conferences as fruitful expressions of collegiality, broadening the outlook of individual bishops by giving them a perspective wider than the boundaries of their dioceses while conveying to bishops of other countries and to the Vatican itself the proportions of a problem in a particular area. Since Vatican II, national episcopal conferences have focused on broad social, political and economic problems possessing moral dimensions that need to be examined closely in the light of revealed principles.

The NCWC was not the first such association of bishops. Latin America had launched a prototype of NCWC in 1899 but the NCWC has been supremely successful in its format and manner of operation; more than fifty other national hierarchies have taken it as a model. As designed by Burke, it was characteristically American in its stress on the voluntary principle. No bishop was obliged to affiliate with it or even follow its recommendations. It possessed no law-making power, no authority to suppress abuses or settle controversies, no sterile legalism. Its aim was simply to promote free and fair discussion of problems of the day and offer information and guidance to Catholics on current issues. Possessing no coercive authority, it was welcomed by lay organizations (which affiliated with it) and was considered no threat to the authority of any bishop, except a few prelates whose groundless fears will be described below.

Surprisingly, the occasion of the creation of this association of bishops was the First World War. When the United States was swept into that conflict in 1917, American Catholic disunity was appalling. The American bishops had not met in formal assembly since 1884. There were 15,000 Catholic societies but almost no communication, coordination or cooperation among them. Taking the cue from Cardinal Gibbons, who immediately endorsed President Wilson's declaration of war in 1917, and following the lead of the hierarchy who promised the President mobilization of Catholic resources for the war effort, Burke presented to Gibbons a proposal for the coordination of war activities of Catholics. It was accepted by Gibbons and the other cardinals, Farley and O'Connell, and the National Catholic War Council was born. The Council was so successful that the hierarchy transformed it into a permanent organization after the war. Burke remained general secretary until his death.

His role as general secretary brought him into contact not only with clergy and laity but with government officials as well. He won the respect of five presidents, including the friendship and admiration of Franklin D. Roosevelt, and he was highly regarded by numerous high-ranking State Department officers. With American Ambassador Dwight Morrow, John Burke brought about a *modus vivendi* between the Mexican bishops and Mexican President Plutarco Elias Calles during the savage persecution of the Catholic Church in Mexico in 1928. This was no mean achievement because Burke and Morrow had to cope with powerful American and Mexican interests, Catholic and non-Catholic, who saw American armed intervention as the only effective way to overthrow the Calles regime.

Yet this priest who felt very much at home with government leaders was not a priest-politician but a mystic who lived an intensely spiritual life. His mysticism flashed through his editorials in *The Catholic World*, which he edited for eighteen years. It seems to me, however, that his editorship showed no startling promise of future greatness, although he once wrote that he considered his NCWC work secondary to his editorship. He was pre-eminently an organizing genius. Like the American industrialists of that bustling era, on the watch for new business methods and managerial innovations, Burke was alert to new methods of organization. He believed that the Catholics of the country needed to organize to protect and defend their interests as a minority, that only through intelligent planning could the vast crowds of immigrants be absorbed into American Catholic life and American society. To a very large degree, the rise of the Catholic immigrant can be attributed to the work of the National Catholic Welfare Conference. Its representatives not only met him at Ellis Island but continued to help him in a hundred ways to realize his potential.

12

This first biography of John J. Burke is not the last word on his career. It is only the first word and deals only with the high spots of his busy life. Hopefully, more competent craftsmen will look into the immense amount of Burke materials now available and publish studies in depth of his work and historical significance. There was a prelude to my writing of this biography. Father Vincent F. Holden, CSP, author of *Yankee Paul*, a biography of Isaac Hecker's early years, anticipating eventual access to the NCWC archives, began to gather information from other sources on Burke. He secured from Mother Helen Lynch, a religious of the Cenacle, three binders (containing about three hundred letters) of messages sent her by Father Burke. She had been his secretary at *The Catholic World* before entering Cenacle. Her successor at *The Catholic World*, Grace Murray, donated to Father Holden for the Paulist archives many letters she had received from Father Burke. Miss Iona McNulty, secretary to Father Burke from 1920 to 1936, furnished hundreds of reminiscences in as many pages to Father Holden; it would not be far from the truth to describe Iona McNulty as co-author of this book. Father Holden died suddenly in 1972 before he could begin the biography but the materials he gathered were intact in the Paulist archives.

In addition to the USCC and the persons already mentioned, I would like to express my gratitude to Mrs. Elizabeth Salmon and Mrs. Mary Bond, nieces of Father Burke, for their help; to Mrs. Elizabeth McKeown for her wealth of insightful information on the National Catholic War Council; to Mrs. Dorothy Mohler of Catholic University; to Miss Nevila McCaig and Miss Constance Larkin of USCC for countless courtesies; to Rev. Lawrence McDonnell, CSP, archivist of the Paulist Fathers for his generous help; to Rev. James McVann, CSP, for his ready information about John Burke, and to all the Paulists at St. Paul's College in Washington; to Archbishop Karl Alter, Rev. John A. O'Brien, Rev. David O'Brien, CSP, and Rev. Thomas F. Stransky, CSP, president of the Paulist Fathers.

chapter 1

A New Yorker goes to Washington

The era in which John J. Burke was born, on June 6, 1875, was a cynical, disorderly period marked by gross political scandals and economic unrest. The American people had managed to survive a tragic and disastrous struggle between the Confederate rebels and the Union forces, a fratricidal bloodbath followed by a breathing spell of prosperity in the North. Factories sprouted up like mushrooms all over the landscape, new railroads thrust gleaming tracks up hill and down dale, conscienceless profiteers worked hand-in-glove with political influence-peddlers connected with a federal regime headed by Ulysses Grant, the war hero who talked endlessly about the need of "practical politics" as he smoked his fat cigars. Why should he bother about the graft and corruption surrounding him? He had soundly thrashed the reformers who tried to unseat him in the 1872 elections. Surely that landslide victory gave him a mandate. A mandate to keep business booming, not to preside over a prayer meeting! But then came the crash in 1873, a panic that lengthened to a depression that lasted six years, throwing millions out of work.

The economic crisis hit the Irish immigrants hard. Factories that had been utilizing the manpower provided by waves of immigrants coming from Ireland to New York now laid them off as the first victims of the job squeeze. Employers, believing in a free-market economy with a vengeance, fired help unmercifully. The Irish immigrants around New York had their political machine but Daniel Moynihan has pointed out that the Irish politicos never thought of politics as an instrument of social change. So the immigrants suffered in silence.

This was the atmosphere and these were the facts of life in 1875 New York. The horizon however was not all dark. There was talk of sweeping social reforms and, under all the unrest and corruption, an irrepressible national pride was emerging. Patriotic societies blew the bugles, waved the flags and talked about this great American nation, endowed by God with vast natural resources and moving upwards and onwards to a destiny greater than that of any nation in history. Many of the Irish immigrants shared this optimism, revering the Constitution with its pledges of religious liberty and equal justice under law.

Patrick Burke and Mary Regan came from "the ould sod," met in New York City, married and settled on the West Side. Not far away in one direction St. Patrick's Cathedral was under construction; in the other direction was an area someone had called "Shantyopolis." John, one of the nine children in the family, was born in the house near the Cathedral but shortly after his birth, the family moved to Seventh Avenue near 56th Street, close to the site of the present Carnegie Hall.

John's father was a horseshoer, an occupation considered a notch above the common run of trades, perhaps because it brought the blacksmith into contact with "the carriage trade." In that era it was not at all unusual for an Irish immigrant looking for work to find himself staring at a sign which read, "No Irish need apply." This was especially true after the Civil War draft riots, for which the Irish were often blamed. Mr. Burke, however, had a regular clientele and during the great depression of 1873 his family did not undergo the hardships suffered by the Irish factory help. Yet his trade, respectable as it was, could not be considered richly remunerative. His talented wife Mary supplemented her husband's income with proceeds from her needlework, for which she had a regular clientele among the New York families of wealth.

Patrick Burke's blacksmith shop was next door to his home

on Seventh Avenue. (Today a store located on the site bears a sign, "Sandwiches to Take Out.") A quiet man was Patrick, undramatically mustached, not tall but strong as an ox, a fine broth of a man. He came from Trim near Dublin, and had received little formal education in contrast to convent-educated Mary who came from Mallow, near Cork, from the parish of the then widely known novelist, Canon Sheehan. Her photo shows a strikingly handsome face with a touch of the aristocratic about it, and with a firmness of feature one associates with venerable mothers superior of religious orders in pre-Vatican II days. From interviews with surviving relatives and friends, I take it that she was a remarkable woman, presiding over her household graciously but firmly. "Herself," as the Irish would say, was the queen of the family, encouraging the Burke children, without coercion, in the pursuit of excellence in their chosen fields. Reading her son John's letters, one cannot help but sense the affection he felt for her along with a sort of intuition that she was a mysterious presence lent for a while to a dreary world. One of John Burke's nieces has remarked that she was a "sweet" person, not syrupy but considerate, sympathetic, kind. She was unquestionably a *definite* person, a quality she communicated to John. *Definite* was his pet adjective; he reserved his choicest criticism for fuzzy, murky language, his accolades for clear-cut distinctions and precise conclusions.

Young John attended local public schools. The family home at Seventh Avenue and West 56th Street was within the boundaries of St. Paul the Apostle parish, served by the Paulist Fathers, but the parish had no elementary school. He attended the Sunday School faithfully. Publicized in Catholic magazines as a model school, it numbered at one time some 2,000 students. Here John formed close contacts with certain Paulist Fathers.[1] The Paulist community had been founded in 1858 by Father Isaac Hecker and three other converts for the express purpose of winning converts to the Catholic faith.

The archives and other records of the Paulist community unfortunately contain very little information that would shed light on John Burke's early years. In the archives however there is a faded brown copy-book reporting the minutes of a parish organization initialed SPABC. What these initials signify is an enigma: a plausible guess would be St. Paul the Apostle Boys' Club but parish records make no reference to any such club.

John J. Burke's name appears frequently under the title of "duplicating secretary." The meetings must have been as hilarious as meetings of the local Irish political clubs. SPABC conclaves were carried on in strict parliamentary fashion festooned with well-worn parliamentary clichés and a grandiose, awe-inspiring pomposity of language, especially in formal reports from committees. One (undated) report of the constitutional committee sounds like an address to a national political convention: "In voting on the admission of gentlemen as members, let us not consider our own friendliness toward them nor alone the pecuniary benefits they might afford us, for it is not solely on account of dues that we wish to have members, it is not on account of a big surplus in the treasury, on the contrary there is a higher and nobler motive. It is the bond of companionship and friendship." The signer of this committee report is none other than John J. Burke. Knowing his adult talent for pranks and jokes, one suspects he may have been writing tongue-in-cheek. The book of minutes gives no clue to the organization's life-span but in this report young Burke notes that SPABC has now existed almost five years.

Apparently only altar boys were eligible to belong but this did not prevent some meetings from degenerating into donnybrooks. Members were required to "give the cry" in the sacristy after the feast was over but the book of minutes does not say what the cry was, nor why it was cried on a feast. The members wielded the weapon of impeachment more enthusiastically than does our Congress. On December 21, 1889, the club president was duly impeached and expelled with great solemnity, whereupon the vice-president resigned in a huff. At the December 21, 1890, meeting the motion carried that "we buy boxing gloves," without specifying whether they were to be used within or outside the sacristy.

June 7, 1891, was a night to remember. Young John Burke was holding forth as duly elected president when O'Brien moved he be impeached. According to the minutes:

During the discussion, the president made a short speech to the house which took such an effect on them and on Mr. O'Brien that he immediately got up, advanced to the secretary's table, asked how much he owed, threw down half a dollar, asked for change, resigned and left the room. His resignation was immediately accepted by the president and his motion was dropped. Whereupon Mr. John Brown, excited by the proceedings and nearly beside himself with rage, stood up and delivered a stinging speech about the president's misdemeanors during the last few years but about every ten words cost him five cents and after his fines had amounted to a half a dollar he disgracefully resigned. His resignation was accepted by the president.

The same book of minutes mentions that John Burke was elected captain of the football and baseball teams of SPABC in 1891 but sports seem to have taken second place to forensics on his schedule. In those days, young Irish Americans cultivated their oratorical talents avidly (and flamboyantly) as prelude to a legal, political or priestly career. The SPABC held debates at their meetings and the topics listed often related to the Civil War, e.g., "Was Antietam Fiercer Than Gettysburg?" or "Who Was the Greater General, McClellan or Grant?" These debates helped to spark in young John a life-long interest in the Civil War, so much so that he became a Civil War buff familiar with every inch of the Gettysburg battlefield.

That the sons of Irish immigrants should become engrossed in Civil War history was to be expected. All youngsters unfortunately like guns and shooting wars but young Irish-Americans had special reasons, if they were New Yorkers, for favoring the Union side. There were many Irish-American regiments in that war such as "the Fighting Sixty-ninth," and companies such as the Emmet Rifles, the Hibernian Rifles, the Sarsfield Guards. Many bishops in the North took a firm pro-

Union stand, notably Archbishop Hughes of New York, who even journeyed to England to prevent British interference in the war, and to Ireland to counter the charge that Irish and German immigrants were being unfairly conscripted into military service by the North.[2] Rev. James A. McVann, CSP, in an unpublished account of John Burke's life, said: "At a presentation of colors in May 1891 the fifteen-year-old boy gave an ardent speech on loyalty to the American flag, printed afterwards in the parish calendar."

The teenage orator made his high-school course of studies at St. Francis Xavier High School, a Jesuit institution on the Lower West Side, and then took his college course at the College of St. Francis Xavier located near the high school. The program for the semi-annual literary exercises of the senior debating society of the college (March 21, 1895) reveals that young John was still involved in verbal hassles and literary polemics. That night he took the affirmative of the topic, "Is the English Prose Literature of the 18th Century Superior to That of the 19th?" These debates and elocutionary contests, a staple of Jesuit education, belied Henry Ward Beecher's concept of "the ignorant, the poor, the uninstructed Irishmen." The stereotyped stage spalpeen of the 1890s was an illiterate, shiftless whelp training to become an adult drunkard. Yet an amazing number of John Burke's friends, at St. Francis Xavier's or elsewhere, became successful surgeons, judges and businessmen. These untypical first-generation Amerirish were literate, brainy and full of ambition. And John Burke's elder brother, Thomas, became an internationally known preacher and superior general of the Paulist Fathers; his brother James was a vice president of Guaranty Trust Company.

After graduating from college in 1896, John began his seminary studies at the Paulist seminary in Washington, D.C., on the campus of Catholic University. He had admired the Paulists while he was a parishioner at St. Paul the Apostle Church in New York, the mother-church of the Paulist community, and had undoubtedly seen and heard Father Hecker many times since Hecker lived at the church rectory until his death in 1888, when Burke was 13 years old. It was the American spirit of the Paulists as well as Hecker's own mysticism that attracted John to the community. He once said that two Paulists, Hecker and Elliott, exercised a greater influence on him than did any other men in his whole career. When a reactionary French cleric in later years attacked Father Hecker's theology, Burke sizzled in high dudgeon at this affront to his hero, "The author of this article absolutely, thoroughly and completely misrepresents, twists and perverts Father Hecker's teaching with regard to the Holy Spirit and the guidance of the Holy Spirit in the individual soul."[3]

Records of John Burke's seminary days are unfortunately not extant. Some of the seminary atmosphere can be recreated, however, by reading the names of men who were his instructors or personal friends: outstanding men like Bouquillon, Kerby, Pace at Catholic University where Burke studied; Finn, Conway, William Sullivan at the Paulist house. Modernism was in the air and Tyrrell, Loisy and von Hügel were contributing articles to the priests' magazines read by seminarians. It is interesting that in the Burke memorial issue of *Catholic Action* (December 15, 1936) Father James Gillis singled out the young seminarian's humor for special praise. Summers the Paulist seminarians spent at Lake George, and Gillis as fellow-student enjoyed John Burke's practical jokes, his storytelling and mimicry. "Not that his laughter was loud or his manner boisterous, but when he gave one of his popular imitations—for example, of a candidate for office on the last day of his campaign, haggard, dishevelled, so hoarse that his voice seemed to have been torn to shreds, making one last desperate plea to the loyal voters of the 15th district to bury the opposition under a landslide, it was we who made the waters resound with laughter" (p. 24).

When the time arrived for John's ordination as deacon, he was deferred because of a technicality about his age, which prompted his mother to register a vehement protest in a face-to-face confrontation with Father Searle, the Paulist superior general. It was a battle of wills, the astronomer-priest just as adamant in holding his position as she was in urging hers. Her own vehemence seems to have taken her by surprise and she often commented in later years about her "definiteness" on that occasion.

After completing his seminary course in three years, John Burke was ordained to the priesthood by Bishop Alfred Curtis, a former Anglican rector received into the Catholic Church by Cardinal Newman. The ordination ceremony took place on June 9, 1899, at the University Chapel, Catholic University, Washington, D.C. He stayed at the University two more years, receiving his licentiate in sacred theology, at that time equivalent in requirements to a doctorate.

These two years provided him with a glorious opportunity to strengthen and deepen his friendship with Father William Kerby. As a seminarian Burke had taken courses under Kerby, newly arrived from his studies in sociology in Europe. Kerby had been profoundly impressed by Leo XIII's *Rerum Novarum* (1891), had gone to the University of Louvain and had received his doctorate in social and political science from the University in 1897. He returned to teach at Catholic University for 40 years, there founding the National Conference of Catholic Charities in 1910. His Louvain dissertation dealt with socialism in the United States, a highly combustible controversy. Kerby inspired in Burke an intense interest in the whole field of social action and social reform, the classroom encounters leading to the beginning of a life-long friendship, each contributing to the other a great richness of mind and heart as well as valuable insights and advice in moments of crisis. It was an extraordinary and wonderful friendship. (When John Burke remarked that Hecker and Elliott exerted the greatest influence on his life, was he perhaps referring only to their shaping of his vocation?) Burke wrote a eulogy of Kerby in the *Catholic University Bulletin* (Kerby Memorial Issue, September 1936) that reveals as much about Burke as it does about his deceased friend. He says, for instance, that Kerby was a quiet worker, a stranger to polemics and the aggressive, never sought leadership, loved the best in English literature, wrote with a rare discrimination in words. Again he held the mirror up to his own approach to social action when he quoted Kerby: "The assumption that one may disassociate service of the poor from religious truth, religious motive and religious inspiration strikes at the unity of life and at the harmony of the revelation of Christ."

After obtaining the licentiate, Burke engaged in parish work in various cities and in giving parish missions. Away from an academic atmosphere, he felt right at home communicating Christ in word and sacrament to the people. While conducting a mission in Iowa, he was notified of his appointment to the staff of *The Catholic World*, the most notable journal at the time in Catholic circles but a far cry from the high-level intellectual magazine established by Hecker in April 1865. For one year, he acted as assistant to Father Alexander Doyle, a remarkable man in many ways but hardly an editor in the Hecker tradition. Yet John Burke learned much from Doyle, an indefatigable worker for the poor and for the conversion of America. At his death in 1912, letters of condolence poured in from prelates and presidents and ordinary citizens of all creeds. None was more appreciative than Father Doyle's good friend, former President Theodore Roosevelt, who said that he had never known any man to work so doggedly for the underprivileged. Acknowledging that in his own speeches he had drawn largely on the accumulated experiences of Father Doyle, Teddy wrote, "I mourn his death not only because he was my friend but because he was so fearless and resolute a worker for the betterment of mankind."[4]

When he assumed the editorship of *The Catholic World* in 1904, John Burke found himself chafing with an almost pentecostal impatience on the threshold of a new century, looking out at a vast country teeming with natural resources and bustling with energy, initiative, enterprise. What was on his mind?

It was not business or belching factory chimneys or the stock market. It was not the establishment of a national episcopal conference that would set the pattern for more than fifty other national hierarchies. He had a few items on his agenda such as sprucing up the format of *The Catholic World* and modernizing Columbus Press (later called Paulist Press). But more importantly, he had a dream: it was the dream of converting America to Catholicism. He envisioned it as a conversion to the living Christ, not a European Christ but a Christ congenial to all that was best in America—democracy, freedom, equal justice under law, all the master themes inspired by the Holy Spirit in the minds of the framers of the Constitution.

Dreamer that he was, he was realistic enough to be painfully conscious of one gigantic obstacle to the conversion of America: the immigrant. Native Americans saw the immigrant as a threat to civic virtue and community welfare, an impoverished, lawless fellow given to brawls and drunkenness, lacking all the civic responsibilities of a good American. Aware that most immigrants were Catholic, Burke knew that the squalor of immigrants in a big city like New York was a standing indictment of the "Romanism" they brought with them from decadent Europe but he was also aware of the efficacy of the American way of life. Given a fair chance and the benefit of equal justice under law, they could become good Americans. The inscription at the base of the Statue of Liberty said it all. The woman with the lighted torch was calling to the ancient lands on behalf of their emigrants, "Give me your tired, your poor, your huddled masses yearning to breathe free, the wretched refuse of your teeming shore." Given equal justice and equal opportunity, the immigrants could revitalize America with fresh blood and become a display window of Catholic life and American loyalty.

A favorite scriptural verse of John Burke's was, "He that puts his hand to the plough and looks back is not worthy of the kingdom of God" (Luke 9,62). He was future-oriented. Although he loved to read history he was more anxious to make history by way of spiritual progress and social reform. Never look back but forward! There is an entry in his diary in which he crystallizes his thoughts about social reform: "The worth of the individual man as such—the sense of personal responsibility—the proper decent personal standards of living—education for all—restlessness and determination to improve and progress—these are the moving powers of the world." These, wrote Burke, "the Christian cannot neglect." He did not live to see the conversion of America but he did witness the Americanization of millions of Europe's poor, the huddled masses who came here yearning to breathe free . . . and in that process of Americanization he played a major role.

chapter 2

The articulate editor

Under Father Alexander Doyle *The Catholic World* had been a popular magazine, reported as having a monthly circulation of over 100,000. Burke realized the circulation would drop as his magazine developed in depth but he simply could not in conscience publish a pietistic journal any more than he could bring himself to succumb to the muckraking craze then in its heyday—retailing scandals ranging from medicine frauds to trafficking in women. He aspired to publish a quality magazine, emulating the best features of top-level periodicals like the *Atlantic Monthly* and *Harper's*.

Burke was editor from 1904 to 1922 but surprisingly, he wrote no formal editorials until October 1909. Possibly the managerial side of his work took up a disproportionate amount of his time. Expanding the printing plant's facilities, modernizing the pamphlets and directing production of *The Leader*, a monthly for juveniles, consumed big swatches of his time and attention. In his early editorials he seemed to be feeling his way gingerly. Was he cautious because Pope Leo XIII had condemned "Americanism" in 1899, rejecting any new methods of preaching the gospel that seemed to verge on compromise with error or which made concessions to the spirit of the times? Pope Leo did not name names, made no specific references to the Paulists, but certain conservatives fastened eagle eyes on the Paulists as being the offending innovators. As a Paulist editor, Burke was conscious of the critical scrutiny focused on his magazine by anti-Americanists.

Then too Modernism had been condemned in two Vatican

documents in 1907 and clerical vigilanti were busy thereafter ferreting out suspects. Possibly one tends to read too much into these early editorials but the Paulist editor did seem to be walking on eggs when he ventured into theology in the course of these editorials. Even in later years, he remained cautious and circumspect when touching on questions of faith and doctrine, unadventurous not out of fear but because of his profound respect for the magisterium. The chill that settled over Catholic intellectual life with the condemnations of Modernism also affected Burke's choice of articles for publication, as well as his choice of book reviews favorable to new scripture themes. Before 1907 he had published several articles by George Tyrrell and other theologians in which they discussed whether or not Catholic doctrines bind Catholics absolutely to the thought patterns of the age in which they were formed. After 1907 this was considered a "dangerous approach." Burke's instinct was to publish articles showing the Church alert and alive, attuned to the times, but bishops had been instructed to search out priests promoting Modernist ideas; so after 1907 Burke published no more articles that might be suspected of such an approach. We can only speculate as to the editorial heights he might have attained in an atmosphere free of institutional immobility and intellectual inflexibility.

Ecumenism was not popular in Catholic circles during Burke's time as editor. To try to find in his editorial policy an ecumenical flavor would be absurd. Convinced as he was of the need of a new approach to Protestants, he did not for a moment doubt that there was only one true Christian church and it was the Catholic Church. In 1910 he apparently still felt that the conversion of America was not far off and in his September 1910 editorial he called attention to Father Robert Hugh Benson's article in the August *Atlantic Monthly* which suggested that "the tide is surely turning toward Catholicism." Burke agreed, saying that "the world almost in spite of itself is preparing to welcome Catholicism." He seems to have miscalculated the staying power of Protestantism as did Isaac Hecker and

Orestes Brownson. Before his death in 1936, however, he had apparently become resigned to religious pluralism in America. An unsigned article in his papers in the Paulist archives in New York, dated 1930 and written definitely in his style, says: "If the peoples of the world are to live in peace they must be prepared to live with one another in justice and in peace and in charity. The world is not of one religious faith nor are there any signs that it will be in the memory of living man."

In dealing with social questions, Burke showed none of the restraint he displayed in touching on theological questions. In the area of social justice he spoke out boldly in advance of most Catholic editors of the day. In the May 1910 editorial, for instance, he made a strong plea for clerical involvement in social action and social reform. Politics or no politics; he insisted that unsanitary housing, the labor of women and children, oppressive conditions of labor, and insufficient wages were concerns that should lead the clergy to act and speak boldly. He suggested not only that a specialist in social sciences be added to seminary faculties but also that students with special aptitudes be allowed to arrange their work in such a way as to incorporate social and economic training into their theological courses.

Did his advocacy of social reforms have a substantial impact on his readers? Probably not at the time. Besides his own editorials on social justice, men of the stature of William Kerby and John A. Ryan wrote innumerable articles on social reform during Burke's editorship. Both clergy and laity however had little interest in social justice before the 1930s when the New Deal sent Catholics scurrying to Leo XIII's *Rerum Novarum* of 1891 and Pius XI's *Quadragesimo Anno* of 1931. Burke, Kerby and Ryan were trailblazers but it took a nationwide depression to awaken most American Catholics to the importance of social justice and the need for social reform.

In his eulogy at the funeral of Father Burke, Bishop Boyle of Pittsburgh spoke of the curious way in which "this strange and unperturbable man . . . bound himself to those with whom he came into even casual contact." Chesterton said that anyone who met St. Francis soon realized that the saint was interested in every minute of this person's life from birth until that very moment. Father Burke took a personal interest, exotic as it may seem in an editor, in the cultural and spiritual development of his co-workers. When he hired Helen Lynch at *The Catholic World* in 1905 he told her, "I will try to give you what Catholic University gave me" and he began with a little course in French. This "caring" for others drew praise from Burke's successor when 1922 saw Burke retiring from the editorship. In an editorial tribute to his predecessor, Father Gillis summed up Burke's concern for his employees: "He drew to him every worker in the establishment, talked with them personally, and taking them as he found them, by example, by counsel and command, he nerved them to the realization of their powers in a spirit of devotion second only to his own." Did they resent all this attention? Few men in history have had a staff of co-workers as dedicated to the work as were his employees at *The Catholic World*.

Most of his co-workers were women. In a sense he had an exalted view of women. Not that he saw them as angelic beings but he felt that women were usually more serious and dedicated than men. Mary Hawks, an assistant to Burke at *The Catholic World* and later president of the National Council of Catholic Women, wrote in her unpublished essay on John J. Burke that he never displayed the slightest condescension to women. "He believed in their equality of ability, mental and spiritual." He never hesitated to entrust them with serious responsibilities. He sent them overseas as social workers after World War I and he relied on women to help him and Father Kerby organize the National Catholic School for Social Service in Washington. When the United States Government awarded him the distinguished service medal for his work during World War I, he presented the medal to Grace Murray, his assistant at *The Catholic World*, who had functioned in his place at *The Catholic World* during the war years thus enabling him to carry on the war work at Washington. (Grace graciously returned it.)

Burke's attitude toward war went through a tortuous evolution in the years following the outbreak of the global conflict in 1914. "The guns of August" initiated the ugliest butchery the world had ever known but the Paulist editor, in his August editorial, made no comment. In September, he quoted Pope Pius X's dying appeal for peace but without aligning himself with either side. As the French and British made overture after overture in an attempt to persuade the US to take part in the slaughter, the majority of Americans opposed American involvement. Some readers of *The Catholic World* thought that the "Recent Events" column in the following months was slanted toward the British side but Burke maintained a neutral stance editorially. In December 1914 he editorialized that the peaceful man is heroically faithful and indignant at any violation of justice: for once, he was vague and indefinite.

Then in his January 1915 editorial he deplored the war in general, saying that the human heart must protest; there is a better way to resolve differences than by resorting to slaughter. In February he declared: "War is not a necessity of human nature. War is by no means a Christian tradition. Indeed our very profession of Christian means that we are pacifists." As the war dragged on, Burke went through an agony of conscience as he heard stories of German atrocities and when he learned of the sinking of the Lusitania by German submarines, on May 7, 1916.

When America finally entered the war in April 1917 Burke endorsed the declaration of war unconditionally. Writing the lead article in the May 1917 issue entitled "The Call to Patriotism" he asserted: "We stand a united people, determined to push this war to a successful issue with all our power but the long months of patient waiting have shown more and more clearly, and now with a clearness that admits of no question, that we have set out on a war that is eminently just." This sudden turn was paralleled by a corresponding turnabout by anti-war Protestant clergy. Randolph McKim, from a Protestant pulpit in Washington, declared it a holy war: "It is God who has summoned us to this war . . . This conflict is indeed a crusade. The greatest in history—the holiest. It is in the profoundest sense a holy war."

Burke saw in the war a marvelously providential opportunity for American Catholics, including the immigrants, to display their loyalty as a means of adding luster to the public image of the Catholic Church in America. In his August 1918 editorial he said:

Upon our shoulders alone rests the apostolate of Catholicism: upon our shoulders more than all others rests the apostolate of Americanism, for the great majority of the foreign-born among us, who lack education in American life and American institutions, are our brethren in the faith. Never was the need for Americanization more vital than today: upon it our future national life depends.

Since the presidency of John F. Kennedy, Catholics no longer need to prove their national loyalty but Burke, throughout his entire life, was haunted by an awareness of this nationwide mistrust. It was no product of his imagination but a colossal sociological fact. During the First World War he felt confident that the bravery and loyalty of Catholics on the battlefield, as witnessed by the large number of Catholic casualties of immigrant stock, would dispel once and forever this deep-rooted anti-Catholicism. The supreme expression of Burke's confidence in the war as a test of Catholic loyalty was his own cooperation in the war effort through his role in the formation of the National Catholic War Council (cf. Chapter 3).

With the passing of time, however, John Burke became progressively disenchanted with American involvement in the war. In his last editorial, in September 1922, the exaltation of "making the world safe for democracy" had disappeared, the glow had gone. He observed that the soldier despises history.

He knows that at least that part of history which is made on the field of battle is wholly sordid and ugly and brutish. But

30   NEVER LOOK BACK

when the horrible fact has been worked over by the historian, it becomes beautiful, stirring, romantic, perhaps even poetic. We wonder if Napoleon would have recognized the Waterloo of Victor Hugo.

He went on to say that we who had read the news day after day, before, during and after the war, could never again credit the historians. Citing a book by Philip Gibbs, Burke said, "The best of the special correspondents on the war gave us *Now It Can Be Told*, a large volume of important facts deliberately suppressed from his first account of the conduct of the war." Burke also told the story of a Louvain professor who met a German officer-friend during the war and asked him, "What will the world think of these atrocities when the history of them is written?" To which the German replied brazenly, "Germany is going to win the war and when Germany has won the war, Germany will write the history of the war."

By curious coincidence, Burke's successor as editor of *The Catholic World*, Father James J. Gillis, also became disillusioned as a result of reading *Now It Can Be Told*. In 1920, on his way to South America, he read Gibbs' account of the chicanery and hypocrisy connected with the waging of the war and the negotiating of the peace. Gillis jotted down in his diary that he was specially concerned about the callous clergy "who praised God as commander-in-chief of the Allied Armies and had never said a word before the war to make war less inevitable." His concluding sentence was, "I have read this book principally because I am concerned that I must henceforth preach against war as long as I live, or can speak, and I am ashamed of some of the things I said in public during the war."[1] Was it Gillis who persuaded Burke to read this book or was it the other way round?

John Burke was no professional Irishman yet he never forgot the injustices suffered by his ancestors any more than the assimilated American Jew forgets the Nazi murder of the six million Jews. In April 1919 he editorially assailed the British for refusing to recognize Ireland's right to self-determination after the war. He was less belligerent in his criticism of President Wilson even though it was Wilson who asserted that "guarantees of political independence and territorial integrity to great and small states alike" were the most important of the Allied war goals, the famous "Fourteen Points."

John Burke read books avidly but with discrimination, agreeing with Nicholas Murray Butler of Columbia University that life is too short to read anything but the best. His taste reflected the literary proprieties of the time—disdain for shockers and trivia but an almost sombre reverence for the classics. No comstockian or prude, he sought out thoughtful works on religion, sociology, literature and did not spend time condemning objectionable books.

Burke's love of poetry was obvious in his hobby of writing short poems, a practice he may have developed at St. Francis Xavier College. Of his thousands of quatrains, many paid tribute to Mary, Mother of God, and are happily devoid of the saccharine Mariology of the time.

Henry Adams hailed Mary the Virgin in his *Mont-Saint-Michel and Chartres* (1913), as a way of protesting against the gray drabness of his time: loving color passionately, he was jubilant over the warmth, color and mercy in the windows of Chartres. Burke's quatrains do not compare artistically with Adams' masterwork or his poem, *Prayer to the Virgin of Chartres*, but they are splashed with bright colors. Burke sent these quatrains, often in the style of Father Tabb, to his friends as Easter greetings or on important occasions in their lives. They were simple, cameo-like in their clarity. He had no intention of producing literary masterpieces; he merely sought to convey an evangelical message of faith and hope. That his verses brought a transcendent note into many lives can be inferred from thank-you notes such as this from Robert Speer, secretary of the Board of Foreign Missions of the Presbyterian Church, USA and fellow-member with Burke of the Committee of Six (see Chapter 3): "I have often quoted the lovely little Christmas verse which you sent me, 'This night this hut all secrets hold' and have never found it to fail in laying a hush on the hearts of those who hear it, calling forth a response from their spirits." The full verse was:

This night, this hut all secrets hold
Come, strengthening cup or chastening rod!
My soul is justly overbold
Since Christ has brothered us in God.

On the other hand, a staff member of the apostolic delegation in Washington thanked Burke in prankish brevity for an Easter verse: "Dear Father Burke. Thanks for your work."

In the Paulist archives in New York are two talks on literature, delivered by Burke apparently in 1923, to students at the National Catholic School for Social Service, in Washington. Both talks dealt with American literature. He praised Daniel Webster and Abraham Lincoln, even Thomas Paine and Benjamin Franklin. Emerson he singled out as a pernicious philosopher bearing many a snake in his bosom, dangerous for his lack of depth. (Was it because Hecker could not abide Emerson at Brook Farm and Concord?) Burke considered Emersonian transcendentalism as lying outside the stream of American thought, a foreign import from Kant and Hegel. The greatest American novelist, according to Burke, was Hawthorne—meditative, mercilessly analytical and magnificently American. Whitman was an egoist identifying himself with the universe, prattling about democracy without knowing its heart and center. Among the poets, Burke viewed Edward Arlington Robinson and Sidney Lanier with special esteem. His over-all conclusion was that in American literature, as in no other, one could find a forward drive to the recognition of human equality and the common brotherhood of all men.

Birth control and church authority were two dominant issues in John Burke's career as editor and later as general secretary of NCWC. His editorials on these subjects faithfully reflected the theology of the day, emphatically so in regard to birth control. At NCWC, much of his time was taken up with efforts to persuade legislators to retain laws, already on the books, forbidding the sending of birth control devices or literature through the mails.

If Burke's native land was America, his native climate was mysticism. Nowhere did he feel as much at home as he did at prayer. He once confided to Helen Lynch that he could not have ploughed through his work at NCWC were it not for prayer and the sense of communion with God that sustained him. There is a certain resemblance between the UN life of Dag Hammarskjold, secretary general of the UN, and the life of John Burke, general secretary of NCWC. Hammarskjold described his book *Markings* as "a sort of white book concerning my negotiations with myself and with God." The first and last entries in his book are poems of his own composition, the other entries represent a *via contemplativa* in the midst of a *via activa*, embracing periods of spiritual growth, self-questioning, resolution. Burke's jottings in his memoranda as well as in his letters reveal a man trying intensely to live a mystical life at the extreme limits of mental and physical exhaustion. (During his last five years at *The Catholic World*, despite fragile health, he had to shuttle back and forth weekly between New York and Washington to attend to his NCWC responsibilities in addition to his editorial tasks.)

Among Burke's literary and theological works were several translations from the French, notably *The Doctrine of the Mystical Body of Christ* by J. Anger. The doctrine of the Mystical Body runs like a golden thread through all his spiritual writings. During his career he saw sordidness in the Church, self-seeking, venality, jockeying for ecclesiastical advancement —all the facets of a human institution. But he also saw Christ as the head and source of the divine life in the Church. The coordination that should exist among members gave him the cue for talks to the NCCW and the NCCM in the early days of organizing these branches of NCWC. He even used the Mystical Body as a set of code words when his associate, William

Montavon, journeyed on a special mission to Kansas City in 1928. The code was; Holy See, head; Calles, foot; Burke, heart; Morrow, ear; bishops, hand; Mexico, body; papal delegate, nose.

Retiring as editor of *The Catholic World* in September 1922, after eighteen years as a journalist, John J. Burke had no intention of ending his public career at the age of 47. His editorship had broadened his knowledge of national affairs as well as his grasp of church concerns: his writing had developed his ability to communicate an idea forcefully, succinctly, lucidly. He was leaving the editorial chair for a role of immense influence. For the first time in history, the United States Government and the Catholic Church were in direct liaison at the highest level in the person of the general secretary of the National Catholic Welfare Conference. Fortunately for future historians, Burke kept a personal record of his NCWC activities in the form of a daily memorandum, a practice to which he faithfully and scrupulously adhered.

chapter 3

The War Council

In January 1917 the German Government announced its program of unrestricted submarine warfare, proceeded to sink eight American vessels and the United States found itself involved in the European struggle. On April 6th President Wilson issued a formal declaration of war to which Cardinal Gibbons, dean of the hierarchy, responded with a pronouncement that it was fitting for every American citizen "to uphold the hands of the president and the legislative department in the solemn obligations that confront us."

Gibbons and the hierarchy realized that again, as at the beginning of other wars, American Catholics were standing trial, the issue being Catholic loyalty to the American Government. At the third plenary Council of Baltimore, thirty years before this outbreak of hostilities, the American archbishops had promised that if the American heritage of freedom were imperiled at any time in the future, American Catholics would stand forward "as one man" to pledge their lives, their fortunes and their sacred honor. Once again, this time on April 18, 1917, the American archbishops pledged their support and that of the whole Catholic body: "Our people, now as ever, will rise as one man to serve the nation. Our priests and consecrated women will once again, as in every former trial of our country, win by their bravery, their heroism and their service new admiration and approval."

To pledge the support of almost twenty million Catholics was a lot easier than to deliver it. There was an enormous war potential among these Catholic millions, civilian as well as military; as Secretary of War Newton Baker pointed out, wars are fought by the whole nation, the army at war being only the point of the sword. But to organize and coordinate these

NEVER LOOK BACK

twenty millions, including some 15,000 Catholic societies, was a task of incredible magnitude. Some central controlling agency was needed to synchronize activities and avert overlapping of projects. "To rise as one man" was easier said than done, especially in view of the fact that the majority of these twenty millions were second and third generation immigrants, many of them with a strong sentimental attachment to their homelands. They had come here to make a living, not to make war, and in the case of German immigrants (from 1914 on) they had tended to accept German propaganda at its face value.

There were two large Catholic organizations[1] on hand at the outset of the war, ready to spring into action, the Knights of Columbus and the Catholic Young Men's Union. The Knights stepped forward with immense power, experience as welfare workers during the Mexican border troubles in 1916, and with a nationwide membership. Just eight days after the declaration of war, their Supreme Board met at Washington to pledge the support of 400,000 members of the order and on June 24th they approved a drive for one million dollars "to be expended for religious and recreational purposes for the benefit of all men in the service." The collections for this War Camp fund eventually exceeded ten million dollars and with the approval of the secretary of war, buildings for social purposes were erected in the army training camps, the chairman of the Commission on Training Camp Activities welcoming their great concern for "the moral hazards surrounding a young man's life." Before the war ended, the Knights had opened some 360 recreation centers in camps at home and an equal number abroad, staffed by about 2,000 secretaries, assisted by 27,000 volunteer workers.

In one sense this was embarrassing to the bishops of the country. As Aaron Abel notes in his *American Catholicism and Social Action*, "Not until America's entry into World War I did the Catholic bishops of the country assume in measurable degree direct responsibility for thought and action in the social field." They had permitted Catholics to take part in social movements, confident that they would not go "radical," but they did not promote social action. The result was that there was no official church agency or organization in 1917 to centralize and coordinate the war efforts of Catholics. The K of C therefore stood in a unique position because of their previous social and recreational work with the US Army and National Guard at the time of the Mexican border troubles.

John Burke, in the very month in which the war began, organized the Chaplain's Aid Association to meet the ever-increasing needs of the Catholic chaplains in the Army and Navy. The Association served as a supply bureau for everything necessary for the chaplains' ministry to the servicemen. Money contributions came in generous proportions, enabling the fifty branches which had sprung up throughout the country to furnish Mass equipment, New Testaments, prayer books and other spiritual aids. For four years before the war, Father Lewis O'Hern, CSP, had acted as official Catholic representative in dealing with the US Government in the appointment of chaplains: there were however only twenty-four Catholic chaplains in the Army at the beginning of the war, four in the Navy. Before the war ended, there were 1,525 in the services. One of the most difficult angles of the chaplaincy problem was that most camps were located in the South, the very section where priests were fewest, making the recruiting of chaplains or auxiliary chaplains a monumental task.

Father O'Hern went to New York to talk it over with Father Burke at *The Catholic World*. This meeting was followed by other and similar meetings attended by Dr. William Kerby, founder of the National Conference of Catholic Charities; Charles Neill, former Secretary of Labor; Father O'Hern and Father Burke. Neill had been appointed a member of the Commission on Training Camp Activities, a group formed by the Government to handle questions of morality at the camps, especially the consumption of alcohol and the problem of prostitution, the ancient fellow-traveller of armies. Neill had been a confrere of Kerby at Catholic University and was a progressive, socially and politically.

By June the four collaborators had decided that a national organization must be formed to cope not only with the problems of social morality in the camps but also with the hundreds of other problems confronting Catholics in wartime. A few weeks later, armed with a plan, Father Burke arranged to visit Cardinal Gibbons in Baltimore to discuss the plan and ways and means of implementing it. The first step of the plan would be a national meeting of American Catholic leaders.

What was the plan? Was it simply a general outline of the main suggestions that were broached at the meetings of the four friends? Or was there a very specific plan that had a history predating these meetings? Helen Lynch, Burke's secretary from 1905 to 1913 at *The Catholic World*, claimed that she had often seen him working on a plan in his office years before the visit to Gibbons.[2] She contended that it was this "diagram" that he presented to Gibbons, and which Gibbons blessed with his hearty endorsement, "This is from God, John!"

In her *Full Circle*, Loretta R. Lawler tells the story of the National Catholic School of Social Service, of which Burke was co-founder. She asserts that Burke had scrutinized the situation of the Church in America and "had even occupied himself with a scheme of organization for some sort of ecclesiastical agency through which Catholic action might be provided. . . . It would take a world war to afford him the opportunity to lift this plan from the limbo of the academic. Meanwhile the thinking behind it became part of himself" (p. 7). Various writers of tributes to Burke in the Burke Memorial Issue of *Catholic Action* (December 15, 1936) referred to the "idea" Father Burke submitted to Cardinal Gibbons or to his "plans" assembled by the time of the war. Very Rev. John F. Fenlon, SS, secretary to the administrative committee of the War Council, referring to Burke, alluded to "the idea, original with him, I believe, of the National Catholic War Council."

Was John J. Burke the founder of the National Catholic

War Council and of its end result, the National Catholic Welfare Conference? In a juridical sense, no; he did not possess the requisite canonical authority. But in a very real sense he did found NCWC. It was he who conceptualized the basic idea and developed and directed its implementation. In a letter to Iona McNulty, his secretary at the National Catholic Welfare Conference, he disavowed any personal credit for creating the organization but his key role in creating it was obvious:

The NCWC was not thought out by me: it was given to me. From the beginning it was like a self-evident proposition. Granting Christ and the Church, it is nothing but Himself living in the Church and we living in the Church and we living in Him and her. So far as I could, it was for me to work it out. As you say, I gave all that I had to it. It probably cost me my health and some years of life but has it not also saved me? (June 10, 1924)

John Agar, financial officer of the War Council, wrote in a letter to Burke: "How the organization you created has grown . . ." (December 31, 1926). On one occasion, Pope Pius XI wrote to Archbishop Edward J. Hanna, chairman of the administrative committee of the NCWC, endorsing NCWC and praising Burke. In passing the good news along to Burke, Archbishop Hanna wrote: "May God bless you with the health and strength to continue to use your ability for many years for the greater good and glory of the piece of machinery which you have builded for the Church in America" (September 19, 1927).

Far more important than the title of "founder" was the great and lasting impact of Burke's visit to Cardinal Gibbons that historic day in 1917. Gibbons listened carefully to Burke's account of the discussions held by the four friends, cautiously weighing the feasibility of Burke's proposal that a national meeting of Catholic leaders be convened to coordinate all these exuberantly proliferating Catholic activities. Gibbons gave his endorsement to Burke's plan for a national meeting but requested Burke to present the proposal to Cardinal O'Connell of Boston and Cardinal Farley of New York. Having secured their approval, Burke proceeded to send a letter (July 17, 1917) to every diocese, citing the Cardinals' approval of a national meeting and asking each Ordinary "to join us in this work and to appoint at once one cleric and one layman as your representative at this national meeting." The meeting was to be held at Catholic University, August 11th and 12th. Similar letters of invitation went out to the officers of all Catholic lay societies of a national character and to Catholic press officials; each society was asked to send at least two representatives.

One hundred and fifteen delegates attended the meeting, including clerical and lay representatives from 68 dioceses and national Catholic organizations as well as men from the Catholic press. The delegates were sincere, earnest eager-beavers but the meeting was a medley of misconceptions, zeal for vested interests and various contentions about all manner of irrelevancies. They tried to focus on the main purpose of the gathering but galloped off in all directions with recommendations, queries and *obiter dicta* as to the right way to solve their problems. In his *American Catholics in the War*, Michael Williams tells how Burke arose in this farrago of cross-purposes and rivalries to deliver "an address which cleared the atmosphere, clarified the issues and presented a definite and positive programme" (p. 116). It was quite obvious that he had been organizing his ideas for many months, so detailed were his suggestions—even down to the needs of the libraries in the reading rooms of the recreation halls at the camps. He was wrong in one item: he said the spiritual care of these men at the camps would require five million dollars. The total expenditure came to more than fifty millions. He had not anticipated that the total American Catholic contribution to the armed services would be one million men.

A committee on resolutions was appointed, the resolutions were approved unanimously and a committee of seven devised a plan for organizing the National Catholic War Council along the lines suggested by Burke. He was elected first president of the Council: the executive committee was to consist of two delegates from each archdiocese to be selected by each archbishop, also the head of the K of C and the head of the American Federation of Catholic Societies.

Reading the text of Father Burke's address today, one is impressed less by its blueprint of logistics and utilization of manpower than by its appeal to religious motivation. He said that America, in this struggle, is looking for a force that will give her "the security in eternal truth of that democracy which she seeks to make safe in this world of men and nations." He is presenting once again his dream of converting America.

If her searching eyes see the whole body of American Catholics reflecting clearly the truths that our Church teaches, if to a man they are unreservedly, without restriction of any kind, devoted to her welfare; with singleness of purpose not only willing but eager to sacrifice every interest and every possession that she may live, then their deeds will prove the justice of her divine claims and America's children will recognize the Church as the teacher that is of God.[3]

At about this time, Burke began to receive reports of lurid behavior and carnal temptations on French soil. He wrote to the Federal Council of Churches, in his office as president of the War Council, asking for their cooperation in persuading President Wilson to protest to the French Government, "requesting the latter to take such measures for the moral welfare of our troops 'over there' as we have taken here." Protestant and Jewish leaders as well as the Federal Council responded favorably and an interfaith committee was formed, called "The Committee of Six." Burke was appointed chairman and before long the Secretary of War made it an official advisory committee to the War Department, Burke being chosen as permanent chairman. In addition to Burke, the members were: John R. Mott, grand old man of the ecumenical movement; Bishop James DeWolf Perry of the Episcopal Church; Dr. Robert E. Speer and Dr. William Adams Brown of the Federal Council of Churches; Colonel Harry Cutler, head of the Jewish War Commission.

Largely through his work with the Committee of Six, Burke developed a warm friendship with Secretary of War Newton Baker.[4] In 1931 Baker thanked Burke for his photograph and asked him to drop into his office on his next visit to Cleveland. Referring to the photograph, Baker wrote: "Amid my generals and statesmen, foreign and native, it hangs to testify that our association too was a part of the great work, and that the friendship which grew out of it is still a precious memory to me." Unlike the general in World War II who said he was interested in morale, not morals, Baker and Raymond Fosdick, head of the Commission on Training Camp Activities, were genuinely concerned about the morals of the troops. Their concern was not a facade to soothe the fears of worried mothers. Baker had been mayor of Cleveland, a successful reformer in cleaning up gambling and prostitution; Fosdick was a New York reformer of police. Certain Catholics condemned Burke for working along with the Protestant leaders in the Committee of Six but when Burke wrote to Gibbons asking if he should continue, the Cardinal urged him to do so.

In November, the board of archbishops decided, at the suggestion of Cardinal Gibbons, to take over control of the National Catholic War Council to further centralize authority. They realized that neither Gibbons nor Burke nor the Committee of Seven had proper authority to establish the War Council but agreed that the actual management of the organization should be entrusted to an administrative committee of four bishops: Patrick Muldoon of Rockford, Joseph Schrembs of Toledo, Patrick Hayes of New York (auxiliary), and William Russell of Charleston; Bishop Muldoon was named chairman.

Certain archbishops had become uneasy about the expanding power and prestige of the Knights of Columbus and this probably brought about the radical reorganization. The aim was to make a clear distinction between the spiritual wartime activities of the War Council and the K of C social work in the recreation centers. It was Cardinal Gibbons who persuaded the Knights to accept a subordinate role in Catholic wartime activities. The eventual line-up was the administrative committee under which were two subcommittees: the Knights of Columbus Committee on War Activities and the Committee on Special War Activities.[5] This latter committee directed all Catholic wartime activities except the work being done by the K of C. Father John Burke was named chairman of this committee. In short, all war work not in the province of the Knights was under the direction of Burke's Committee on Special War Activities.

He had the direction but not control of these Catholic wartime activities; he was to coordinate and promote but not to rule. "Not all of the bishops" says Elizabeth McKeown, "were willing to commit their hopes to a national Catholic organization or to trust the conviction of the War Council organizers that a new era of opportunity had dawned for the American Church if only Catholics would seize it. Burke and his associates therefore were faced with the great task of re-educating their fellow Catholics."[6] Many bishops feared the War Council might lead to interference with their own autonomy, other sincerely felt they could serve their country better through their own diocesan projects.

Michael Williams says of Burke's committee: "The Committee on Special War Activities was the managerial center, the wheelhouse of the ship, or if we may change the figure, the dynamo of the plant" (p. 154). Yet he was not a free hand: he was responsible to the administrative committee and ultimately to the fourteen archbishops. In August 1918 moreover, the War Council became an officially recognized agent of the US Government, entitled to have its committee records printed as part of the government record and to share in the collections of the United War Work campaigns. Burke was thereafter under the control of the Government as well as of the bishops; fortunately he enjoyed the trust and confidence of government officials. "For the first time in its American sojourn the Catholic Church mustered the necessary strengths to establish itself at the seat of national government as a special-interest group, determined to make its influence felt in the shaping of the national consensus."[7]

Father Burke had seven subcommittees functioning under him: men's activities, women's activities, chaplains' aid, Catholic interests, historical records, reconstruction and after-war activities, finance. The subcommittee on women's activities operated visitors' houses in training camps (especially for women who came to visit soldiers), established community houses in large cities with special attention to girls who came to cities to do special war work, and started the National Catholic School for Social Service to train social workers. Father Burke took a very personal interest in this latter project and in fact lived at a house next to the school for many years. After the armistice some of these girls were sent abroad to staff community houses, residence clubs, etc. Father Burke conducted the first retreat for the first overseas unit, Kerby and Cooper giving the later retreats. "Father Burke's girls" as they were called had to sign a contract stipulating that they would not touch liquor, smoke, use paint or powder and would dress in the uniform of the War Council. On one occasion Raymond Fosdick, head of the Commission on Training Camps, cabled the assistant secretary of war: "The women workers sent over by Father Burke's special committee of the National Catholic War Council are excellent and more could be effectively used suggest you take up with Burke advisability of sending in reasonably large numbers."

The subcommittee for men's activities promoted war work among various Catholic societies, staying out of the bailiwick of the Knights whose province was recreational work in the camps. In cities and towns near camps, service clubs were established for men in uniform; they were operated under the local management of diocesan councils and, surprisingly, the need for these service clubs intensified after the armistice. At these clubs men about to be demobilized could obtain information about employment, war risk insurance, hospital aid and vocational training. This subcommittee also promoted Student Army Training Corps branches on Catholic campuses and formed units of Catholic Boy Scouts.

The history of each one of these subcommittees really deserves a full-length book, but the subcommittee on reconstruction and after-war activities attracted very special attention. Even after the war ended, the War Council continued in existence for some years and on February 12, 1919, the War Council published a pamphlet called "Social Reconstruction: A General View of the Problems and Survey of Remedies." The document is said to have consisted (to some extent) of a speech written by Dr. John A. Ryan. He had intended to deliver it at a gathering of the Knights of Columbus at Louisville, Kentucky, but deciding it was too long and detailed, discarded it. Father O'Grady, secretary of the subcommittee on reconstruction, asked Ryan to edit it, then gave it to the administrative committee (of the four bishops) who changed it slightly and published it as their own pronouncement on Lincoln's birthday. Scores of other proposals for reconstruction were offered throughout the country but, according to Aaron Abell, this "Bishops' Program," as it was generally called, became the most widely known of all the proposals for postwar social reconstruction. *The Nation* commented editorially (June 28, 1922) that "the program is far and away the most significant social pronouncement made by any church in the United States. . . . Its publication shook the assurance of many non-Catholics that an authoritarian church which had officially condemned Modernism in theology could ever assume an effective leadership in a social democracy." The Bishops' Program supported labor's right to organize, distribution of ownership as far as possible among the workers, adequate representation of both capital and labor to bring about harmony in employer-employee conflicts, a family living wage, government planning to help discharged soldiers and sailors establish themselves in cities and on farms, equal pay for women doing the same tasks as men, high wages and high purchasing power by the masses as a guarantee of prosperous industry.

Bishop Muldoon and Father Burke were keenly disappointed to find as the years went by that "not a single remedial or transforming proposal in the 'Bishops' Program'," as Aaron Abell wrote, "was adopted during the 1920s." In the anti-Bolshevik hysteria after the war, many frightened Americans feared that all reformers were Bolsheviks or at least dupes of revolutionary agitators, John A. Ryan being considered a socialist or worse. The administrative committee saw this as proof of the grave need of economic and social education and therefore put a heavier stress on the War Council as a continuing peacetime agency. Throughout the explosive controversy generated by the Program, Burke supported Ryan and in *Social Action* (December 15, 1936) Ryan affirmed that Burke was one of his staunchest defenders in that stormy time, his whole record in social action being unimpeachable. Burke and Father Ryan were always good friends but not in the degree of intimacy that existed between Burke and Bishop Muldoon, or between Burke and Monsignor Kerby.

The War Council played a key role in the United War Work drive in 1918. At first the YMCA, the YWCA, the War Camp Community Service and the American Library Association planned to run this drive's first phase to collect 133 million dollars; then the War Council, the Salvation Army and the Jewish Welfare Board were to conduct a second drive for their purposes. Burke saw this as divisive of the unity that had existed among the cooperating agencies and secondly, as the practical-minded Muldoon expressed it, "those who had the first collection would get the cream." The administrative committee, accompanied by Father Burke, protested in person to Secretary of War Baker on the ground that the double drive would give the people the impression of national disunity. The outcome was that President Wilson ordered a single drive "so that in their solicitation of funds as well as in their work in the field, they may act in as complete cooperation and fellowship as possible."

The War Council, with the aid of bishops and clergy, was able to furnish more than 500,000 adult workers for the drive whose goal was set at 170 millions. Although the armistice occurred the very first day of the drive, the public was well aware of the pressing needs of demobilization and reconstruction and the total collected was 188 millions. Of this the War Council received almost 33 millions. Burke felt that the success of the drive not only helped the War Council's reconstruction program for Europe and postwar America but also showed the American public's approval of Catholic America's war effort.

Revitalized by funds from the United War Work drive, the committee on reconstruction and after-war activities inaugurated some prodigious projects. It established schools for illiterate veterans, maintained some 39 employment bureaus to help veterans find jobs, and opened out-patient and social service departments in 15 Catholic hospitals for the after-care of discharged veterans and their families.

One project that drew special attention was the Americanization of the immigrants. It would seem that by 1919 the conversion of America, related in an intimate way to the immigrants, was receding into the dim future—as far as Father Burke's hopes were concerned—but he was still very much interested in this problem of molding millions of newly arrived immigrants into a practical American Catholicism. The War Council launched a nationwide civic education program aimed particularly at the immigrants to guide them away from subversive radicalism. The lecture materials were written mainly by John Lapp of the War Council, whose published civic education materials were translated into 13 languages with a circulation of over a million copies. While the approach was designed to divert immigrants from affiliation with radicals, the tone of the program was positive and the contents consisted chiefly of basic American principles.

Important as the Americanization of the immigrant might be, Burke felt that the more important item was the preservation of the faith of the Catholic immigrant. Brownson, in the last century, was ordered by Archbishop Hughes of New York to stop trying to make Americanism and Catholicism compatible but Hecker insisted they were not only compatible (for the most part) but complementary. Burke agreed with Hecker's theme but realized that the assimilation of the immigrant presented grave threats to his faith. How to become American without loss of Catholic identity? This was the problem.

In her *War and Welfare* Elizabeth McKeown delineates the dilemmas of Catholic leaders at the beginning of the century and cites the solution for these problems offered by Father William Kerby in an article in *The Catholic World*, January 1907, entitled "Reinforcements of the Bonds of Faith." Kerby pointed out that the Catholic could expect no reinforcement for his faith in the social atmosphere of America; therefore he must look to his Church for reinforcement. "Specifically" says Elizabeth McKeown, Father Kerby in this article "encouraged church leaders to improve upon the modes and opportunities for association among Catholics and the development among them of group feeling and common viewpoint. Rational adherence to dogma and even participation in common sacramental and liturgical functions were not enough."[8] In short, Kerby insisted that a sense of Catholic identity could be preserved by intensifying Catholic group consciousness.

It seems that Father Burke's handling of the immigrant question reflects this article: Kerby was an intimate friend of Burke and indeed it was Burke who published this article. He agreed with Kerby that Catholic leaders should improve and make more attractive the numerous Catholic associations and societies so that the immigrant could have a sense of pride in identifying with the Church. Burke had no desire to suppress the 15,000 Catholic societies in the US but he did want to develop them and encourage them to communicate with other Catholic organizations as well as with the secular world. He agreed also with Kerby on the need of giving the laity a larger role in church affairs as a means of developing a tighter Catholic group consciousness but he realized this was something that could not be imposed.

In *Catholic Action*, December 15, 1936, Dr. T.E. Purtell,

president of the National Council of Catholic Men, spoke of Burke's vision of the laity. He speculated that more could have been accomplished with the laity "if those of us who were laggard in appreciating the vision had been regimented" but then he added that an imposed unity would have been a failure, "that if growth were to have any permanency it must be from within." Precisely because he believed in individuality and personal freedom Burke was successful in promoting among American immigrants a sense of their Catholic identity in a pluralistic society. The National Catholic War Council, operating on the voluntary principle, was a supreme example of a Catholic association that fostered a sense of Catholic group consciousness and at the same time adapted the immigrant to American culture.

The previous pages of this chapter presented a brief summary of the nature, aims and history of the National Catholic War Council until the end of the First World War. What was the War Council office like in its day-to-day operation, in its "existential reality"? Mary Dineen wrote a letter to Father Vincent F. Holden, CSP, dated January 25, 1951, recounting some of her experiences with the committee on special war activities, in its office in Washington, D.C. She was secretary to Father Burke (1917-1919). The following has been excerpted from that letter:[9]

Father Burke, as he will ever be to me, was at once the greatest and kindest man I've ever met. He thought well of all men and distrusted none. . . . At first we were located at 932-14th Street, N.E. over a tire store. . . . As for the physical setup of the office, lest I forget, the rats decided to make it their home and the shrieks and screams indicated whose desk had been occupied during the night. A pest control company was called and they put in weasels to run out the rats. . . . Remember, we didn't have any money and were operating on a shoestring. . . . No one had any hours. We worked far into the night many a night when the occasion demanded: we never knew a holiday or a Sunday—many nights at midnight I was taking dictation as Father Burke made ready to board the midnight for New York. At that time he would spend 3 days in Washington, 4 days in New York at *The Catholic World*. Going up to New York he would read manuscripts: returning he would study programs for the War Council. We didn't mind working long hours, it was exciting, we were young. It was a crucial time for our country and a critical time for a new offspring of Catholic thought. We were deeply, honestly interested because of the dynamic power of divinely inspired Father Burke. . . . Issues with the War Department became hot and heavy. They had no index on how to fight on foreign shores nor here at home with modern equipment and men. . . . Meantime he had his troubles from within his own organization and the rumblings backstage were loud and long. It was all so new that many did not want to change the old setup, but he went doggedly on his way, constantly supported by Cardinal Gibbons. . . . historic decisions were made, and Father Burke was challenged much and often as to his views, and being one among many he had to battle for men's souls while they battled for their bodies. When it was apparent that the draft would drain off the seminarians and cause a gap in the ranks of ordained priests, Father Burke went to Baker and asked that all registered students in a qualified seminary be exempt. He was given the permission.

I remember Father Burke dictated, pacing back and forth with his hands clasped behind his back, and in a hurried moment had to have the paper to be read before this august body at the War Department. So I speeded up and in my hurry transcribed "britches of the government" instead of "breaches of government". Father Burke read it as written and the whole committee got a huge laugh and it broke the tension, so I got by as Father Burke got a real laugh too. Father Burke loved nature and in the fall when the leaves fell heavily in the park he would walk through the leaves instead of on the walkway, saying he liked to hear the rustle. He never ate properly or at regular hours. Many a lunch I brought from a nearby hotel and while interviewing somebody or listening to some tale of woe he would try to snatch a bite. Time was so short and the war was so hard. He smoked a brand of cigarettes named, I think, "After the Show" but I always asked for "Between the Acts."

To him must be given the credit for establishing a platform from which the bishops of America could speak. Never in the history of the Country did they all gather together to discuss matters pertaining to their special calling. And when the "Bishops Program for Social Reconstruction" was issued the controversy ran high, even behind the scenes and back of the headlines, and through it all serenely and sedately walked Father John J. Burke. Father Ryan was also most helpful at this particular time. . . . We must remember the promulgation of social consciousness was entirely new in 1918. These men were pioneers in advocating many truths now become commonplace and many others not yet accepted. This alone is a monument to Father Burke and Father Ryan. How Father Burke worked against bigotry, against lawlessness, always for the honor and glory of God—with utter disregard for self: how his huge frame would sag with almost utter defeat only to rise and keep on fighting for what he knew to be right: how his very own stabbed and cut but he carried no rancor and I was ready to use the hatchet on many a titled head, and in my heart I did. . . . His positive approach to a question, and his triggerlike mind to an answer which had included all sides was amazing to his colleagues and confusing to many a bureaucrat of 1918. . . . Would that he had lived to see the vast accomplishments of his daring and the gigantic results of his planning but the heartaches and the hardships he endured then were the foundation stones. That the structure has engraved itself upon the face of the nation today is proof of his careful attention to the blueprint put out during those fateful years of 1917 to 1936.

Pardon the many mistakes. It has been nearly 32 years since I have used the typewriter so that it is like my memory, out of date. With every good wish to all of you who carry on so valiantly in the steps of one who gave his all.

(signed)
Mary D. Coyle

If Mary Coyle reflects the admiration and veneration Father Burke's women employees cherished for him, the following is a sample of the loyalty of his male coworkers. It was written by Michael Slattery, one of Burke's assistants in establishing the War Council and later in promoting nationwide the NCWC's

National Council of Catholic Men. He was also a member of the resolutions committee at the August 1917 meeting at Catholic University that led to the creation of the War Council. A Philadelphian, he had worked for seven years for Archbishop Ryan of that city, then became a successful gold prospector in Mexico. He was present in Mexico City the day in 1910 when Madero fired the first shot of his revolution. When the churches were looted, nuns attacked and bishops hunted down, he began to wonder how this could happen in a 95 percent Catholic country, eventually coming to the conclusion that the people were Catholic one hour on Sundays but had no Catholic organizations to keep them interested. In 1917 he met Father Burke. In 1922, during a low point in the NCWC's history, Slattery wrote Burke a letter from which these excerpts have been taken:[10]

I have tried to serve you and in serving you I felt I was following the leadership of the only man who had a real vision of the needs of the Church in the United States. . . . You have blazed the trail. You have given hope to many who were anxious to serve and in so doing you have created jealousies and animosities. It is ever thus with all great men. I told you on one occasion that I have given up everything to follow you. Opportunities to go back to my old profession have been many but I feel that if I made enough to live and educate my two boys properly I would stick until the last. . . . My Katie idolized you and prayed for us both. She is praying before the throne of God today for us and it is because of my faith in her that I have never lost hope for the future of NCWC. . . . I will serve you as God gives me strength. . . . If I have been sentimental in this letter please remember my pen is only scribbling what my heart is dictating.

Always faithfully,
(signed) Michael

These two letters reflect the enthusiastic support Father Burke received in his War Council work from some Catholics but the letters also hint at some of the opposition he received within Catholic ranks. A notable example of this was the strong criticism directed at the Bishops' Program by conservatives. They considered it dangerously radical and the administrative committee tainted with socialism. John A. Ryan, the actual author, was suspected of being a Marxist sympathizer, and a National Civic Federation committee studying socialism spoke of priests who are in important positions in Catholic organizations and who "sympathize with, foster and aid" Marxist-oriented philosophy. In view of a situation that developed in 1922, it seems probable that a few bishops were among the critics of the War Council but John A. Ryan did say that no bishop publicly attacked the Bishops' Program.

It is not uncommon in Catholic history that powerful movements of change in the Church come from the lower levels rather than from official sources. Father Thomas T. McAvoy notes in his *History of the Catholic Church in the United States*: "Actually this National Catholic War Council had no real authorization because neither Father John J. Burke nor Cardinal Gibbons had any real authority to call the convention that created it."[11] McAvoy says that the initial meeting represented more or less the feelings of the patriotic mass of Catholics led by the Knights of Columbus in their desire to do their duty in the war effort. The War Council was the crystallization of a movement that came from below rather than from top official levels in the Church. Father McAvoy's statement, however, underplays the key role of Father Burke in organizing the meeting at Catholic University. The Knights of Columbus did invaluable work during the war but it was a priest who planned and organized the initial meeting on that August day in 1917, and it was a priest who sent out the invitations from his *Catholic World* office in New York.

True, the War Council lacked official approval at the outset but the archbishops supplied their authorization when they assumed control of the War Council in November 1917. The Council continued to exist for some years, even after the war itself ended, until the Council had fulfilled its various commitments. In a letter (May 8, 1931) John Burke informed Bishop

John G. Murray of Portland, Maine that a court order dissolving the old National Catholic War Council had finally been received. Its total expenditures were $36,000,000.

chapter 4
The beginning and sudden suppression of NCWC

When the armistice brought an end to World War I hostilities on November 11, 1918, the cessation of slaughter found a serious lack of unity in the American Church at its topmost levels. The War Council had grappled with the communications gap between dioceses but approached it from the angle of increased efficiency in the war effort, not from the standpoint of increased unity in the official Church organization. This lack of organizational unity served to make more ludicrous the rumors that arose from time to time to the effect that the American Catholic hierarchy was a smoothly functioning, highly synchronized apparatus working day and night to take over control of the American Government.

It had been the custom for the archbishops to meet together once a year, a custom followed faithfully since 1884, the year of the Third Plenary Council of Baltimore, but in all those 34 years the American bishops had not once gathered in formal assembly. In the early history of America, of course, Catholic bishops and archbishops had been conspicuously absent from public gatherings, due to the prevailing anti-Catholic prejudice. In 1765 Catholic laymen in Maryland warned the Jesuit provincial in England that the presence of a bishop in Maryland would furnish a pretext for persecution, and in 1771, a Father Ferdinand Farmer, a missionary in Philadelphia, roused by the suggestion that a bishop be asked to come down from Quebec to administer confirmation, wrote that the arrival of a bishop "would create great disturbances, with the danger of depriving us of the paltry privileges we are now enjoying."[1]

In the twentieth century, however, the situation had radically changed and bishops could appear in public without creating a riot. But each diocese had very little communion or contact with its neighbor diocese. Each bishop entertained a clear, sharply defined concept of his relationship to his own diocese and to the Holy Father but it was not until Vatican II that the doctrine of "collegiality" was elucidated, affirming the principle that all bishops belong together to an episcopal "college." *The Constitution on the Church* (article 23) says that all bishops should promote the welfare of the whole Church, instruct the faithful in love for the whole Mystical Body, foster every activity common to the whole Church and finally "in a universal fellowship of charity, bishops should gladly extend their fraternal aid to other churches, especially to neighboring and more needy dioceses, in accordance with the venerable example of antiquity."

The isolation of diocese from diocese, visible in 1918, was a striking contrast to the sweeping national trend toward centralization then beginning to develop in the American Government. The War Council had promoted Catholic participation in a gigantic war effort that had become "the greatest promotion and public relations program the American Church had ever known" but Father Burke feared that when the Catholic soldiers returned home, each diocese would soon be back at business as usual, back to antiseptic insulation from other units of the American Church. This might not necessarily mean each diocese would lose contact with secular developments outside its borders, but it would mean breaking contact with Catholic life and thought in other parts of the country and withdrawal from the ever-expanding task of defending Catholic interests in legislation proposed in Congress. The situation, in Burke's judgment, needed a permanent national Catholic office in Washington to protect the interests of the Catholic minority.

A golden jubilee unexpectedly provided a response to the problem. On February 20, 1919, seventy-seven bishops gathered in Washington, D.C., at Catholic University, not as an official assembly, but to celebrate the golden jubilee of Cardinal Gibbons' episcopal consecration. Archbishop Bonaventura Cerretti was on hand as representative of Pope Benedict XV. He addressed the audience in the chapel of Caldwell Hall at the University, praising the Cardinal for his work during the war and then speaking of the Pope's own prewar efforts to prevent, and his wartime efforts to end, the recent conflict. (The bishops were aware of the American critics who had been accusing Pope Benedict unfairly of favoring enemy countries such as Austria, where Catholicism predominated.) Cerretti praised the Pope's impartiality and expressed the hope that the American bishops would join the Holy Father in working through some form of organization for a just and lasting peace and in his efforts to promote Catholic principles in the area of education and social justice.[2]

That very day Cardinal Gibbons appointed a committee to determine how best to implement the Pope's wishes, and the following day, at the meeting of the archbishops, it was recommended that the entire hierarchy assemble annually, including the auxiliary bishops. Gibbons then appointed the four bishops of the War Council administrative committee, along with himself, to supervise general Catholic activities and interests at least until the next meeting of the hierarchy, which would be held in September. At this meeting, the Cardinal would propose that a permanent committee be elected by ballot. On April 10, 1919, the Pope wrote Gibbons, praising the decision to hold annual meetings and stating that the direction of the bishops might be helpful in the social and educational movements of the day.[3]

On September 24-25, 1919, ninety-two of the one hundred and one ordinaries of the United States met at Catholic University, the largest meeting of bishops in American history. On the 24th, by official resolution, they launched the National Catholic Welfare Council (changed in 1923 to "Conference") and Cardinal Gibbons was happy to inform the Holy Father: "In this way the hierarchy is now well organized to care regularly and efficiently and immediately for every important Catholic interest in the United States, and to this work of organizing the bishops gave most of the time and the wisdom of the meeting."[4]

At this meeting the bishops elected seven members to the administrative committee of NCWC to transact business between annual meetings and carry on the work. Archbishop Hanna of San Francisco was named chairman, to be assisted by Archbishop Dougherty of Philadelphia, Archbishop Dowling of St. Paul, Bishops Muldoon of Rockford, Schrembs of Cleveland, Russell of Charleston, Canevin of Pittsburgh. At a meeting in December 1919 Father Burke was elected executive secretary of the administrative committee (changed to "general secretary" on April 14, 1920). It was to be his responsibility to preside over the headquarters in Washington.[5]

Not every bishop was elated over the creation of NCWC. At the September meeting, clouds of future trouble cast their shadows over the discussion, causing considerable distress to Cardinal Gibbons. Bishop Charles McDonnell of Brooklyn suggested that such an organization would conflict with the principle that no bishop should exercise jurisdiction in the diocese of another bishop without special papal permission. He added that the Pope's letter recommending the annual meeting had not been prepared in Rome but in the United States, intimating forgery of his signature. Muldoon cheered up the Cardinal, assuring him of a happy outcome, and the bishops voted down the objections.

Burke, not the Cardinal, was disturbed by criticism coming from the editor of the Cardinal's diocesan paper, the *Catholic Review* of Baltimore. On December 20, 1919, an editorial in this paper assailed the YMCA, the K of C and the War Council for its lavish expenditure of millions during the war. "Where have they gone?" The editor proceeded to say, "Give us the old-fashioned Catholic methods of looking after man and his welfare and we know that much good will result." This was an attack on the War Council, the K of C and Father Burke but was also advance warning about future NCWC expenditures. Burke protested to Gibbons but the cardinal did not seem to be particularly displeased with his editor's viewpoint and merely suggested to Burke that he write the editor about his criticism.

The National Catholic Welfare Council was often referred to as a continuation of the National Catholic War Council. The latter was created however as a temporary organization to fill a wartime need; the Welfare Council was a distinctly new organization of a permanent nature. In fact, the War Council continued to exist for several years after the Welfare Council was formed, the two organizations running concurrently. Burke looked upon the Welfare Council as a distinctly new organization and felt that he should not affiliate himself with this new venture. When the superior general of the Paulists was asked by Gibbons to give Burke to NCWC full-time, the request was granted and Burke moved to Washington, albeit not gladly. The superior general was Burke's own brother, Thomas. He was jubilant not only for the good name of the Burke family but also for the honor accruing to the religious community he headed. John, however, had remonstrated with his brother, asserting the appointment would mean the end of his life as a Paulist, might mean the ruination of his health and the loss of peace of mind. Reluctantly he consented.

How deeply he felt about becoming involved in this new enterprise is obvious in a letter he wrote (April 2, 1920) to Grace Murray, his secretary at *The Catholic World*:

I don't want the Welfare Council work. I'm not fitted for it. I never went into the priesthood for it. I don't think I'm called in any way to direct the national work of the Catholic Church in the United States. It's a pain and just now little short of an agony to accept it. One wants someone else to understand him: it is well and comforting to put it to God, and yet there is extreme loneliness unless another soul knows. The honors come thick: people consult me: I've looked forward to this and that —but all that doesn't give my soul a bit of comfort. . . . My days have been cut off from those I love most. I miss my home: my days have been cut off from those—yourself, Gertrude, Mary, the men in the house to whom I was devotedly attached, whom I love, with whom I worked and loved to work just as one of themselves. They loved me and were devoted to me. It is not so nor can it be in the new work. I brought you faith. I haven't always been to you what I ought to be but I've given you the best in me and trained you carefully, if somewhat harshly—in a very high way. My heart was in the work. Nor do I think I would mind it so much if I were taken away to another work for which I thought I ought to be fitted. The telling me that another priest was coming was welcome—and yet it seemed to fix more surely what I dread—the other work. . . . You say but you knew it: you knew the national work must be done. Yes, I knew it and I saw it but while the vision may be for me, I don't think the achievement is. Or rather the achievement as a personal thing has no charm for me. It has no stimulation. The vision has, but whatever I do, the vision is beyond the achievement. Someone else ought to have been chosen and I would gladly have served in my own way. . . . Who else would take it, you ask. I don't know. Why did I take it? I suppose because of circumstances. I wept when the invitation was given to me. I wept when I read your letter today and my heart knows no joy. For all the courage you have and will show I thank you immensely. . . . I see the big things I ought to do and my soul is not going to quake nor go back. It is going to push ahead with the same courage, the same determination, the same single, absorbing love of our Savior Jesus Christ. I want that love to consume me and burn me up on the altar of his sacrifice. But I do want you to know—or rather, my heart wants to tell you that it is all costing me a great deal; for my mission is to lead others. . . .

> Your father in Him,
> J.J. Burke

Augusta, Georgia

This is the letter of a man harassed by a collectivity of painfully disquieting factors. In the Paulist archives there is another letter from Augusta, Georgia, undated but apparently written about the same time as the above letter. In it Burke writes Grace Murray that he is not well, that he has been impatient and irritable but "as the doctor said, I was at least sensible in giving heed to the warning." Undoubtedly his fragile health was one reason for his reluctance to take on the new work. Another reason was that he realized all too clearly that permanent residence in Washington meant breaking his ties to his Paulist friends, his family, and his friends at *The Catholic World*. Again, he did not feel happy about getting into administrative work once more, perhaps disenchanted by the outcome of his work with the War Council in connection with the war effort. The war to make the world safe for democracy had a bitter taste. But most importantly, he was motivated by a very positive factor: he felt that his destiny was to direct and guide persons aspiring to sanctity. All his life he considered spiritual direction "the art of arts" and was never so happy as he was in developing the life of Christ among followers of Christ.

Reluctantly but yet whole-heartedly Father Burke assumed his duties as general secretary, focusing on his favorite theme—unity. "The genius of the National Catholic Welfare Conference," he said at a later time, "is our active unity that shows forth to the world the faith from which that unity is born, and which it must express." Yet like the Church itself, the NCWC experienced trials and troubles within as well as without. Some of its officers questioned the wisdom of particular policies, some personnel became involved in personality conflicts.

Dr. John M. Cooper, noted anthropologist and expert in child care, had worked closely with Father Burke as executive secretary of the War Council's women's activities committee before becoming an official of the National Council of Catholic Women, a unit of the NCWC department of lay organizations. He resigned this latter post on March 8, 1920, in Burke's words, "in anger and disappointment." Burke wrote to Muldoon (March 9th) saying that Cooper's displeasure seemed to be with the way things were run at NCWC. "Father Cooper does not believe I am honest in the general acceptance of the word." Cooper, moreover, according to Burke, admitted frankly that he did not believe women were capable of running their own organization. Then on March 15th Monsignor Splaine of

Boston wrote Burke, at the instigation of Cardinal O'Connell, to complain about remarks made by Dr. Cooper to Mrs. Slattery, the Cardinal's representative at a convention of Catholic women. Splaine said that Cooper must make a fitting apology if further cooperation was desired. "Please write me as fully as you can because His Eminence anxiously awaits a complete and early reply." Burke undoubtedly saw the humor in this request to jump through the hoop at the command of Cardinal O'Connell just as he saw the humor in the resignations touched off by Cooper's resignation. He wrote to Muldoon, "Father Cooper thought it incumbent on him to call all the stenographers in when he resigned and ask them not to resign (which reminds me of the avaricious priest who told the rich lady in a devout tone, 'Next Friday is my birthday. Kindly say a prayer for me'.)"

Burke apparently had many reverses and disappointments in the early months of NCWC's existence. On June 18, 1920, he wrote to Helen Lynch, formerly his secretary at *The Catholic World* but later a Cenacle religious, that he had difficulties in getting the organization on its feet but now felt that the lines had been laid for the future work. "I have had much of sacrifice, of disappointment, of bewilderment and of bitterness." At Christmas, however, he wrote Mother Lynch in a different vein. "This work grows beyond my dreams. It is Christ manifesting the unity of the Church and the power of his word before men."

It is quite obvious from the correspondence that Bishop Muldoon felt a special regard and affection for Father Burke and this was reciprocated. At Christmas 1921 Burke wrote to Muldoon, "What is difficult to say I wish you to understand— my appreciation, my gratitude and my personal affection." Writing to the apostolic delegate (April 6, 1921) to urge that Muldoon be given a papal honor as assistant at the papal throne, Burke said that Muldoon has held the post of chairman of the administrative committee of the War Council "to the entire satisfaction of the hierarchy of the United States." On another occasion Burke said he would "lay down his life for Muldoon." Schrembs and Burke were also close friends. The former wrote Burke when he was ill (December 30, 1921), "God grant you may soon be your old self again. I am looking forward to the day when I shall see your smiling face again and feel the warm pressure of your hand."

Burke's references to Cardinal Dougherty, on the other hand, were quite formal and remote. The cardinal was head of the department of legislation at NCWC. Burke wrote, in a memo for his own use (April 23, 1921), that the cardinal seemed uninterested in Catholic education during a recent visit made by Burke and Dr. Pace to Dougherty for the purpose of discussing upcoming legislation on education. Nor did he show any interest in the Welfare Council. But he did perk up at the mention of Philippine independence. Having been a bishop in the Philippines, the cardinal launched into a disquisition on the islands, inveighing against their independence. Then Burke mentioned that Archbishop Hanna had been elected vice president for the coming annual meeting of the bishops: immediately the cardinal showed intense interest. The welfare of the Church, noted Burke, became secondary to who should preside at the September meeting, Dougherty contending that Curley of Baltimore should preside. "As we left we had various strange thoughts on the sense of values entertained by some leading churchmen."

While Burke was a strong advocate of a responsible role for the laity in the church, he did have his troubles with laity from time to time. On February 23, 1921, he wrote Hanna, criticizing the Knights of Columbus for holding themselves out as the officially accredited representatives of the mind of the hierarchy whereas the administrative committee was the hierarchy's agent in matters of national importance. Burke feared that this K of C tactic would lead to disastrous confusion and dissension. He told Hanna that the K of C's support of Hoover's 33-millions fund for European Relief had been interpreted by the relief administrator as the official approval of the Catholic

Church for this postwar project but, according to Burke, "we are anxious to make sure the money will not be used for proselytizing purposes." Burke then added, "I went to see Hoover in this matter and he treated me as if I were the head of some sodality. He said that the approval of the K of C meant the approval of the Catholic Church." Burke concluded that the work at NCWC would be impossible unless the administrative committee informed the Knights that they were not the voice of the hierarchy.

In the *Formula* Burke presented to the administrative board of NCWC on February 25, 1936, he summarized the principles obtaining in regard to laity-NCWC relations. Every Catholic lay organization was asked to affiliate with the department of laity, NCWC, but affiliation was a voluntary matter. It could be nothing else, according to Burke, because the NCWC and its administrative board had no canonical authority. "As the whole NCWC was established as the voluntary co-operation of the bishops, so must the note of voluntariness, willingness, go through its whole structure." The NCWC was not founded as a hindrance either to responsibility or initiative but the proper order, said Burke, was for Catholic lay organizations to contact the NCWC as a clearing-house for information and find out the mind of the bishops before speaking out categorically on a matter that would affect the whole country.

In the early 1920s Burke was anxious for the laity to concern themselves with national affairs, especially with the burgeoning power of the federal government which even under the "do-nothing" administration of President Harding was reaching out for more and more control of the individual. "Legislation is not only becoming more and more federal, legislation is becoming more paternal" he wrote in a *Catholic World* editorial. In response to a suspicious-looking bill for education of immigrants, Burke obtained the approval of the administrative committee to release the following statement to the press:

The growth of bureaucracy in the United States is one of the most significant after-effects of the war. This growth must be resolutely checked. Federal assistance and federal direction are in some cases beneficial and even necessary but extreme bureaucracy is foreign to everything American. It is unconstitutional and undemocratic. It means officialism, red tape and prodigal waste of public money. It spells hordes of so-called experts and self-perpetuating cliques of politicians to regulate every detail of daily life. It would eventually sovietize our form of government. The forward-looking forces in our national life must resolutely stand against further encroachment on individual and state liberty. The press, the home, the school and the church have no greater enemy at the present time than the paternalistic and bureaucratic government which certain self-seeking elements are attempting to foist upon us. (Release to press approved by administrative committee, NCWC, January 26, 1922)

Burke was disturbed not only by evidences of expanding bureaucracy in Washington but also by the economic distress in Germany and Italy. Economic unrest spawns dictatorships and potential dictators were on the prowl in Western Europe as a result of the recent war. At the NCWC, on the contrary, the future was bright with promise. The new organization had established an enviable record of accomplishment. Whereas the Federal Council of Churches had formerly been regarded by lawmakers as the voice of American religion, NCWC was now generally accepted as the voice of Catholics in national affairs. President Harding thanked Catholics for organizing it since it gave him a reliable means of sounding out Catholic opinion, and Congress itself came to regard NCWC as authoritative. The new organization watched over Catholic interests in relation to new laws being proposed and secured from the executive branch of the Government benign interpretations of existing legislation. The prohibition law, for instance, at first barred priests from obtaining any wine for mass; Burke arranged for a less absolute interpretation of the law. In view of the extraordinary success of NCWC we would have good reason to expect the Vatican to send a message of sincerest congratulations to

NEVER LOOK BACK

the infant organization. A message came but it was a shocker.

It was a papal decree, sponsored by the Consistorial Congregation at Rome, suppressing the National Catholic Welfare Council. Dated February 25, 1922, it was sent to all the ordinaries of the American hierarchy by the apostolic delegate, Giovanni Bonzano. Not only was the NCWC suppressed but the annual meetings of the bishops were banned as well. The most important and probably the most progressive project in American Catholic history had been struck down in mid-career just when it was attaining a remarkable momentum. The bishops were stunned. The decree was as follows:[6]

Sacred Congregation of the Consistorial

A Decree on Episcopal Gatherings in the United States

In the United States of America, the custom has recently arisen that all diocesan ordinaries assemble, even from outlying provinces, to treat of some matters which seemed to require assembled deliberation. Furthermore, in order to settle other matters which may occur during the year they have determined to establish a certain committee of bishops called the NCWC.

But now, because circumstances have changed, some bishops in their own name and that of others have decided that the procedure and this establishment is no longer needful or useful; so they have asked the Holy See that steps be taken.

When, therefore, by direction of the Holy Father, Pope Pius XI, this matter was taken up in the full committee of the Sacred Consistorial Congregation, on February 23rd of this year, the eminent Fathers decided that the rule of the common law be wholly re-established, and, therefore, such general gatherings be not held anymore, except for reasons reviewed and approved by the Holy See in each case, in keeping with Canon 281 of the Code. Likewise, the eminent Fathers have cited that the office and activity of the above NCWC committee should cease, and what is laid down about conferences and provincial councils in Chapter VII of Book II of the Code and in the decree of the Congregation of July 25th, 1916, be observed.

The Holy Father sustained and confirmed this decision and ordered that it be made known through the Apostolic Delegate to all the Ordinaries of the United States of America.

Given at Rome, in the office of the Consistorial Congregation, February 25th, 1922.

C. Card. De Lai, Bishop of Sabina
Secretary

A. Sincero,
Assessor

The old ecclesiastical maxim had it: "When the heavy hand of Rome strikes, you must kiss it." Burke did not kiss it. Immediately on receiving the bad news, he went to work. He wrote to mothers superior of religious orders of women contemplatives requesting prayers for "a critical situation" without describing or identifying it. Rumors of all kinds hovered over the NCWC offices. Burke, on March 27th, addressed the employees, referring to "a rumor" without stating it but suggesting that "it is our solemn duty not to accept the rumor as fact and not to discuss it with outsiders, even priests or dignitaries of the Church." He apparently thought it was an error caused by some misunderstanding but the employees understood the "rumor" as a threat to their jobs. He told them he could give no assurance of their retention of employment but must wait for the decision of the administrative committee. Once again he asked them to remain silent: "This is a time that tries your soul and my soul. I beg of you again to make the resolution before God not to talk. . . ."

Archbishop Dowling of St. Paul felt that it was futile to attempt to fight the decree. He wrote Burke (April 1st) that the Welfare Council could not be saved and "we shouldn't try to." Rome had spoken authoritatively and crushingly; not to submit would be to justify the accusers and to recreate the NCWC would be impossible unless with the backing of the largest dioceses, which was not forthcoming. Dowling thought the only real question was: how to announce its demise? "Should the scandal and odium of it be allowed to fall on the Holy See or be distributed among the American representatives of the sacred college or fall on the bishops of the country?" One thing was certain, in Dowling's mind, and that was that "we must proceed to liquidation at once." His conviction was that NCWC's enemies "will eat us alive" as soon as they find out how defenseless we are. There is a curious ambivalence, however, in the letter. Dowling was resigned to defeat and yet he urged that Schrembs take the case to the Holy Father personally. He advised Burke, "You are young and will live to smile at this. Don't lose sleep. The Church has a way of muddling through somehow." As for the bishops, Dowling said they were inexperienced and timid, possessing "little sense of the crisis that is here." In another letter to Burke (this time undated) he retained his defeatism but said that the administrative committee must show it has not been "the coryphaeus of a schism in the United States." Meanwhile Father Burke had wired Archbishop Hanna, chairman of the administrative committee: "Positive reasons lead me to believe matters should be taken at once to the highest authorities. Definite immediate action will certainly ease and may save a most critical situation for Church and country."

On April 6th the members of the administrative committee met at the residence of Schrembs in Cleveland, Burke also being present. They proceeded to send a cable to the Holy Father saying that "legal and business obligations make it imperative to continue the work," referring to works begun publicly with the approval of Benedict XV and also to commitments to the US Government for immigration and Russian relief work. They asked for a suspension of the decree, non-publication in *Acta* and permission to continue their activities until a full report could be sent to the Holy See. Press reports of the condemnation of NCWC, a renewal of Masonic attacks on the Church, and proposed federal legislation that would imperil the parochial schools caused considerable consternation among Catholics. The committee requested an early reply so they would know how to act. The cable was signed by Hanna, Muldoon, Dowling, Schrembs, Walsh, Russell and Gibbons (of Albany).

On April 8th came the reply sent by Cardinal Gasparri: "Holy Father received telegram. Decree will not be published in *Acta*. Fuller information will shortly be given by apostolic delegate."

This reply gave the committee time to plan its case. Bishop Schrembs was deputed to journey to Rome to present the committee's case. Dr. James A. Ryan, head of the education department of NCWC was to act as his aid. Pope Benedict XV having died on January 22, 1922, Bishop Schrembs would present the *relatio* to Pius XI, elected on February 6, 1922. Schrembs scheduled his departure for April 25th. In the interim, Burke, Muldoon and Father Fenlon drew up the *relatio* and, having spent long days and nights on it, entrusted it to Archbishop Moeller who left the US after Schrembs' departure but would deliver the *relatio* to him on joining him in Rome. Moeller, however, was not a member of the administrative committee. The episcopal trustees of Catholic University on April 26th also prepared a petition[7] (April 26th) asking the Holy Father for a suspension of the decree until a full investigation could be made: they sent the petition to every American bishop, asking him to sign. The trustees who signed were Archbishops Glennon, Moeller, Mundelein, Shaw, Hayes, Curley and Bishops Lillis, Nilan, Shahan. Cardinal Dougherty absented himself at midday to keep an appointment with the apostolic delegate. Before leaving he said that he had been in Rome but that all he knew about the decree was that it had been handed to him before leaving by a subsecretary of the Consistorial Congregation who told him that the reason for the decree was that NCWC was not in accord with canon law. (Eventually eighty bishops signed the petition.)

On April 26th, after meeting with the Catholic University trustees, the administrative committee called on the apostolic delegate, Bonzano, to keep him abreast of developments. On that occasion he denied any role in the making of the decree. He said he had not been consulted and had written to the Holy See protesting the decree. The decree, at this time, prompted some amateur detective work and much speculation as to who was the culprit and "who got Rome into this mess?" Russell of Charleston, a member of the administrative committee, put the accusing finger on Cardinal De Lai of the Consistorial Congregation. Writing Muldoon (April 9th) Russell said he thought De Lai was "the master hand of the plot," a plot to get an accredited US diplomatic representative to the Vatican, and perhaps wind up with the apostolic delegate presiding at the meeting of the hierarchy. Next to this letter from Russell in the NCWC archives is a carbon of a letter from an unidentified correspondent (perhaps Russell) addressed "Dear Archbishop" and lamenting "Italian ecclesiastical politics" while asserting he would prefer persecution from honest but prejudiced Americans rather than Italian domination. Burke, at this time, did not hint at some American prelate's involvement in the suppression, as accomplice before the fact, nor did he venture a guess, but in a letter to Rev. Lantry O'Neill, CSP, at Rome (May 1, 1922) he said that some of the trouble arose from the fact that "at the last meeting of the hierarchy the bishops showed they were very unwilling to have as their head the Cardinal of Boston." Several of the bishops, however, suspected Cardinal O'Connell of having a hand in the suppression. Explaining that he had been out of the country for a few months and knew nothing about the situation, O'Connell wrote Muldoon (May 3rd) asking about reports that the "condemnation" had caused "consternation" among Catholics. On May 9th Dowling wrote Muldoon saying he was dubious about giving O'Connell a detailed answer to his "interrogations." Said Dowling, "You may be sure he will put an artful twist on whatever you say. . . ." But Muldoon did finally respond to O'Connell (May 22nd) stating that the first press reports spoke of a "condemnation" but that this was later corrected by Rome. Muldoon then went on to inform him in no uncertain terms that there was widespread consternation and bewilderment among Catholics that an organization blessed by Benedict XV should be dissolved without warning.

On May 9th Schrembs reported to Burke from Paris that Cardinal Cerretti "now knows all." (It was Cerretti who spoke as personal representative of Benedict XV at the golden jubilee of Cardinal Gibbons.) "Dougherty as well as O'Connell are at the bottom of affairs."[8] Cerretti was very sympathetic and his support so enthusiastic that Schrembs wrote, "I hope to be able to persuade him to go to Rome." Schrembs also added in this letter to Burke that Cerretti felt that Cardinal De Lai was the man who put the whole thing over and that the Holy Father really knew practically nothing about the matter. An undated letter from Burke to Muldoon quotes Fenlon who said he had a long talk with Bernardini, consultant to the papal delegate, in which Bernardini declared the decree was the work of "the two American cardinals" who had persuaded Cardinal De Lai who in turn persuaded other members of the Consistorial Congregation. The American cardinals, said Bernardini, had given the impression that there was a grave danger of schism in the US because of NCWC. Another letter from Burke to Muldoon (undated) had it that Dougherty told someone in the Welfare Center at Paris that he was hostile to NCWC and that it "would be killed in its youth." Then, in a handwritten note (May 10th), Burke informed Muldoon confidentially that he had succeeded in having President Harding send word to the Vatican, through the American ambassador, that he would be much displeased and disappointed if the NCWC were suppressed. "No one knows of this except Senator McCormack and he and I have pledged secrecy." (And no one in the NCWC office except Iona McNulty, Burke's secretary, was aware of it.)

Meanwhile Burke had been in touch with Schrembs in Rome. He wrote Schrembs, stressing the imperative need of NCWC as a means of protecting Catholic interests, asking him to emphasize this point and to get a special letter from the Holy See approving NCWC and urging American Catholics and Catholic organizations to support it. He insisted to Schrembs that he should not be content with a mere *tolerari potest*. In the letter (May 7th) he expressed his trust and confidence in Schrembs and ended the letter on a note of optimism about the outcome.

Shortly after his arrival in Rome after seeing Cerretti in Paris, Bishop Schrembs had his first audience with the Holy Father, an *ad limina* visit in which he requested a special audience to discuss the decree. He was thrilled to hear the Pope say, "Do you think I am a man who can be believed? If so, I tell you as the Holy Father that I did not know what the decree meant. . . . I promise you on my word as the pontiff that I have been deceived and that I shall carry out justice for the bishops of the United States. . . ."

Bishop Schrembs then began preparations for his coming audience with Pope Pius, attempting to inform and persuade as many Vatican personnel as possible. James H. Ryan (later rector of Catholic University) was his confidant and helper. Ryan wrote Burke a series of almost daily reports that were superb in their on-the-scene description of every significant development relating to the suppression. Possibly no other reporting of a major Vatican episode has ever been written with as much dash and go and interpretative commentary.

Ryan's first letter to Burke was dated May 25th. He tells how Bishop Hickey of Providence made a strong plea to the Pope, and also to De Lai who remained intransigent.

I saw O'Hern [rector of the American College]. He says all will be settled to the satisfaction of everybody. O'Hern belongs to the Del Val crowd. Everybody realizes a mistake has been made. . . . Bishop Turner [of Buffalo], I hear from Bishop Schrembs, has sold us out. He took a program to the Pope which he said the bishops would accept . . . I do not know where he got it nor who coached him unless it is a certain clique trying to get power. This clique, according to Pucci [Roman correspondent of the NCWC press department] is made up of Del Val, Van Rossum, De Lai and Pompili and are making war on Gasparri [secretary of state]. Bishop Schrembs will stand his ground, he says, and insist that the decree die a natural death. Tomorrow we will take our documents, books and pamphlets to Monsignor Pizzardo to hand to the Pope. Bishop Schrembs has written a letter which explains thoroughly that the 80 signatures [the signatures of the American bishops who signed the petition asking for withdrawal of the decree] represent 9/10 of the hierarchy. Bishop Schrembs will have his audience about Tuesday. . . . The opposition claims NCWC would destroy the autonomy of each bishop. It's the old stuff.

These dispatches from James Ryan are too lengthy to permit of verbatim reproduction here. The following synopses convey something of the spirit and movement of Ryan's reportage.

May 30th. Moeller has had an audience with the Pope at which Ryan was present. The Pope was very gracious. Moeller presented the *relatio* and the petition along with a letter from Schrembs. The Pope told Moeller of the need for NCWC, that the decree was all a misunderstanding and the affair would be settled satisfactorily. The papal delegate's letter has not arrived yet and the Pope will not do anything until it arrives. If the delegate has written to De Lai, perhaps it has been pigeon-holed. . . .

June 1st. The battle has begun in dead earnest. Moeller saw Cardinal Bisletti who said he knew nothing of the whole affair; Moeller told him the decree was all wrong and should be withdrawn. Next, Moeller saw Gasparri who claimed everything would be settled satisfactorily, without saying how. In the afternoon, Schrembs had an urgent summons to call on De Lai Friday at 9:30 A.M. Last evening, Moeller and Schrembs visited Cardinal Sbarri, member of the Consistorial Congregation. Apparently he had not seen the decree; there is no doubt that few if any of the Cardinals saw the decree before or after it was issued. Sbaretti complained of "certain secretaries speaking in the name of the hierarchy." Pucci, NCWC correspondent, came in with a "feeler" proposing meetings of the bishops "whenever necessary," which made Schrembs jump on him with both feet and almost scare him to death. The fine hand behind these compromises (according to Ryan) is that of Bishop Turner of Buffalo, very close to Gasparri. Schrembs says that if we are beaten, it will be due to Turner.

June 1st. Ryan went with Schrembs to the Consistorial Congregation: had an hour with Cardinal Sincero, the big gun of the Congregation. Schrembs was simply wonderful, inexpressibly so, explaining the copies of the *relatio* he was giving Sincero, the nature of the NCWC, etc. The secretary and Sostituto were called in, Schrembs met all objections, the usual about vast expenditures and laymen speaking for the hierarchy. Sincero deprecated the decree and said it would be retracted. Here was Sincero, the assessor, saying this and that NCWC would rise stronger than ever. "My name is Sincero and I am now sincere in this promise, not only in word but in fact." Ryan exults, "Isn't it glorious! They feel they have been sold by Boston and Philadelphia and they are now going to the other extreme." Gasparri is under Turner's influence, thinking annual meetings are not necessary, but he will not take a strong position and Turner will be left holding the bag. If Hickey, Schrembs and Moeller had come a week later, the whole cause would have been lost.

June 3rd. Hickey had a glorious audience with the Holy Father last night. He told Hickey to inform all the bishops he was blessing the NCWC. Schrembs saw De Lai this morning, came away crestfallen but not without hope. De Lai was like a rock of Gibraltar. Sincero was stunned by De Lai's attitude and promised to write a letter. Ryan and Moeller went along with Schrembs to see Turner at the American College. He has changed in the last few days. Whilst not enthusiastically for us, he is mildly so. . . .

June 5th. De Lai was a bear in his last interview, has convinced himself the NCWC is against canon law . . . O'Hern,

Turner and Sincero went on a week's outing at Monte Cattini, near Florence. We do not get the significance of this "outing". . . .

June 6th. Yesterday we saw Father Ledochowski, superior general of the Jesuits. Kind and helpful. He and Schrembs spoke in German. He told Schrembs not to get discouraged if things go slowly: he will say a good word for us if he gets the chance. He gave us an insight into the mental attitude of the Big Four, especially Del Val: "They still see Modernism in everything and are afraid of every movement." . . . Then we called on Cardinal Boggiani, Schrembs speaking in Latin, and the cardinal asked if McNicholas had signed. Schrembs triumphantly produced his signature to the document and the cardinal was much impressed. He had not attended the plenary session, had not seen the decree and knew nothing about it although he is a member of the Consistorial Congregation. Where does De Lai get that "plenary meeting" anyway?

June 9th. The battle goes on merrily with victory appearing in the future. . . . Rome does not like to be pushed, to be made to fight, and we have carried the fight to her, and put the issue up to her. Everybody, except De Lai, admits the justice of our cause but he is unalterably against us. But everybody wishes to save the face of the sacred congregation and they do not know how to do it and recall the decree. Every Cardinal with the exception of Del Val has been seen . . . It was evidently a one-man meeting and a one-man decree. In the afternoon, Schrembs had an engagement with Pizzardo, substitute of the secretary of state. He suggested an interpretative decree as a solution but Schrembs attacked furiously. Pizzardo said the honor of the sacred congregation must be safeguarded, to which Schrembs responded, "And how about the honor of the American hierarchy?" Schrembs then showed how not one cardinal had attended the so-called "plenary session" and he ended up with saying that the decree had as many lies as sentences. Schrembs said *mensonge* (lie) is not a diplomatic word

NEVER LOOK BACK

but it expresses what I mean. "You must save the honor of De Lai and what about the whole hierarchy of a great country?" Schrembs was livid, Pizzardo absolutely cowed. Then Pizzardo mentioned the Holy Father. "Do not mention his name in this matter" said Schrembs. "He was deceived. We love the Pope, we will do whatever he says, but his name must not be brought into this discussion." Pizzardo could see no way out except a new decree. Schrembs suggested a pontifical letter. Pizzardo jumped at the idea and asked Schrembs to sketch out a letter. He did, and Pizzardo will propose it as a possible solution. Schrembs made good use of the argument that the hierarchies of England, Ireland, Germany are allowed to meet. Why brand us as suspects? We trust in God but keep our powder dry. If we lose, it will be a defeat with honor.

June 11th. The ex-general of the Conventuals, Father Dominic, saw the Holy Father on Friday, brought up the matter of NCWC and the Pope stopped him and said he would find a satisfactory solution. He was nettled, no doubt fed up on the whole affair. We saw Pizzardo again yesterday. He saw the Pope and was told that the Consistorial must reopen the case, study it and hold a plenary session on June 22nd. De Lai is irreconcilable and will try to bring in an unfavorable report. Pizzardo insisted that Schrembs prove to the Cardinals that NCWC does not mean introduction of parliamentary methods into the government of the American Church. Here it is a fight against straw men, fears, misgivings, intangible nothings, shadows—that is what we must fight.

June 11th. (Sunday afternoon) At noon Schrembs and Ryan attended the Trinity dinner of the American College, Schrembs next to Cardinal Bisletti. He was much impressed by the fact that 80 American bishops signed.

June 12th. Schrembs called on Bisletti, who was very gracious. There is little doubt of the fact he will vote favorably at the plenary session on the 22nd. Next, Schrembs saw Cardinal

Pompili who asked, "Look me in the eye and tell me frankly why are the two American cardinals opposed?" Schrembs answered, "Eminence, I will reply with a question. Why is the majority of the bishops opposed to the two cardinals?" Pompili got the point. He will not oppose us, we feel. Pucci said today that if De Lai keeps up his obstructionist tactics, the Pope will surely ask for his dismissal. It looks very much like the fall of De Lai or the fall of the NCWC, with the odds in favor of NCWC.

June 13th. Schrembs saw De Lai. The latter suggested a compromise but Schrembs tore into him, asked why every other hierarchy could meet but not the Americans. Then De Lai let the cat out of the bag, "You have such a large country, so many bishops, the power of them, etc." There it is in a nutshell. Schrembs gave De Lai a piece of his mind and De Lai retracted and apologized. They are always talking about the autonomy of the single bishop. It's a smoke screen. What they mean is that it is easier to deal with one bishop than with a hierarchy. . . .

June 19th. The resume of arguments in favor of NCWC will be in the hands of each cardinal by Thursday, in time for study before the plenary session. Last night Schrembs had a private audience with the Pope. He did not give any explicit promises but kept saying, "Can't you read what is in my mind?" There is no doubt he is favorable but he must wait on the Consistorial Congregation. Schrembs told the Pope he could not wait all summer and the Pope promised an early answer. De Lai is not really against NCWC but he has been told it is a dangerous movement to destroy the hierarchy and erect in its place parliamentarianism. The Pope kept repeating, "Can't you read my mind?"

June 20th. Cardinal Sbaretti has a bomb to explode at the plenary session. Canon 250 of the Code says *coetus epis-*

coporum matters belong to the Congregation of the Council, therefore the consistorial decree is invalid. Schrembs saw Del Val: he was like ice at first but he warmed up and they parted like old schoolmates. He had been stuffed by Boston. Del Val will not be for us but he will not be violently against us either.

June 20th. (afternoon) Gasparri is with us. He has been charged by the Pope to tell the Consistorial Congregation that His Holiness wishes the NCWC to continue and will not support the decree of suppression. Yesterday we saw Cardinal Boggiani, the one man we feared after De Lai. He had a letter from Bishop McNicholas, *amicus devotissimus*, in which McNicholas praised the NCWC. Boggiani will be with us to the bitter end. Scapinelli still has some difficulties with NCWC but he will not support the decree. As it stands, only De Lai and Del Val can be said to be opposed but they see the decree cannot stand.

June 23rd. The old NCWC is still standing and its enemies retreating. It was a great day. Our friends fought for us valiantly. Monsignor Bernardini called in the morning with the good news that Gasparri had been to the Pope before going to the meeting. He brought to the meeting a message that the Holy Father would not accept the Consistorial Congregation's judgment if they approved the decree. At 1:30 P.M. Pizzardo's servant came to tell Bishop Schrembs the cause had won, and at 4 P.M. Bernardini confirmed the good news. Schrembs then called on Pizzardo who rushed into his private room, brought out a beautiful palm and gave it to Schrembs, the palm of victory. Then Schrembs called on Gasparri: the Congregation by a great majority had voted that there is no longer any decree and that instructions for the further conduct of the work are to be awaited from the Pope. Gasparri fired the first gun at the plenary session, saying that only fools refuse to admit error, that surely the Consistorial did not want to put itself in the same class with Pilate who wrote, "*Quod scripsi, scripsi.*" The

Holy Father will sign the document this afternoon: he was happy with the outcome. Cardinal Boggiani threw syllogisms at the eminent fathers and Cardinal Sbaretti gave a long speech, primed along the lines of the famous Canon 250. . . . The forthcoming Instructions will be prefaced by praise for the American bishops and their work. These Instructions will solidify the position of the NCWC and will express the hope that it shall become a model organization for the whole world.

June 25th. Everything is lovely. The victory is complete. Schrembs saw the Holy Father last night. The Pope told him he could publish the decision but that the NCWC should not crow over the victory. Our great trouble, said the Pope, was that no one knew of us here. He blessed the NCWC and Schrembs in a special way. He said the United States was the hope of the Church.

A newspaper clipping in the NCWC archives (NCWC dispatch but undated) tells of Schrembs' farewell to the Holy Father: "I wish I might take Your Holiness in an aeroplane to America." Pope Pius replied: "Ah I wish I could go. I love to travel. I like nothing better than to be in a small compartment on a train with two or three companions of the heart. I would enjoy seeing America. I have always longed to see it. I had made up my mind fully to go there but now that is all past. I shall never see it." His Holiness and the Bishop spoke in German. The Pope gave Schrembs this message for America:

I love America better than any other country. Especially do I love the youth of America for I know that the world must look for the solution of the problems which now affect the nations. The youth of America has a great responsibility, a great opportunity for service to the world and I send them my blessing and ask God's benediction upon them that they may be the better fitted for the great task that will be theirs to perform.

Bishop Schrembs was of course the stalwart protagonist who

gave the coup de grace to the De Lai faction's handiwork but others should not be overlooked. James Ryan was immensely helpful to Schrembs, and Ryan wrote that Bernardini was the direct cause of Gasparri taking the NCWC side with vigor. At the August 11-12, 1922, meeting in Chicago, the administrative committee approved letters of appreciation to Schrembs, Ryan, Fenlon and Burke. Bishop Gibbons of Albany praised Burke (June 27th) for "this great victory, won largely by your splendid effort." Muldoon (June 23rd) extolled Burke for the way he handled the whole affair and suggested: "If I was nearby I would induce you to violate the 18th amendment" (the reference being to the prohibition law). McGrath, head of the NCWC press department, said he realized what the victory meant to Burke: "The rest of us were only employees but you were the father of the child."

Father Burke however was still uneasy for weeks after the news of the revocation had been received: the Instructions had not yet arrived. He went to the Paulist general chapter in July but could not attend sessions due to a sudden illness. A contributing factor to his uneasiness was the news of a revival of bigotry in many quarters. *The World* (July 14th) announced formation of a society, headed by the president of the Baptist World Alliance, to fight "the Romanist evil." Described as the biggest movement since the days of Martin Luther, it aimed to compel every child to attend a public school and offered prompt information about raids on city or state treasuries by papal agents as well as information on "utterances against the 18th amendment or against any of our laws or institutions." A few months earlier, Burke had heard from Bishop Noll of a sudden proliferation of anti-Catholic groups, including a college in Georgia intended to enlighten Americans about Catholicism, ready to open with 2,000 students, thanks to the Klan.

According to an NCWC release (August 14th) the bishops finally received the text of the decree reinstating NCWC through Archbishop Bonzano, apostolic delegate. The decree itself was short:

In a plenary session held on the twenty-second day of the month of June, the Sacred Consistorial Congregation, acting on new data, has decided that nothing is to be changed concerning "The National Catholic Welfare Council"; and that, therefore, the bishops of the United States of North America may meet next September as is their custom, in accordance, however, with the instructions given below.

Given at Rome at the Office of the Sacred Consistorial Congregation on the twenty-second day of June, 1922.

> C. Card. De Lai, Bishop of Sabina
> Secretary
>
> A. Sincero,
> Assessor

The instructions, covering several pages, followed immediately after the text of the decree.[9] Among other points, they provided that the bishops should discuss whether or not their meetings should be held at longer intervals than once a year, that the meetings would have no legal force but were to be held as friendly conferences, that the participating bishops should be furnished beforehand with a summary of topics to be discussed. One item contained the suggestion that the bishops discuss the wisdom of choosing some other name for the Council. Obviously any name was acceptable provided it did not identify the NCWC with the hierarchy.

The restoration of NCWC seems to have evoked Cardinal O'Connell's ingenuity. On December 16th he wrote Hanna, chairman of the administrative committee, that he objected to the word "Council" in the NCWC title (the implication being that the word connoted a quasi-Council or threat to episcopal sovereignty). He contended that he had received a communication from the Holy See in which the Holy Father said he wanted the name changed to "Committee" rather than "Conference." Hanna replied adroitly that he was only too ready to honor the Pope's desire if His Eminence would let him have that part of the papal communication expressing the desire for "Committee."

At the January 12, 1933, meeting of the administrative committee, Hanna reported that he had not as yet received an answer from the Cardinal of Boston. The administrative committee then agreed to recall to the Cardinal's memory the decision of the bishops in regard to the change of name of the NCWC. Bishop F. T. Hurley, in the article on "National Catholic Welfare Conference" (*New Catholic Encyclopedia*, 1967) succinctly summarized the history of the organization's change of name. The administrative committee, through correspondence with the Holy Father (after receiving the Instructions relating to the decree restoring NCWC), clarified certain points about the nature of NCWC "but its name still left some lingering doubts." The Holy See, therefore, requested that the term "Council" be changed to "Conference."[10]

The identity of the bishops who actually opposed the continued existence of NCWC is not altogether certain but Schrembs, in an undated letter to Pope Pius XI, named seven: the two cardinals (Doherty and O'Connell), Archbishop Keane of Dubuque, Bishops Byrne, Rhode, Morris, and Walsh of Trenton. One bishop thought NCWC would never survive after the Instructions were received: this unnamed bishop wrote Dowling in August, "The NCWC is coming home to die in its bed rather than on the gallows." Dowling reported this to Burke but added a pinch of his own pessimism, "The ironed-out instructions are full of broken glass." The future was to prove him a poor prophet. In a short time, NCWC was back in full stride.

What was the basic reason for the opposition to NCWC in the United States?[11] Father Burke probably comes close to the heart of the matter in a letter he wrote to Archbishop Mitty of San Francisco, chairman of the committee of reorganization of NCWC (April 2, 1935). He focuses on the charge that it was a powerful bureaucracy destroying the sovereignty of bishops in their individual dioceses:

The old charge that the NCWC would be an *imperium in imperio* carries no longer any weight with anybody. It was the fear that the NCWC might take up ecclesiastial matters and be used as a preliminary to a plenary council, or take the place of a plenary council, that led some to oppose its establishment. And I think it is always well to bear that fear in mind.

He then shows how totally voluntary the NCWC actually is. No bishop is bound by its rulings: a bishop may even vote at a general meeting in favor of a measure, yet oppose it in his own diocese. Some bishops have asked that the administrative committee bring in "conclusions" to the general meetings of the bishops but Burke says this practice would tend to make the bishops' meetings a cut-and-dried affair, diminishing the voluntary nature of the discussions. The administrative committee's practice has been, on the contrary, to propose subjects of discussion rather than "conclusions," thus giving the bishops a free hand. It was precisely because of his deep respect for the conscience of every man that Burke refused to coerce the conscience of any man.

chapter 5

The golden twenties

The decade of the 1920s was a busy, challenging era for Father Burke and the NCWC. It was an era of unprecedented prosperity, an era of neurotic anti-Communism, a tumultuous Jazz Age in which many old moral rules went by the board but American life and habits became standardized. Burke's major accomplishment, as peacemaker in Mexico, occurred toward the end of the era and will be detailed in chapters six and seven. In this chapter, some of his responsibilities will be described. He worked hard to block federal control of education, playing an important role in the Oregon Case of 1925. The scope of his concerns was vast: his reports to the administrative committee touched on Russian relief work, the Church and the American Occupation administration in the Caribbean, the Volstead Act, the peace movement, the rise of the Nazis, Philippine independence.

Bishop Schrembs, at a meeting of the administrative committee on September 25, 1922, gave a jubilant account of his triumph at Rome. The mood of the meeting was one of soaring optimism. The NCWC seemed to have clear sailing ahead: Rome had vindicated and blessed the aims and purposes of the organization. Michael Williams, however, saw clouds on the horizon. Williams, who founded *Commonweal* in 1924, wrote Burke on September 20, 1922, that certain critics regarded NCWC as a bureaucratic colossus grasping for a monopoly of ecclesiastical power. This was a familiar cry but Burke valued Williams' judgment and Burke himself had been worried by the threat of expanding bureaucracy in the federal government. In fact, he had released to the press in January his own statement on creeping bureaucracy in federal government which might eventually "sovietize our form of government." Williams claimed that certain Catholics saw in NCWC a reflection of this burgeoning federal regimentation.

This fear of federal control was undoubtedly due in part to the anti-Bolshevik hysteria of the time. The "red scare" of 1919 had not entirely disappeared: there was less talk of "madmen" and "assassins" but more concern about the growing arrogance of Communist Party officials, vowed to the extermination of all religion. Paradoxically, the NCWC, suspected of arrogating more and more power to itself, was now confronting problems arising from the Communist threat, e.g., the morality of recognizing "red Russia," the relief of starving Russian peasants, the task of coping with the all-out war on religion.

At the August 11, 1922, administrative committee meeting at Sherman House, Chicago, Burke reported the appointment of Father Edmund Walsh, S.J., as representative of NCWC, Russian Relief. The appointment of Walsh as papal representative in Russia for relief work was made apparently by Pope Pius XI and approved by the Jesuit superior general. Entering Russia on March 22, 1922, he crisscrossed the country for eighteen months to help relieve the misery caused by war and the revolutionary upheaval. In the foreword to his *Fall of the Russian Empire*, written some years later, Walsh said that the Russian people in 1922 faced the worst famine in their long and sad history, twenty-three millions on the verge of starvation, of whom six millions perished despite the best efforts of the combined relief agencies.

The colorful Father Walsh injected a somewhat theatrical note into his frequent, cryptic, secret-agent communications to Burke. Writing from Rome before entering Russia, he said, "I have now seen Cardinal Gasparri and yesterday Pius XI but I would wish that you say nothing of these matters only that I have been nominated by you as 'representative of NCWC for Russian Relief'." The message was in Latin, the date March 10, 1922. On March 27th he wrote Burke from Moscow claiming all other relief organizations were on the scene except the Roman Catholic. "Please mention to no one my being authorized to act for Holy Father. We are not ready for that yet. I am here now solely on the American Committee representing the National Catholic Welfare Council." (He underlined the first sentence.) On April 12th Burke wrote Walsh that he had just received word that the NCWC must go out of existence. If it should go out of existence, said Burke, the Hoover Relief Administration would have to recall Father Walsh at once and terminate his official status as NCWC representative on the American Committee.

Walsh wrote Burke (April 23, 1922) from Moscow that the purpose of the whole Communist movement was the gradual extinction of all religion. "I believe it would be a service to humanity if the US hierarchy would come out in a ringing statement to that effect." He went on to say that he had begged the Vatican to permit him to voice the answer of the American clergy right here in Moscow, in their teeth, cost what may, but he had not yet received the necessary approbation. It would seem that Burke, fed up as he was with the secrecy and subterfuges of the Consistorial Congregation, would cast a cool look at this furtive correspondence but he did not tip his hand about his reaction. Possibly the administrative committee was suspicious. They instructed Burke, at their April 27th meeting, not to make any public announcement that the Pope wanted NCWC to be a central office of information and literature for the proposed collection for papal relief in Russia, which collection the Holy See was allegedly planning to have taken up in every diocese.

Walsh was in Rome when he wrote a letter to Father Burke[1] on July 5, 1922, saying that he saw Cardinal Gasparri on June 29th and was informed that the decree of suppression had been withdrawn and that the NCWC might function as publicity agent for the Pope's appeal. So Walsh told Burke to go ahead with organizing the program for Russian Relief. The papal appeal itself was to be sent in a week or so—to the apostolic delegate. Hoover ought to be consulted in order to assure unity of action but "our program will not necessarily be governed,"

Walsh said, by the wishes of Hoover, Bonzano or the ordinaries. He said that he had his final conference with the Pope, June 30th, showed him the "poster" and again the Pope gave full authority for NCWC to act as publicity agent and coordinating organization in the campaign. He instructed Burke regarding the "poster": (1) that the Pope be not shown as holding out his hand to America; (2) let one hand be holding back the four horsemen of the apocalypse and the other protecting the Russian men, women and children in the background; (3) that it be clear that the Pope is interested in the Russian people, not the Government.

Walsh wrote again from Moscow (October 30, 1922) about a Dr. Farrell and a Dr. Breen who would get in touch with Burke in the States before going to Russia as Walsh's assistants. Walsh added that he had been in a railroad wreck and that the American Relief man, Shields, had been found with three bullets in his back, his body hidden under a pile of stones. Burke responded (November 29th) that Breen and Farrell had arrived, that he had helped them obtain passports and assigned them as assistants to Walsh on the NCWC staff. In the meantime Burke received a cable from Walsh asking him to hold Breen, which Burke did, but Farrell had already sailed.

On June 7, 1923, Father Walsh sent a French and an English account of the trial of Archbishop Jan Cieplak, requesting Burke to let him know "in a guarded way" if he received them and suggesting that he refer to them as "those interesting English and French documents regarding the Russian Easter celebration." He had visited the archbishop twice in prison, being allowed to see him about once every two weeks. Walsh concluded his letter by asserting "it is high time Soviet propaganda should be fought in the US." His last note in the NCWC files (June 14, 1923) said, ". . . my housekeeper was arrested a few days ago and is now in some unknown hole of the Cheka." His final challenge was that the time had come "to silence those pinks in the USA."

Archbishop Hanna, Bishop Muldoon and Father Burke

called (April 12th) on President Harding to thank him for his services in the State Department in protesting against the execution of Catholic prelates in Russia. A few months earlier, Burke had visited Harding on a very different errand. In a letter to Muldoon, Burke said there was a vacancy on the Supreme Court, Joseph McKenna being therefore the only Catholic on the high court bench. "I took up the matter with the president. He promised to appoint a Catholic to succeed Justice Pitney . . ." Before the year was out, Harding did appoint Pierce Butler. (One wonders how Burke felt about helping an ultraconservative to the Supreme Court.) Chancellor Joseph Dineen of the New York archdiocese had written Burke on September 11, 1922, that Archbishop Hayes was interested in the candidacy of Martin Manton of Brooklyn for the Supreme Court. "Anything that you may be able to do in his behalf will be much appreciated by the archbishop." (A note in the NCWC archives, not in Burke's handwriting, says that Manton's name was mentioned in Burke's interview with Harding [October 18, 1922] but Harding intimated he would not appoint him.)

After the bishops' annual meeting on September 27, 1923, the administrative committee held a meeting in which they made a resolution that seems to have been inspired by Burke. They approved the plan of establishing a Catholic daily newspaper in New York or Washington and recommended that it be kept before the Catholic mind and public opinion for realization as soon as conditions permit. This was a familiar dream to Burke: Father Hecker had started to collect money to buy one of the big New York dailies but the project died when he became ill. And Burke's friend, Michael Williams, in his September 20, 1922, letter to Burke had urged the publication of Catholic dailies "like the Christian Science Monitor." After this meeting, the administrative committee and Burke visited the White House at President Coolidge's request. Burke seems to have been on friendly terms with Harding, Coolidge and Franklin D. Roosevelt. There was a cool formality about his relations with Herbert Hoover and Woodrow Wilson; he felt Wilson had let Ireland down after the First World War. Cardinal Hayes of New York admitted his feelings about Wilson in a letter to Burke (February 19, 1924): "Thank you very much for your word about the statement I issued on the death of the late President Wilson. I must confess that I found it very difficult to write it. He certainly was not sympathetic to us."

The intense concern about the growing bureaucracy in federal government manifested by Father Burke in 1922 focused very largely on his fear of federal control of education. In the early months of 1924 however he felt more confident about the defeat of bills that might lead to federal monopoly of education. On February 9th he wrote hopefully to Archbishop Hanna about the demise of the Sterling-Reed Bill. Then he began to fix his attention more intensely on the current immigration bill which would radically reduce quotas for Southeast European countries, Italy's quota facing a potential drop from 40,000 to 3,800. During the following year, Admiral Yamamoto,[2] a leading Catholic Japanese, requested help in killing the bill excluding the Japanese. Yamamoto feared that Japanese mobs would attack Catholic institutions if nothing were said by Catholic Church officials in Washington about the bill. The apostolic delegate recommended that Burke convey merely a statement on international friendship, not on the merits of the bill, in responding to Yamamoto.

In the course of a letter to Muldoon in 1924 Burke made some interesting distinctions about bigotry in the House and the Senate.

Significant and universal is the great respect in which the Church is held. Yet hand-in-hand with this goes a feeling and at times a deep-seated conviction that the Church does not work with, or works against the country. With the respect there is fear: and of the fear is born suspicion. In other cases, the opposition is not born of conviction but is expressed and registered as a matter of political expediency. It may sound paradoxical but it is true that the anti-Catholic feeling was never so

NEVER LOOK BACK

extended, and yet it has been far more deep and more dangerous.

Precisely because of this latent suspicion of Catholicism, an interview with Cardinal O'Connell published in the Boston *Herald* was potential dynamite. In the interview, O'Connell said that he had been named papal legate for the first national Holy Name Society convention held in Washington in September 1924 and had been received as papal legate by the authorities at Washington. ". . . it is to be remembered that the Pope is still acknowledged by all the European powers as a royal sovereign, quite apart from his spiritual character as pontiff." Justin McGrath, head of the NCWC press department, reflected liberal Catholic reaction when he wrote irately to Burke (October 18, 1924) that O'Connell had implied that the Vatican was a political as well as spiritual sovereignty. On October 24th, McGrath brought the interview up again for discussion, contrasting O'Connell, who claimed the right to be received as "a prince of the blood" with Carroll, the first American bishop, who strenuously objected to dependence on Rome in the matter of appointment of a superior because he felt it might expose the Catholic Church in America "to the reproach of encouraging a dependence on a foreign power."

Archbishop Dowling of St. Paul, on a trip to Rome in February 1924 investigated certain rumors to the effect that the Vatican had changed its attitude toward NCWC since its restoration but, Gasparri assured him, "there was absolutely nothing against the NCWC." Dowling also asked De Lai, who had masterminded the dissolution in 1922. He grinned and commented, "They do good." Burke apparently reported this to Schrembs who replied, "I am especially pleased that the old grizzly bear, De Lai, is satisfied at last that we have no sinister intentions of destroying the Church or becoming popes."

Rome also occupied some of Father Burke's attention in regard to the acquisition of the church of Santa Susanna as "the church for the Americans" in Rome. On March 21, 1921,

Burke wrote to Muldoon that Gasparri had been helpful to the Paulists in their endeavor to acquire possession of the church and "the Holy Father had approved everything." Paulist possession of the church was held up temporarily by litigation because it was the cardinal church of the Archbishop of Bologna but the understanding was that, as soon as the litigation was settled, Gasparri would request the archbishop to ask the Paulists to take title. At the end of the letter to Muldoon, Burke added, "So it might be well for me to give up the Welfare Council work and go to take charge of this church in Rome but as I don't know Italian this is very unlikely." This undoubtedly was only an expression of Burke's old yearning for pastoral work. Muldoon, his confidant, knew well what aspirations lay dormant in his friend's mind and heart.

The Paulists provided religious services from this time on at Santa Susanna's but it took several years and persistent urging before they received legal and canonical title. Father Joseph McSorley, vicar general of the Paulists, wrote Burke on August 9, 1924: Rumania was at the time drawing up a concordat with the Holy See and wanted possession of Santa Susanna's incorporated into the agreement. A Roman cardinal (Gasparri?) suggested that prominent Americans might be helpful to the Paulist cause if they would endorse the Paulists. McSorley asked Burke to sound out the apostolic delegate for suggestions, and Father Thomas Burke, John's brother and superior general of the Paulists, indicated that a friendly word from the US Government might help. Burke, therefore, went to see Secretary of State Charles Evans Hughes but Hughes said that the Government would not interfere in religious matters at home or abroad, having already done all it could when President Harding, at Burke's request in the matter, recommended the community highly. Burke explained to Hughes that he had no intention of asking him to do anything out of line with his duties as Secretary of State, whereupon Hughes said that Mr. Child, American ambassador to Rome, was on his way back to the United States and that he, Hughes, might speak to Mr.

Child in a personal and private way. Hughes did follow it up. On March 25, 1927, Burke wrote a memo to the effect that he had been chatting that afternoon with F. M. Gunther, head of the Mexican division of the State Department, who had been in Rome and knew the Paulists. He told Burke, "Why, certainly I knew them: it was through the efforts of Mr. Child and myself that the church of Santa Susanna was saved permanently to the Paulists and not taken over by the Rumanians." Burke added in his memo that Gunther's spontaneous recollections "revealed what effective work Mr. Hughes did in the matter."

Another item pertaining to Paulist community affairs came up in a letter sent by Father McSorley to Burke on September 9, 1924. McSorley reported that at the last community chapter, the sentiment of the delegates favored the custom of Paulists living together in community. Would it be practicable, therefore, if Father Burke were to live with either of the two Paulist communities in Washington, that at St. Paul's College or the community at Mission House? Burke responded that he had been sensitive to the dangers that living apart from the community might mean in the way of his love, fidelity and loyalty to the community but he could conscientiously say that none of these fears had materialized. "And as proof of this, I place myself unreservedly under the will of the community as expressed by yourself, whatever that will may be." (He had been living for some years at 2405 20th Street, N.W., Washington, D.C., not far from his office, along with several other priests.)

He explained to Father McSorley that moving to a Paulist house would adversely affect the work of NCWC and his work as general secretary. In that work, he personally represented the administrative committee, which in turn represented the hierarchy. Were he to live in a Paulist house, he would be thought of as doing work for his community rather than for the Church in general, the representative character of his office being obscured thereby. Three priests, he said, now lived together at the staff house on 20th Street and bishops were accustomed to stop there on visits to Washington, the house being only a block away from the apostolic delegation. The delegate did not hesitate to call Burke from time to time, asking him to drop into the delegation to see him about important matters, which would not happen if Burke were not in the vicinity. Oftentimes dignitaries, according to Burke, came to his home for conferences, likewise other persons who could not come to the office. It would be inappropriate to ask them to go out to St. Paul's College, for instance, as conferences with the staff were frequently necessary. Burke concluded by adding that his work included the spiritual care of the Social Service School next door with its schedule of daily Mass, courses in Christian doctrine, confessions and conducting the yearly retreat.

Father McSorley responded on September 18th in a very cordial note expressing concern about Father Burke's health and stating: "There is no disposition on the part of the Council to do anything that would limit your usefulness in the position you now hold."

The Oregon School Case decision was the great event that overshadowed every other item in NCWC history in 1925. In the case, *Pierce v. the Society of Sisters*, the NCWC and Father Burke personally scored a magnificent victory: it was to Catholic education what the 1954 desegregation decision of the US Supreme Court was to civil rights. The Court ruled unanimously that the parent is the primary educator, striking down as unconstitutional an Oregon law that made attendance at public schools mandatory for children. This law had been conceived and promoted by the Scottish-rite Masons of Oregon and was vigorously supported by the Ku Klux Klan.

The NCWC administrative committee, along with other bishops, certain educators and lawyers, met at Chicago on January 11, 1923, to plan a campaign for the invalidation of the Oregon law because similar legislation was pending in several other states; they resolved to make this a test case. The first step was to solicit $100,000 from the bishops of the country to publish pamphlets dealing with the rights of parents under the Constitution. The federal district court upheld the

Oregon law but Governor Pierce appealed to the US Supreme Court. The noted William Guthrie, aided by a stellar array of counsel, contended that the law was unconstitutional. On June 1, 1925, the unanimous court ruled against the law: "The child is not the mere creature of the state: those who nurture him and direct his destiny have the right coupled with the high duty, to recognize and prepare him for additional obligations." It is doubtful that any words in any other high court decision have been quoted as frequently as these. Pope Pius XI in his *Christian Education of Youth* lauded the decision and the UN's *Declaration of Human Rights* (article 26) reflects the influence of this historic opinion. Pope Pius had followed the case closely. When Father Burke had an audience with him in 1929, the Pope brought up the Oregon case in conversation. Burke remarked that the Supreme Court had handed down a unanimous decision, "which practically makes it a part of the organic law of the United States." And when Burke said he had worked for two years to defeat the law, the Pope said, "I know you did."

At the previous administrative committee meeting on September 22, 1924, Burke was given permission for a vacation, his doctors and religious superiors having ordered him to rest and having advised him to travel, appointing James Ryan to act as general secretary in his absence. In reading his report to the committee on April 22, 1925, in relation to developments in the Oregon School Case, one wonders what happened to the vacation, so well-informed was the report. He traveled to Puerto Rico, San Domingo, Haiti and Cuba but he seems to have been busier than ever in his dealings with government officials and bishops in these areas. He found in Puerto Rico only one priest per 18,000 souls but a good clergy and a governor sympathetic to the Church; in Haiti, although clergy and teachers were miserably paid the Breton priests were zealous despite the people's tendency to voodooism; in Cuba, no parochial schools, cohabitation without marriage prevalent, little religious instruction and less priestly zeal. In San Domingo also the conditions were bad. One of the by-products of the visit to Haiti was that he was selected to discuss with the US State Department a problem relating to Haiti's concordat with the Holy See. Gasparri and the Holy Father as well as the Haitian bishops had all agreed that Burke was the right man for this task.

After lunch on April 22nd, the committee received Admiral Benson, Mr. Denechaud and Mr. Dolle of the National Council of Catholic Men. Benson said the condition of the organization was critical but he was receiving no help from the hierarchy that created it. He asked for help or permission to let the organization die but later submitted suggestions for improving its situation, focusing on keeping the parish unit as the goal, thus allaying the fears of national Catholic organizations. Benson saw a great missionary work awaiting the Church in America. "Millions of Negroes could, with proper planning and zeal, be brought into the Church."

The independence of the Philippines was an extremely controversial topic at this time, a topic of special interest to Catholics because it was a predominantly Catholic country. A bishop from the Philippines, Bishop McCloskey of Jaco, had assured Burke that independence would mean that the American bishops would be driven out and the Church taken over by native clergy but Senator Osmena of the Philippine Senate, at a meeting of the administrative committee, asserted that the desire for independence was universal among Filipinos, clerical as well as lay, and that any action by the hierarchy that might be interpreted as hostile to independence would do the gravest injury to the Catholic Church in the islands. He asked that the hierarchy take no action in the matter. At an administrative committee meeting on September 14, 1925, Burke sounded out the members as to their reaction but they decided they would prefer not to make a statement at that time though they sympathized with the movement for independence.

So too with the question of the Volstead Act banning alcoholic beverages: the committee refused to make any statement regarding the enforcement of the law. Burke had encountered unbelievable difficulties in trying to arrange with the Government an exemption from the prohibition law whereby priests could obtain wine for Mass. Finally in 1926 he did succeed, through a new federal regulation requiring priests to file a special form 1412. The administrative committee's reluctance to approve enforcement of the law was undoubtedly influenced by the uncertainty of John A. Ryan of the NCWC social action department, the leading moral theologian of the time.[3] In April 1925 he published an article in *The Catholic World* stating that if the Volstead Act was more breached than observed, the duty to obey it lost force. The next month he published another article on the topic claiming that manufacture, possession and transportation of liquor for private use were lawful but that sale of liquor was morally wrong, (*The Catholic World*, May 1925). Two years later, Ryan had changed his views on "the noble experiment." His studied conclusion after watching the almost total failure of enforcement was that this failure was so dismal as to warrant a reasonable man in holding that the Eighteenth Amendment was an unnecessary, unwise and unjust enactment.

At their annual meeting in September 1925 the American bishops had decided "to make no propaganda" against new education bills unless some grave situation might demand that they take strong action. In mid-December, Burke saw Father Wilfrid Parsons and Father Paul Blakely of *America*, informing them that there was no need to be overzealous about any education bill and that advocacy of federalization of education had been steadily losing ground. Then just before Christmas, Burke visited Archbishop Curley in Baltimore. The sturdy defender of all that is good and holy told Burke that he had written a strong article condemning Father John A. O'Brien, advocate of Newman Clubs at secular universities, and that he was also preparing to attack the Curtis-Reed education bill. Burke reminded Curley of the decision of the bishops the previous September directing NCWC not to agitate for or against such bills but to watch and wait: the archbishop, on the contrary, told Burke that it was the mind of the bishops that Catholics should be positively opposed to such bills. When Burke told him that President Coolidge, only a week before, had informed him that no new education bill would pass the present session of Congress, Curley changed his mind and promised he would make no public pronouncement on education bills.

Curley was not the only Catholic leader who objected to the new strategy of toning down opposition to new education bills because they were already losing ground. In its January 2, 1926, issue the magazine *America* attacked the Illinois University Foundation and, in an editorial entitled "An Alarm and a Warning," the editor said that certain "guardians of our Catholic interests" were possibly betraying the Church. Bernardini at the apostolic delegation told Burke he felt the editorial had the NCWC in mind. So Burke sent a special delivery letter to Father Parsons, the editor, asking him to publish an admission of his error—if NCWC was meant.

Burke speculated that *America* was making a concerted drive against the attendance of Catholics at state universities and linking it up to a parallel drive against any and all bills favoring federalization of education. In assailing the Illinois University Foundation, thought Burke, *America* was really striking at Father John A. O'Brien, Catholic chaplain at the university, who was suspected of encouraging Catholic students to attend secular universities. Moreover, Father O'Brien and the Knights of Columbus were collecting one million dollars for a Catholic foundation at a secular university. Some Catholics at the time felt that this diverted Catholics from their primary duty, the support of Catholic education.

Burke wrote on January 2nd to Muldoon asking him if he, Burke, should write a protest to the Jesuit Father Provincial, if no satisfactory reply came from Parsons. The response from the Jesuit editor was rather evasive but Burke apparently dropped the matter at that point, perhaps with the crushing defeat of the Curtis-Reed Bill in February. The NCWC summoned expert talent from all classes, creeds and professions in opposition to the bill, the administrative committee having decided on a tactic of active opposition to the bill. Burke's opinion was that the presentation was so effective that it would set back federal education for years to come. Burke wrote Muldoon (February 26th) that Father Parsons was at the hearing, "as conspicuous as a nervous hen. . . . probably *America* will have led the fight single-handed."

On September 12, 1926, Father Burke had a memorable interview with Cardinal O'Connell at the Oblate House, Catholic University: the Cardinal was in Washington for the annual bishops' meeting. The conversation ranged over a wide variety of topics but Burke never did discover why the Cardinal had called him for this discussion. The first topic, after O'Connell's comments on a book on the Western Schism which he had been reading, touched on the Phipps Bill. What had Burke done about it? The Cardinal had heard rumors that Burke had "sold out" on the education question, yielding ground to forces working for federal control of education. Burke informed O'Connell that Archbishop Dowling, head of the department of education, NCWC, had approved the Phipps Bill as a lesser evil than the Curtis-Reed Bill. His Eminence asked how this fact had been publicized, and Burke replied that it had been published in the Catholic press. The administrative committee, moreover, had approved Dowling's action.

In his memo of this September 12 meeting, Burke tried to report the conversation objectively but one could read between the lines what was on his mind. The cardinal passed from the Phipps Bill to His Eminence's views on two schools of thought among American Catholics: those educated in America and those educated in Rome. "To know the Catholic Church and to have those Catholic traditions that enable one to keep the faith intact, one must have been in Rome: have had international experience." Dowling was a good man but his zeal, lacking the solid traditions of Catholic practice and positions, led him and men like him to surrender unknowingly on matters of principle.

They were brought up in America and had a minority complex, unknown to themselves. Then the cardinal recalled Leo XIII's *Testem Benevolentiae* (the condemnation of "Americanism"). Anyone reading Hecker, Ireland or Gibbons in 1926 would have to admit they didn't know the fine distinctions of Catholic teaching. Burke apparently sat impassive but patient. "America is a Protestant country" continued His Eminence, "expressive of Protestant traditions, not Catholic." Therefore the Catholic must always suspect the Government, be on his guard, aware that anyone looked upon with favor by government officials is *ipso facto* suspect. "There are certain principles on which Rome never yields" and while she sometimes seems cruel in condemning individuals, she is really kind in protecting principles. In the course of the discussion, Father Burke happened to mention that the Paulists suffered from the inroads of Modernism, to which O'Connell responded that they did not receive Roman training.

The conversation returned to the Phipps Bill, that one could not accept the Phipps Bill in order to defeat the Curtis-Reed Bill since it was never allowable to accept a lesser evil in order to avoid a greater evil, the evil of surrendering a Catholic principle. His Eminence then turned to the Mexican question. "What was there we could do? We could intervene or use physical force." As for the exiled apostolic delegate, Caruana, he should have worn his Roman collar. (Archbishop Caruana had entered Mexico in secular dress.)

After lunch, O'Connell got on the education question again, touching on the need to hold to principle. As for NCWC, that was just a committee of bishops and wouldn't last: nothing like that ever lasted. The Catholic Church is organized, why get up another organization? The NCWC was a work of supererogation, dangerous unless properly directed. Its agents went far beyond their authority. For example, John A. Ryan actively supported the child labor amendment, delivering a talk in favor of it when he knew that His Eminence was opposed to it. "His arguments reached Massachusetts. What the devil right has he anyway to favor the child welfare amendment and drag in the name of NCWC? He might speak as a Catholic University professor. That would be bad enough." (Burke notes here in his memo that the cardinal earlier had frowned upon the idea of having a Catholic university at the capital of the nation, a situation likely to make the university subservient to government authority and influence, according to His Eminence.)

Then the cardinal stated that his own representative, Mrs. Slattery, had been flagrantly insulted by Burke or by Bishop Schrembs and particularly by Miss Regan. When Father Burke asked His Eminence when it was that he had insulted Mrs. Slattery, the cardinal could not cite details. Agnes Regan, mentioned by the cardinal, was executive secretary of the NCCW. As the interview ended, the cardinal's parting salvo was: "Father Burke, no government has ever used a priest without squeezing him dry as a lemon and then throwing him out. Goodbye, Father John, come and see me in Boston."

Archbishop Curley continued to make headlines in the latter part of 1926. He had begun his blasts against the American Government (cf. chapter 6) in February and had kept up his campaign in the following months by supporting various congressional proposals and protest meetings designed to bring about some positive action by the State Department as regards Mexican Catholics. His talks embarrassed the NCWC and Father Burke because the severance of American diplomatic relations with Mexico, one of Curley's aims, might easily involve the United States in a war with Mexico. His inflammatory speeches were also embarrassing to Burke because he feared the State Department would think he was behind Curley's agitation and criticism whereas Burke was vehemently opposed to any American Catholic protest meetings; nine Mexican bishops had served notice that such meetings would only injure the Catholic Church in Mexico. An added concern for Burke was that Curley had consulted the apostolic delegate before launching his February attack on the American Government, and Burke began to wonder if the Vatican was supporting a policy of belligerent intervention.

In November, the loquacious prelate trained his oratorical guns on the NCCM and the NCCW in a talk to the Catholic Alumnae of Maryland. Walter Johnson, head of NCCM, wrote Burke lamenting the archbishop's well-publicized tirade in view of the fact that "the lack of success in his own diocese is due primarily to his own indifference and lack of recognition and support. If the archbishop would give the NCCM and NCCW the same support constructively as he has all the time rendered in passive tolerance or direct opposition it now seems we might easily have accomplished similar work in Baltimore to what has been done in Cincinnati, Cleveland etc." (November 7, 1926). Burke replied to Johnson that the criticism as published in the Baltimore *Review* was inaccurate and unfair to NCCM and NCCW leaders, and he praised Johnson for the manner in which he met the criticism. Bishop Schrembs summed up the whole episode succinctly in a letter to Cardinal Sincero, assessor of the Consistorial Congregation at Rome:

Unfortunately His Grace, the Archbishop of Baltimore, has lately grown displeased with the central office of the National Catholic Welfare Conference because we did not support him in his vitriolic attacks upon the President and the Government of the United States in the conduct of the Mexican policy. He blamed Father Burke, our general executive secretary, with assuming to dictate the policy of the Catholic Church in America and when he was told at the meeting of the bishops that, as a matter of fact, Father Burke had acted only on the unanimous advice of the seven bishops of the advisory board, he came to the conclusion that the National Catholic Welfare Conference is a failure and there is scarcely a week passes by without some bitter attack upon us in his diocesan paper. These things are unfortunate because there was never a time when we needed a unity of head and heart more than today. . . . It is very easy for men sitting in their rooms without full knowledge of complications to criticize and to attack but it is quite another thing to bear the responsibility for the tremendous evil consequences that are bound to come from ill-advised and inconsiderate action. (March 25, 1927)

Some months earlier, Schrembs had written Burke about the incongruity of criticism of NCWC by the Baltimore *Review*, a paper fed by the NCWC news service. In a postscript, Schrembs added: "I believe you ought to go to the archbishop yourself, making up your mind not to lose patience or your temper no matter what he says. The cause is bigger than we are. So, try in God's name." Burke responded, December 2, 1926: "With regard to the Baltimore *Review* articles, I do not think a visit from me to Archbishop Curley would be in order."

In March 1927 a colossal tempest in a teapot arose over a simple prayer alleged to be heretical according to the mind-set of that non-ecumenical time. In the first week of March, the NCWC news service sent out a news item about a dinner addressed by Father John A. O'Brien and a prayer he was said to have composed in cooperation with a Protestant minister and rabbi. Burke was called in by the apostolic delegate. Marella, an assistant to the delegate, at first said the news service had no right to publish the dispatch containing the prayer. Burke defended the news service's right to publish: it was a piece of news and McGrath, as head of the press, had simply used his prudential judgment. Monsignor Marella seemed to accept Burke's position but the delegate was extremely critical of O'Brien. Then Marella seemed to backtrack and said that O'Brien, as a member of the executive board of the department of education, NCWC, enjoyed a certain prestige and should publicly retract the prayer. The Church was extremely sensitive about heresy, according to Marella, and if a member of an organization were suspected of heresy, all other members of the organization would be suspect. Archbishop Dowling, chairman of the education department wrote Burke (March 22nd): "It is open season for heresy hunting and I feel that O'Brien is not the one the Inquisitors are after." He failed to specify whom they were after but he did say he thought O'Brien was indiscreet. To which Father Burke responded, April 7th, that Archbishop Curley had publicly denounced O'Brien as a heretic but that, "Yesterday Father O'Brien had sent a complete answer repudiating the charges of Archbishop Curley." The administrative committee felt that McGrath had made a mistake in sending out the prayer but Burke tended to agree with McGrath's contention that if editors felt the news service was censored, they would distrust it.

In retrospect, the whole episode seems amusing, though it was not amusing to Father O'Brien in his role as trailblazer for Vatican II. The prayer itself was quite innocuous. The questionable part seemed to be the sentence, "Open our eyes to see that as nature abounds in variations, so differences in human beings make for richness in the common life." This was thought to smack of indifference, if not heresy. Father Burke felt that McGrath had simply published an item of news but even he was of the opinion that a priest should be around to make sure no objectionable news appeared; he told the administrative committee that the news service would not print, for instance, the fact that a priest had left the Church. *Tempora mutantur*.

Archbishop Dowling, unfortunately, asked for and received O'Brien's resignation from the department of education, NCWC. There was apparently a prevalent notion, derived from Archbishop Curley's diatribes against O'Brien, that the Newman chaplain at University of Illinois was trying to dismantle the whole Catholic school system whereas O'Brien was simply trying to provide spiritual facilities for Catholics attending secular universities. It was due to this misunderstanding that Curley had described him as a heretic.

Moreover, he did not collaborate in composing the prayer but simply approved its use in Protestant churches—and for a very good reason. The peace of the local Illinois community had been disturbed by the anti-Catholic tirades of a Helen Jackson, an alleged ex-nun, who had packed the local theater every night on her recent visit, pouring out inflammatory abuse against nuns, priests and the Catholic Church. Father O'Brien tried to have the talks stopped but the Ku Klux Klan owned the theater, and fiery crosses were burned before the Catholic churches in the community. A Methodist minister decided to get up a prayer for good will and friendly relations among all classes of local citizens, and Father O'Brien collaborated only to the extent of approving the prayer for use in Protestant churches. In a letter to his bishop, Edmund Dunne of Peoria, he stated that he did not write a word of the prayer nor did he use it. Apparently, the saying of the prayer did help considerably to put a quietus on Klan bigotry in the area.

In a letter to Mary Hawks, head of the NCCW, Father Burke (July 11, 1928) said that the original peace committee of the NCWC was formed with the express approval of the NCWC administrative committee but was not a duplicate of the Catholic Association for International Peace, an organization lacking the official approval of the administrative committee. Thus, he pointed out, a proposition accepted by the peace committee would go before the administrative committee with the corporate approval of the NCCW, NCCM and the social action department. Each of these had a representative on the committee. It was at the request of these three groups that Burke had asked the administrative committee to form the peace committee. The administrative committee on April 23, 1925, authorized Burke to form the new committee.

Father Burke played a part in bringing the Catholic Association for International Peace into existence. Patricia McNeal told the story in her "Origins of the Catholic Peace Movement in the Thirties," *Review of Politics*, July 1973. Burke saw that John A. Ryan was interested in questions of war and peace but relatively inactive in this area. According to Miss McNeal, Burke finally "pushed Ryan in the direction of organizing a peace movement among Catholics. He suggested that Ryan and his assistant, Father R. McGowan 'get leading Catholics together at the 28th annual eucharistic congress to be held at Chicago in 1925' and together they could begin to discuss the issue of international peace." The meeting was held immediately after the congress, the CAIP was organized and adopted the motto, "The peace of Christ in the kingdom of Christ." It educated Catholics on the Catholic viewpoint in international affairs and influenced legislation dealing with war and peace. CAIP had its headquarters in the NCWC building in Washington and used NCWC facilities but it was, according to Miss McNeal, an entirely independent branch of the social action department, NCWC. CAIP therefore was an entity quite apart from the NCWC peace committee which Burke discussed with Miss Hawks and NCWC did not stand sponsor officially for CAIP pronouncements. Within CAIP the general consensus was in line with the traditional just war theory and some members, like John A. Ryan, would not cooperate with pacifists; others steered clear of contacts with Protestant peace organizations for fear of rebuke from the Vatican for such cooperation with Protestants. John A. Ryan, its first president, was succeeded by Father Raymond McGowan, then by Msgr. George Higgins. CAIP was discontinued in 1969.

In his last *Catholic World* editorial (September 1922), Burke had assailed historians who glamorize war (see chapter 2), and this concern about peace showed up in the sermon he delivered (February 13, 1929) at the celebration at Catholic University of the golden jubilee of the priestly ordination of Pius XI. He described how Pius in 1922 had begun his pontificate "in a world sickened by slaughter," a period not much better than the 1929 "state of armed peace which is scarcely better than war itself, a condition which tends to exhaust national finances, to waste the flower of youth, to muddy and poison the very fountainheads of life, physical, intellectual, religious and moral." The message in Pius XI's encyclicals, therefore, as Burke read them, was that the only peace is the living Christ.

The League of Nations had proved impotent at the time but Burke envisioned a unity of nations under the rule of the living Christ. "The unity of nations is a thing spiritual, not material: promoted, achieved by earthly agreements but born of and sustained only by an acceptance and a recognition of the reign of God and his son, our Savior Jesus Christ." The futility of peace efforts without Christ, a growing theme in Burke's mind, was a conviction that derived partly from his Mexican experience, partly from his remembrance of the Versailles peace conference that sowed the seeds of the armed peace that obtained in 1929. Pius XI's conviction, on the other hand, was that the fall of the old European monarchies had prepared the way for war-weary mankind to find peace and true community in the kingdom of Christ. Today we are more cynical about world peace than was Pope Pius or Father Burke and more realistic about an early recognition of the reign of Christ, yet hopeful that Christians and non-Christians, in the post-Christian world in which we live, will work together in the spirit of Pope Paul's plea at the UN, "No more war, war never again!"

chapter 6

Peacemaker in Mexico

In 1913 Governor Venustiano Carranza of Coahuila organized an armed rebellion against President Huerta of Mexico, temporarily subdued other rebel leaders such as Villa and Zapata and gained control of most of Mexico. President Wilson gave the Carranza regime diplomatic recognition on October 27, 1915, a welcome bonanza for a rebel chief hungry for respectability. As chief of the constitutionalist army, Carranza convened a constitutional congress to meet at Queretaro in 1916 to revise the old constitution. Fully expecting his largely middle-class liberal supporters to control the convention, he was unpleasantly surprised when radical voices prevailed and the constitution that emerged in 1917 proved to be totalitarian in spirit, socialistic and belligerently nationalistic. Certain anticlerical provisions of this document spawned the persecution of the Mexican Catholic Church that was to embroil the Mexican Catholics for years in an intermittent civil war, drawing American ambassador Dwight Morrow and Father Burke into the church-state struggle as peacemaking negotiators.

The chief concerns of the doctrinaire radicals at Queretaro seemed to be repression of the Church and transfer of land to the peons. They regarded the Church as the ancient, irreformable enemy of the poor whose miseries could be relieved only by class war and the expropriation of property of the rich. Among the clergy, on the other hand, there were some hard-bitten conservatives resolved to defend the status quo at any cost but most bishops tended to follow Pope Leo XIII's *Rerum Novarum* discreetly, calling for social reforms based not on violent expropriation but on "the just rights" of landowners and appeals to their consciences. The Queretaro constitution recognized no inalienable rights, only privileges granted by the government. Freedom of education was regarded by most of these anti-clerical legislators as a fuzzy platitude designed to help the scheming clergy indoctrinate children with religious fanaticism. Never approved by the Mexican people or even by the federated states themselves, the constitution was promulgated on February 5, 1917. First Chief of the Constitutional Army Carranza then became President of Mexico on May 1, 1917. A moderate, old-style liberal himself, he tried as president to undo many of the harsh reforms prompted by the new constitution but met with radical opposition, especially in his efforts to ease the implementation of anti-religious legislation. Carranza was assassinated on May 20, 1921, in a revolution launched by General Obregon. With Carranza, liberalism also died.

Obregon affected a certain amount of tolerance, anxious to win American support and unify the country, but it took him three years to get American diplomatic recognition. His successor, Plutarco Calles, took over control of the government in December 1924, resolved to clamp down on the clergy, but for various reasons he allowed a year to pass before starting his blitzkrieg against the Catholic Church. The blow-up came in early 1926 when after harassment of the Church by state governors, Archbishop Mora y del Rio, primate of Mexico, announced the bishops would meet and plan a campaign of organized resistance to laws, especially to articles 3, 5, 27 and 130 of the constitution. The persecution was soon underway with a vengeance, Church properties were confiscated, foreign clergy expelled, a national investigation of Catholic schools begun, all clergy required to register. The enforcement of the anti-religious laws was uneven, depending on the policy of individual governors, but in places it was fierce and massive, with the clergy in no mood to conciliate or surrender. The primate retracted his statement that the bishops were planning an anti-government campaign but Calles went right ahead with his campaign to punish the clergy: he intended to fulfill his program even though some states did not follow along.

Father Burke was watching the situation carefully, especially because of the concern shown by many American Catholics. He found that most of the Mexican bishops were not as belligerent as the fiery Manriquez y Zarate of Huejutla who condemned in his pastoral, "Viva Rey," the entire constitution, saying that laws meant nothing to him if they violated the rights of the Church. Most bishops realized a rebellion would be futile: Calles had the support of the army, labor unions, agrarian groups. The administrative committee, undoubtedly at Burke's instigation, sent Charles Phillips into Mexico and published his findings after he had talked with Mexican bishops. (Phillips, a Notre Dame professor, had investigated a somewhat similar situation in Poland.) The nine bishops he interviewed advised against any American Catholic protests on the ground they would only hurt the cause.

Archbishop Curley of Baltimore felt otherwise. In a memo (dated March 22, 1926) Burke writes: "To our utter amazement on February 22nd Archbishop Curley made a public address in Washington in which he calls for a nationwide protest and meetings of protest against the present Government of Mexico." The archbishop then attacked the US Government as being delinquent in its duty and complained that no courageous Catholic body had spoken out, calling therefore upon the "indifferent" Knights of Columbus to rouse themselves to aggressive action. Burke noted that "we" knew nothing of this speech until it was delivered nor were "we" consulted in any way. Later the doughty archbishop published articles in the Baltimore *Catholic Review* affirming that he would pursue his course even if he had to go it alone: his aim was to promote protest meetings in order to force the US to break off diplomatic relations with Mexico. Burke considered this the prelude to war.

A few weeks earlier, Archbishop George Caruana, a naturalized American citizen, informed Burke in Washington that he was on his way to Mexico as the new apostolic delegate to that country. He slipped into Mexico without any publicity and without divulging his office to the customs authorities. He conferred with leading Mexican prelates on how to handle the situation there and also met secretly with men from the Calles Government. One prelate that impressed him was Pascual Diaz of Tabasco: Caruana had him organize an episcopal committee and thereafter all public statements from the Mexican hierarchy came through this committee. In May, the Mexican Government expelled Caruana on the ground that he entered Mexico illegally. Sheffield, the American ambassador, protested this expulsion of an American citizen but took no official action despite criticism from American Catholics. Archbishop Curley complained that the American Government would have taken action if a handful of Methodists were involved and Bishop Kelley of Oklahoma wired President Coolidge a request to break diplomatic relations with Mexico.

Burke began to wonder if something sinister was happening behind the scenes. Here was Curley crusading in spite of instructions from the apostolic delegate and the pleas of the Mexican bishops not to stage Catholic protests north of the border. "That is afoot of which we know not but which we can surmise." Burke's surmise (and he listed his reasons for the surmise) was that the Vatican was pursuing a secret policy designed to wipe out the Calles Government. "Virulent, aggressive action must be the order of the day. Arouse the Catholics of the US to angered protest. . . . Make the US Government uncomfortable. Threaten them with political opposition by Catholics of the US. Have them break off diplomatic relations. . . . Encourage those who would by revolution drive Calles out." Burke wondered if this were the mission entrusted to Archbishop Curley by the Holy See and as a reward, "if he succeeds, it has been promised that he will journey to Rome and receive the red hat." Burke, of course, was only speculating and probably mentioned his fears to no one. He went on to say in this memo that Curley had directed Congressman Boylan to introduce a House resolution framed by Boylan and Curley. He was disturbed by the resolution because he knew that, if adopted, it would mean a break-off in diplomatic relations, which Burke considered tantamount to a declaration of war on Mexico. Was his hunch about a Vatican plot a pure figment of his imagination? Later developments would seem to lend some plausibility to the guess.

After subsiding for a few months, the persecution was on again in full fury. On July 2nd Calles published a decree more brutal than the constitution itself, outlawing religious education in primary schools, banning monastic orders and forbidding any attempt to persuade a person to take religious vows. The Mexican laity responded. The National League for the Defense of Religious Liberty (usually known as the Liga Nacional) decided on an economic boycott of all consumer goods except absolute necessities. Supported by other lay organizations, the Liga sought the help of the episcopal committee and the committee acceded, the bishops convinced that the time for a showdown was at hand. Their weapon was a clerical strike, suspending church services. They agreed to forbid priests to register, one of Calles' demands, and announced that after July 31, 1926, all religious services requiring the presence of a priest would be suspended in churches throughout the country and all parents should withdraw their children from non-Catholic schools. Women were to observe the boycott by wearing black as an indication of their participation in the boycott. The aim of this many-pronged move was to encourage irate parents to pressure the Government into submitting to the bishops' demands. The assumption was that the people felt the need of religious services so keenly that they would exert pressure on the Government when deprived of them. And in the remaining days before the deadline, July 31st, crowds jammed the churches almost as if the world were coming to an end.

It soon became evident that the boycott was a failure. The Liga had visioned the boycott as paralyzing the social and economic life of the nation but the reality was disappointing. The poor peasants had no luxuries to renounce; they were already living close to the starvation level. As to the closing of the churches, the clergy dared not go so far as to deprive the faithful of sacraments that could be administered outside the churches, nor forbid popular devotions in the homes or withhold communion from the sick and aged. Gradually the stark reality emerged painfully clear: the only choice for Mexican Catholics was surrender or armed resistance. By September, the boycott as well as the strike had failed. The churches remained closed. The Liga took up arms in December.

Burke visited the State Department occasionally but found the official policy toward Mexico unchanged. The policy was unmistakable: the US would not intervene in the domestic affairs of Mexico. Religious liberty in Mexico was a Mexican affair, not a concern of the US State Department unless the rights of Americans in Mexico were involved. The most that Burke could expect was that his friends at the State Department might say a word to the Mexican ambassador about the persecution below the border. At a meeting of the administrative committee on September 13, 1926, Father Burke and Bishop McDevitt, a member of the committee, were requested to pay a visit to President Coolidge. The president apparently handed them over to Secretary of State Kellogg who promised he would inform the Mexican ambassador in strong language exactly what the US Government thought of the anti-religious policy of Mexico that was triggering so many protests in the United States. Kellogg did as he had promised. Burke also busied himself with requests to the press for fair coverage of the Mexican troubles. In addition to this problem of biased press coverage, Burke had to circumvent if possible the abundant propaganda being circulated through the country by the Mexican ambassador to the US and some of the Mexican consuls. The K of C further complicated matters for him by starting a one million dollar campaign "to the end that the politics of Soviet Russia shall be eliminated . . . and the ideals of liberty of conscience and democratic freedom may extend to our afflicted fellow human beings beyond the Rio Grande."[1] They followed this up with inflammatory pamphlets proclaiming that "Red Russia shall not, through the mouths of traitors, rule Mexico and the Mexican continent" and imploring the US State Department to intervene and force Calles out of office.

The Catholic laity in Mexico increased their military activity, especially after the failure of the boycott; bands of rebels roamed the countryside carrying banners inscribed, "Viva Cristo Rey!" While it is true that the Holy Father forbade, and the Mexican hierarchy never approved, armed rebellion, a plausible case might be made for the argument that an armed rebellion could be justified since the Calles regime had been imposed by military force and lacked legal sanction; secondly, the Queretaro constitution was null and void, having never received the approval of the people. What dissuaded many Mexicans from actual participation in armed rebellion, of course, was the apparent futility of attempting to smash the well-trained and well-armed government forces under Calles.

During the remainder of 1926, the Cristeros, despite the lack of episcopal support, carried on their rebellion valiantly but feebly for lack of weapons. They talked eloquently about the new government they hoped to see arise in Mexico and maintained occasional contacts with exiles who came over the American border carrying mysterious messages but little more than moral support. The Vatican continued to withhold sanction for armed rebellion but also refused to approve any accommodations to the regime's anticlerical laws, Gasparri calling for "passive resistance" to force the regime to come to terms. On November 18, 1926, Pope Pius XI issued an encyclical, *Iniquis Afflictisque*, lamenting the plight of Mexican Catholics, praising the peaceful resistance of certain Catholic groups and describing the ruling regime's conduct as barbaric.

Almost the entire Mexican hierarchy gathered in Mexico City on November 26th at the home of Bishop Pascual Diaz, the Jesuit who acted as the secretary of the episcopal committee but was suspected by certain bishops of being a pliant ecclesiastical opportunist. The hierarchy met with lay leaders to discuss the Liga's plans for revolution. Diaz told the lay leaders that the bishops had examined the plans but could not give their approval to use of arms. Priests could serve the rebel forces but could not join the fighting. Although in sympathy with the rebels and unwilling to condemn their armed rebellion, the bishops did not sanction armed revolt. As the prelates had not actually forbidden the Liga to join the Cristeros in their fight, the Liga leaders felt that Diaz had given a quasi-blessing to the rebellion and they set to work organizing the rebellion more eagerly. Diaz himself was arrested for allegedly directing Cristero military activities but was exiled rather than jailed. Deported, he journeyed to New York. At the administrative committee meeting on April 26, 1927, Burke informed the committee that Diaz had made clear to him that the Mexican hierarchy did not want NCWC to countenance in any way the promotion of armed resistance in Mexico.

One Mexican archbishop, José Maria Gonzalez Valencia of Durango, seemed to feel that the Pope had been ambiguous in his encyclical. (It was said that he had shown Pope Pius some materials favoring a militant policy, and that the encyclical was written on the strength of these materials.) On February 11, 1927, the archbishop, in Rome, addressed a pastoral letter to his people in Durango, "on the field of battle, front to front with the enemies of Christ." He declared:

We never provoked this armed conflict. But once all peaceful means had been exhausted and this movement began, you, our Catholic sons, rose in arms to defend your social and religious rights. After having consulted with the sagest theologians of the city of Rome, we say to you: Be tranquil in your conscience and receive our benedictions.

He went on to tell his people that the Holy Father had been moved by the account of their struggles. "We have seen him bless your resistance, approve all your acts and admire all your heroisms." In Jalisco, Archbishop Orozco y Jimenez was equally anxious to foment rebellion. Undoubtedly to counteract the militancy of the Archbishop of Durango, Bishop Diaz went to Rome and met with Secretary of State Gasparri. In his conversations with Gasparri, he not only showed his disagreement with the Durango archbishop's viewpoint but also minimized the effectiveness of the Liga Nacional. He contended that the Cristero movement had no future in Mexico. As a matter of fact, the Cristeros lost ground rapidly in March and April 1927, especially through their policy of wrecking railroad trains, which met with public disapproval. The rebel cause continued to lose in mid-summer, so much so that Calles began to discuss the possibility of freeing some rebel prisoners, predicting that the religious controversy would end shortly and certain expelled priests would reenter Mexico.[2]

The situation took a bad turn however when Father Miguel Pro, a Jesuit, was executed on November 23, 1927, for his alleged role in an attempt to assassinate former president Alvaro Obregon, the probable successor to Calles when the latter's term expired. Innocent of the crime, Father Pro was nevertheless executed without trial. Catholics seethed with indignation at this gross miscarriage of justice, their rage rising to fever pitch when the chief of police (stupidly) released photos of Father Pro, executed with arms outstretched like Christ on the cross. Father Pro was executed with the approval of Calles. The prospects for the future were grim: to talk of peaceful compromise was futile, to continue the armed revolution could only result in bloodshed and disaster.

A ray of light pierced the gloom with the appointment of Dwight Whitney Morrow, a partner in J.P. Morgan & Co., as ambassador to Mexico. His daughter Ann later married Charles A. Lindbergh and became one of the most admired writers of her generation. James Sheffield, Morrow's predecessor, had harbored a profound contempt for Calles and his regime and had been sympathetic to the Catholics but he was adamant in maintaining an officially neutral position in order to avoid any appearance of interfering in the domestic affairs of a foreign country, especially in the area of religious liberty. Morrow, on the other hand, less the traditional diplomat, took the position that none of Mexico's problems, domestic or foreign, could be solved unless the religious issue was first disposed of. Yet he did not ignore the Calles regime's law requiring foreign oil companies to surrender their titles to land in exchange for fifty-year leases. This was considered highway robbery by Americans, and some Mexicans, fearing American retaliation by way of intervention, murmured, "After Morrow, the marines!"

Before he presented his credentials to President Calles on October 29, 1927, Morrow had been approached by certain American Catholics who explained to him that while they deplored the persecution, they realized that American Catholics had aggravated rather than alleviated the plight of Mexican Catholics.[3] Among those who approached Morrow were Archbishop Hayes of New York, Judge Morgan O'Brien and Father John Burke. The Paulist met with Morrow on October 13th at the Mayflower Hotel in Washington, D.C. Robert Olds, Undersecretary of State, was present and the talk lasted two hours. Burke pointed out to the ambassador the note Pope Pius XI had written to the bishops of Mexico forbidding the use of arms and partisan political action. Then he said that unless stable government came to Mexico, Calles and Obregon would drive it into anarchy and communism. Morrow and Olds said they would like to see Calles and Obregon out of the way as they were depleting Mexico of many educated citizens by way of murder and exile. Burke responded that it was absurd for American liberals to favor the despotic Calles since his regime would topple in a week if American recognition were withdrawn. "What do you think I can do?" asked Morrow. Burke said it was a tough question but he would keep in touch with Olds in Washington. In his memo regarding the Mayflower meeting, Burke noted that Morrow and Olds knew surprisingly little about Catholicism, the Mexican constitution or religious liberty. He saw, however, that Morrow was a thoroughly honest and dedicated public official. As a matter of fact, Morrow was soon giving long hours to the reading of Mexican history and cultivating an interest in Mexican art and culture so that he was an informed and unprejudiced American by the time he was called on to make major decisions in Mexico City. Burke apparently made a good impression on Morrow who wrote later to Olds that he felt a *modus vivendi* could be worked out if "a liberal Catholic of the type of Father Burke, who talked with us in Washington, were dealing directly with President Calles."[4]

The administrative committee asked Burke to meet with President Coolidge and it was arranged: they met on November 26, 1927. Undoubtedly Coolidge knew of Burke through Morrow, an Amherst classmate of the President. Burke asked Coolidge to notify Calles that his methods did not find favor with the US Government. Coolidge expressed his abhorrence of Calles' cruelties but said that if he protested, the US would probably get a tart reply and we would have to be ready to invade Mexico. He insisted that neither he nor the American people wanted war and said he had told Morrow to try to win the good will of the Mexican Government. Burke then suggested that Coolidge forward, without comment, the protest of a body of American citizens against the outrages. The President replied that he would speak to Secretary Kellogg about it, and would also ask Morrow if something might be done to bring the justice of the protest home to Calles.

On November 28th, Burke talked with Secretary Kellogg who told him that he had reminded the Mexican ambassador how serious the situation was and had given the ambassador the administrative committee's protests as well as other protests, begging him to show them to his Government. On the question of an official protest, however, Kellogg was intransigent: an official protest would mean possible withdrawal of the ambassador—and war! He then told Burke confidentially that Ambassador Sheffield had been asked to resign precisely because he thought that war was the only way out of the mess.

NEVER LOOK BACK

War, said Kellogg, would only fan the flames of anti-Americanism in every Latin American country. On leaving the secretary, Burke gave him a chronological list, 43 pages long, of the anti-religious acts of Calles from February 12, 1926 to November 22, 1927.

Burke had appealed to Ambassador Sheffield when Father Pro was executed but he was informed that the US could not protest the punishment of Mexican citizens. Then he appealed to Coolidge on December 10th on behalf of Archbishop Orozco who had been arrested on suspicion of being implicated in the murder of General Obregon. In a phone conversation with Morrow in Mexico, Olds told the ambassador that Father Burke considered Orozco a Cardinal Mercier of his people: Morrow said he would speak to Calles. The outcome was that Orozco escaped death but was exiled. Morrow told Olds that Calles had informed him the Catholics were rebels he intended to suppress at any cost.

During this period, Burke and Undersecretary Olds became close friends, with Burke a frequent visitor to Olds' office in the State Department. Early in January, 1928 Burke was chatting with Olds at his office when the latter sounded Burke out on the possibility of his going to Mexico City, a proposition deriving from Morrow himself. Burke feared this might embarrass the Holy See but his first step was to consult the administrative committee who in turn asked the advice of the apostolic delegate. The delegate took a dim view of any negotiations with Calles, confiding to the committee that he deemed discussions with Calles futile, that the American Government had no interest in religious issues, and that Morrow himself went to Mexico not as ambassador but as a banker to help other bankers, and that even the State Department knew nothing about catechetics. The bishops however replied that twenty million Catholics in the US resented the failure of the Republican administration to help the victimized Mexican Catholics, and that the Republicans simply had to do something about Mexico in view of the coming elections, especially since the Democratic candidate might be the Catholic, Al Smith. Bernardini of the apostolic delegation thought no harm could come from cooperating with the State Department by allowing Father Burke to work into Morrow's proposal. Finally, the delegate, Fumasoni Biondi, gave his approval, conceding that Burke was well qualified for the mission. Morrow then suggested they meet first at Havana, during the coming Pan American Congress, but privately and without any publicity.

On January 17, 1928, the Paulist and the Protestant ambassador dined together at the Sevilla Biltmore in Havana in Morrow's room. William Montavon, head of the legal department of NCWC, had accompanied Burke to Havana but was not present at this first meeting. Morrow had already discussed the Mexican situation with Calles and in this meeting described him to Burke as a man of strong, obstinate will and "to my mind, a fanatic." He possessed, according to Morrow, administrative ability, a capacity for hard work (12-14 hours a day), a firm conviction that the Catholic Church was his enemy, its hierarchy hard at work stirring up revolution, its clergy generally stiff-necked in their hostility to the real social and economic progress of the Mexican people. Morrow summed up: the Government is Calles, the constitution is a farce, Congress and the judiciary are simply agents of Calles.

Morrow told Burke that Aaron Saenz, bigoted Methodist campaign manager for Obregon, had regaled him with stories of the "rottenness" of the Catholic Mexican clergy, to which Burke responded with praises of them. Morrow then confided to Burke that he was baffled. He had gone to Mexico out of friendship for Coolidge, his Amherst classmate, who had said to him, "Do all you can to keep war with Mexico out of my administration. I don't want war; the people don't want war." Morrow felt the solution was to win Calles over—but how? No point in waiting for Obregon to succeed Calles in December: he was unreliable. But if Morrow was looking to Burke for leads out of his quandary, he didn't get them. Burke reminded him that American Catholics wanted their Government to show more interest in human rights than in oil and property. To make certain that Morrow entertained no false impressions about his credentials, moreover, Burke let him know he came with no authority, no official representation except that the apostolic delegate knew and approved his coming to Havana.

Morrow kept emphasizing Calles' obstinacy but Burke contended that the most practical move for Calles was to recognize the Holy See, allow an apostolic delegate to enter Mexico and the exiled bishops to return to Mexico. (At this time, about twenty Mexican bishops were living in exile.) But Morrow did not seem very hopeful. That night Burke jotted down, "Spent four hours with him and came home disappointed and depressed."

The next day they met again, in the afternoon. Burke hammered hard at the need of allowing an apostolic delegate to serve in Mexico, Morrow finally declaring that it was outside his province but he would do it: he would persuade Calles to allow the apostolic delegate to function even though Morrow himself might lose his ambassadorship in the process. Then he turned to Burke and asked him, "If Calles shows himself willing to receive you and discuss this matter with you, will you come to Mexico to talk with him?" Burke agreed, provided he could get authorization from the Church. The only authorization he needed, said Morrow, was to be able to say to Calles that the Church knew of his errand. (As Burke left, Morrow gave him copies of *The Church and the Modern State* by Figgis and *Men of Destiny* by Lippmann.)

At the next interview, several days later, Burke returned the books and promised to send Morrow an English Benedictine's book on the Civil War. They then discussed commercial treaties in relation to religious toleration.

Burke returned to Washington, Morrow to Mexico City, where the ambassador saw Calles who told him he would be willing to meet with Father Burke but insisted that the Catholic Church was opposing him by armed insurrection and that he was determined to drive it out of politics. They then made arrangements for an interview between Calles and Father Burke. Unfortunately, the interview never materialized. The *New York Herald Tribune* (February 9th) publicized the forthcoming journey by Burke, and Calles decided that the publicity had made any thought of an interview impossible. In a letter to Olds (May 22nd) Burke explained that Archbishop Mora had apparently informed some old regime Mexicans that Burke was to meet Calles. The Mexicans confronted Burke, contending that he had no right to meet with Calles, and that there could be no peace for property owners or the Church until the whole crowd was ousted from the Government. Burke questioned their Catholicity since they put property rights in the same class with the welfare of the Church. Two days later, the news story appeared, and Morrow informed Burke of the cancellation by Calles. But a few days later, Calles expressed once again a willingness to see Burke.

The ambassador made arrangements for the postponed interview, the apostolic delegate this time expressing an anxious desire for the meeting to come about. On March 15th Olds and Burke discussed the trip, Olds warning him that spies were probably watching him as well as the State Department. Burke showed Olds a letter he had received from Walter Lippmann, from Mexico City, reporting that he had a long talk with Calles in which Calles had fixed on two points of controversy in the church-state quarrel, the registration of priests and the allocation of priest quotas, as points that could be interpreted in a sense acceptable to the Mexican bishops.

A discernible change in official American policy on Mexico was daily becoming more and more obvious, due chiefly to Morrow's insistence that the State Department give the religious liberty issue first priority and also to the influence of Walter Lippmann's editorials in *The New York World*. Lippmann maintained there could be no real peace between church and state in Mexico or any real cordiality between the US and Mexico until the religious issue was settled. On March 24th, Lippmann visited Burke at his home and talked with him for three hours. He quoted the Mexican finance minister as saying that the framers of the 1917 constitution wanted to crush the Church but "we are not of that mind today." The noted journalist had held two discussions of the religious issue with Calles shortly before the visit to Burke. Calles had expressed his desire to oust the clergy from politics but not once, according to Lippmann, did he show any bitterness toward the Church. Lippmann asked Calles if he would be willing to write a letter stating that he would consider changes in the constitution—if Burke would write to him. Calles said he would be glad to do so. Lippmann's impression of the Mexican President was that he was intelligent, a slow thinker who was only now beginning to understand the function of an apostolic delegate. Obregon, on the other hand, was unreliable and likely to play a double game but Lippmann said that Calles, for the sake of continuity, would consult first with Obregon before writing the desired letter.

The following day, Burke lunched with Lippmann at the Carlton Hotel in Washington. Lippmann paid tribute to the affectionate hold the Catholic faith had on the Mexican people, especially on the Indians, adding that their Catholic faith was the only thing that conveyed meaning and dignity to a Mexican's life and that Protestantism would never appeal to them. For two hours in Lippmann's room afterwards, Burke and Lippmann worked on a program, Lippmann quoting Calles' assurance to Morrow and himself that he would sign the draft of a *modus vivendi* Morrow had sent to Burke. The following day they met again at the Carlton, Lippmann stating that Calles had done practically nothing to enforce the objectionable laws for nine years and would have left them dormant had it not been for Archbishop Mora y del Rio's blast at the constitution in 1926, and fear of American intervention. This explanation of his sudden burst of anti-religious activity was not only given to Lippmann by Calles at this time but was offered by Calles to others at various times: yet Calles himself told an American reporter of the *New York Herald-Tribune* he would have acted as he did if the archbishop had not made his protest. Moreover, the notion that Calles would make a "show of force" to stave off American intervention is absurd. Lippmann later concluded that the crux of the whole matter was not an incident but the central question "whether the Catholic clergy had accepted the Mexican Revolution (of 1910) as a *fait accompli* and whether the government would believe the clergy had done so."[5] Ernest Lagarde, French chargé in Mexico City, recalling Calles' record in earlier years as governor of Sonora, said: "What is particularly dangerous about him is that he is a man of principle, possessing energy to the point of obstinacy and cruelty, ready to attack not only persons but principles and the institution, and that the system of government to which, by virtue of his philosophical convictions he has become attached, condemns the very existence of the Church as economically and politically nefarious."[6]

Father Burke's contacts with Lippmann in relation to Mexico were very cordial. In a letter written March 24, 1931, Lippmann recalled these experiences with appreciation and gratitude. He wrote Burke from New York that he was sailing for Greece and planned to wander around Europe, then added:

Let me say that no incident in all the time I have ever been on a newspaper gave me as much enlightenment and as much personal pleasure as the time when I felt that in some small degree we were cooperating with you in the Mexican affair.

Lippmann never forgot "the Mexican affair." According to an AP dispatch (*Chicago Tribune*, December 15, 1974) on Lippmann: "At 80, he said the two things of which he was most proud were opposing the war in Vietnam and helping prevent a similar conflict in Mexico during the 1920s."

On March 27th, Burke told Olds he was ready for the trip to Mexico City; he had asked Father James Ryan to substitute for him in delivering the sermons at the Three Hours Agony service at the Paulist Church in New York, on Good Friday. Olds had been hesitant about Burke's journey: the two had

NEVER LOOK BACK

become intimate friends, discovering a common bond in historical studies such as Acton's views on the Mexican clergy's attitude toward the advent of Maximilian into Mexico. On the 28th Morrow proposed a text of a letter to be written to Calles, embodying the basis of a *modus vivendi*, including matters such as the registration of priests and the fixing of priest quotas. The arrangement was that Burke should write it, sign it and have it in Olds' hands by the next day for transmission via diplomatic pouch to Morrow in Mexico. Morrow would make sure that, even if publicity did break, Calles would see Burke. On March 29th, Burke saw Olds, gave him the letter for Calles to be given to Morrow. Due to a last minute change, the plan was to interview Calles at Vera Cruz, not Mexico City. On March 30th Burke left Washington with Montavon as companion.

Two weeks earlier, his friend, Olds, had wondered about the eventual outcome of the journey if Calles did agree with the terms in Burke's letter and the official Church then refused to accept the agreement. "Father Burke, you may find yourself sitting on a limb." Burke, however, experienced no palpitation or apprehensions on that score, now that he was on his way to Mexico. He had an almost unqualified respect for authority and his superior, Fumasoni-Biondi, the apostolic delegate, had urged him to meet with Calles but instructed him that whatever emerged from the negotiations would be communicated to Rome for approval. If Rome rejected the *modus vivendi*, well —he would cross that bridge when he came to it.

In the letter to Calles,[7] Burke stated that he had learned that President Calles never intended to destroy the identity of the Church nor interfere with its spiritual functions but aimed only at keeping ecclesiastics out of politics. The Mexican bishops felt however that the constitution and the laws, particularly the provision requiring registration of priests and the provision granting states the right to fix the number of priests, have threatened the identity of the Church if enforced in a spirit of antagonism. Burke wrote that he was satisfied that the bishops were animated by a sincere patriotism and a yearning for a true and lasting peace as well as a desire to resume public worship, which could be done if they were assured of a tolerance within the law to exercise their spiritual offices. This would leave to the Mexican people, acting within the law, the adjustment of the other questions in dispute. Burke then proposed that if Calles would declare it was not his purpose, nor that of the constitution and the laws, to destroy the identity of the Church, and would be ready to confer occasionally with the authorized head of the Church in Mexico, no reason would exist for the Mexican clergy to refuse to resume their spiritual functions. "It might be well that each in an atmosphere of good will would suggest at a later time changes in the laws which both the republic of Mexico and the Church might desire." In the last paragraph, Burke concluded with the statement that if Calles felt such an adjustment might meet the situation, he would be very glad to come to Mexico to discuss with the president the steps necessary to bring about this adjustment. He signed: "John J. Burke, CSP."

On Monday, April 2nd, Burke and Montavon met Albert F. Smithers, personal representative of Calles, and a Mexican immigration official at Laredo, on the US side of the international boundary. Smithers, a Catholic, knew the purpose of the mission; his brother, James Smithers, would act later as interpreter for Calles. The party passed through Tacuba and eventually included Morrow and his secretary, Mr. Springer, also Dawson of the American embassy staff, the two Smithers brothers and Father Burke. After going through Mexico City, they went to Vera Cruz and on April 4th Burke was taken to a fortress prison in the harbor. Here at this island prison of San Juan de Ullúa, Calles and Burke met, the two Smithers brothers and Morrow being present.

The Paulist opened the discussion with an explanation of the NCWC and his role in it, how the apostolic delegate to the US had asked him to represent him for the purpose of finding out if certain Mexican laws could be interpreted in such a way as to permit the Church to function. Burke gave a somewhat lengthy talk and the tension was almost tangible, especially when Calles responded bluntly, "Father Burke, you are all wrong with regard to the facts." Calles blamed the Archbishop of Mexico City for stirring up trouble by making a hostile pronouncement with the purpose of weakening, and possibly destroying the Mexican Government, an action he claimed was typical of the Mexican bishops. After citing the boycott and the closing of the churches, Calles went into a long list of grievances against the bishops who, he alleged, were aspiring to political control. He denied that he was opposed to the Church but maintained that he must demand obedience to the laws, at the same time lamenting that the bishops had not devoted themselves to work for the poor peons, socially, educationally, morally.

Burke replied that he had no desire to get involved in an argument. He could question Calles' facts just as Calles had questioned his but he preferred only to ask if Calles would allow the bishops to return to their spiritual duties, unencumbered by laws hampering the priests.

After lunch, attention focused on the letter Burke had written as the basis for a *modus vivendi* and Calles' reply to it. Burke explained that he planned to show it to the delegate who would submit it to the Holy See for approval. As to acceptance of an apostolic delegate in Mexico, Calles said he would allow him to function, unless he were foreign born, but would not give him any diplomatic recognition. The interview lasted five hours. Calles signed the letter, handing it to Burke as he remarked, "I hope your visit means a new era for the life and people of Mexico." On the return trip, Montavon left Burke at San Antonio, Burke going on from there to Albuquerque where the apostolic delegate, Fumasoni Biondi, was staying. Burke gave him a full report and the apostolic delegate to the United States expressed, in Burke's words, "modified satisfaction."

Anxious to press for restoration of worship as soon as possible, Burke wrote Calles (May 7, 1928) urging him to make a public statement on this, and along with the statement an amplification of parts of Calles' April 4th letter to Burke, that is, the letter in which Calles thanked Burke for his March 29th letter and the interview. Burke also asked, in this May 7th letter, that Calles issue an official statement to the effect that laws relating to religious instruction were not designed to make religious instruction impossible for children of primary school age.

Meanwhile, Archbishop Mora, whom Calles had blamed for the recurrence of the persecution, died and Archbishop Ruiz y Flores presided at a meeting of the Mexican bishops at San Antonio.[8] He was the only bishop who had been informed of the Burke-Calles agreement and he succeeded in persuading the Mexican bishops there to sign a statement similar in content to the letter which Burke gave Calles and which Calles approved. Morrow now felt that atmosphere was favorable for negotiations so he asked Burke to come down from Washington to Mexico City as soon as possible (tomorrow night) bringing Archbishop Ruiz with him. Calles and Obregon would both be present. When Morrow told Calles of the plan, he objected strenuously that he preferred to deal with Burke and Morrow, that a small but active minority would cause trouble because of Ruiz's presence, but Calles finally gave in. As Burke left for the train (May 12th), accompanied by Montavon and Ruiz, the apostolic delegate, Fumasoni Biondi, urged Burke not to be seen with Ruiz lest publicity might again spoil their plans.

As the train arrived at St. Louis, as luck would have it, Father Burke met a Mrs. Hackett of Milwaukee who recognized him in spite of the secular suit he wore. He explained to her that he was on a secret mission, that it was important that she tell no one, and she did apparently keep the secret without knowing what the mission was. At Nuevo Laredo they were met by vice-consul Aguirre and A. F. Smithers. (Burke noted in his memo that Ruiz saw some doves and speculated that they might be omens of peace.) The party arrived at Tacuba

(May 17, 1928) and stayed at the home of Captain Lewis B. McBride, naval attaché at the embassy. Calles objected to Ruiz's presence at the coming interview but Burke insisted: to isolate the archbishop would certainly displease the Mexican bishops. Burke won out. After long conversations with Morrow, the visitors went to Chapultepec Palace about 4 P.M., along with James and Bert Smithers. Burke noted in his memo that Calles shook hands with all in the party but did not smile at Archbishop Ruiz.

Burke began the discussion (May 18th) by reporting on the meeting the bishops had held at San Antonio, informing Calles that they had asked Burke to find out if Calles would clarify the law on registration of priests, religious instruction and the return of church buildings to religious uses. Calles said the registration law did not interfere with internal church organization, that religious instruction could not be given in primary school buildings at any time, and finally, that the present troubles were caused by the imprudence of some bishops. As for return of church buildings, he would listen to requests for their return but the fact was that some had already been sold. Ruiz then reported on the meeting of the bishops at San Antonio, assuring Calles they were anxious to return to their sees and definitely not intransigent. He then offered to write a note comprising the substance of Burke's letter to Calles of March 29th, inserting a beautiful tribute to the Church made by Casauranc, minister of education, to the effect that the Catholic faith made Mexico great and was the faith of the Mexican people. Calles approved the archbishop's offer and agreed to write a note duplicating the reply he gave Burke on April 4, 1928. The understanding was that as soon as Church authorities ratified this exchange of correspondence, it would be published with the announcement, "In the light of the attached two letters, the Holy See has authorized the resumption of religious worship in Mexico." Religious services would then be resumed on Pentecost.

Morrow and Burke worked carefully Thursday afternoon

and evening, May 17th, on the wording of a long telegram to the apostolic delegate in Washington, describing in detail the contents of the proposed agreement and urging on the delegate the need of cabling the full cable to the Holy See requesting resumption of worship on Pentecost. Some members of the State Department staff in Washington stayed on duty all night to transmit the message to the delegate, send his cable to Rome and send Rome's reply to Mexico City. But the best laid plans of mice and men. . . .

At the delegation the situation was incredible. The delegate was uneasy about so quick a solution, muttering to James Ryan, Burke's associate: ". . . these American are crazy. They want to rush things. It can't be done. Rome does not act in that way. She is eternal." So he decided he would not send the full cable, reasoning that Rome would not act on "mere telegraphic advices." He therefore instructed James Ryan to send a telegram to Mexico City: "Chief wishes party to return immediately. Both of you go across as soon as possible. This is the quickest and only sure way to achieve purpose. Am working on accommodations. Leviathan sailing May 26th. Ryan." This telegram did not reach Burke until the afternoon of May 19th.

The telegram was a crusher. Morrow was depressed. Burke expressed his gratitude to Morrow, told him Ruiz had praised him for his efforts (which pleased Morrow after all the scurrilous letters he had received from Catholics). The ambassador then said goodbye to Burke and Ruiz and they left for Laredo. Arriving at Washington, Burke found that Ruiz was to travel to Rome, the delegate having decided against sending Burke. Apparently he distrusted Ruiz's judgment and did not want Burke involved in any fiasco of Ruiz's making. M. Elizabeth Ann Rice suggests a different explanation, that is, that "Mexico would have considered it an insult to her national pride" if an American priest had reported at Rome the conversations with Calles.[9]

On June 13th, in a visit to the delegate, Burke discussed the

Holy See's delay in approving the agreement and also touched on the matter of a cable the delegate had received from Gasparri, papal secretary of state: "The Holy Father wishes your Excellency to thank Ambassador Morrow for his good offices and to ask him to insist with Calles that he make some acceptable proposition." Burke had been quite unhappy about this lefthanded compliment, which was really an undiplomatic way of saying that Calles should cut out the nonsense and come up with a serious offer. Morrow too felt the cable was most unfortunate when Burke told him about it. It would if implemented, said Morrow, destroy Morrow's good offices, lessen Calles' respect for the Holy See and expose Morrow to ridicule, practically requiring his resignation. Upon hearing about Morrow's reaction, Fumasoni-Biondi protested that Burke need not have mentioned the cable to Morrow at all, that a verbal message simply asking Morrow to work for more acceptable proposals would have been enough. Then Marella contended that the cable should not have been shown to Morrow since in many cases it is necessary to lie in conveying messages received from the Holy See. This kind of casuistry was not Burke's cup of tea: the secretiveness of Vatican diplomacy did not strike a responsive chord in his "Americanism" and his openness was the very quality that endeared Burke to Morrow.

On one occasion, Burke was composing a cable message when the apostolic delegate said to him, "Your mind acts differently from the mind of the Holy Father. You are looking at particulars: the Holy Father looks at generalities. He does not commit himself to anything." Both Morrow and Burke moreover seemed to feel that they were approaching the Mexican problems from an angle different from that of the Vatican. Morrow especially felt that the Vatican was working for a change in the constitution of Mexico while they were only trying for a return of the bishops and resumption of worship. Morrow noticed moreover that Burke, the priest, was chiefly concerned about the Mexican people. In a letter to his friend, John J. Raskob, Morrow wrote:

Father Burke, upon both of his visits to Mexico, made an excellent impression on President Calles. He put the whole Church problem before the president in a different way than the president had heretofore seen it. While he did not give up any of the Church's contentions with reference to its historical and moral rights, he laid all the emphasis upon the help that the Church could render in lifting up the Mexican people, spiritually, mentally, materially. (June 28, 1928)

Archbishop Ruiz in the meantime had arrived in Paris, where he lived up to Fumasoni-Biondi's worst expectations. In a talk to American reporters in Paris he said that Obregon would soon take up the reins of Government and would need the support of the Church, that Calles had seen "the trouble which has followed our exile and we have reason to believe he favors reconciliation." Whatever might have been the reason for his garrulity, the fact now was that the negotiations were no longer a secret, Calles was infuriated and militant Catholics redoubled their efforts to stave off a settlement. Ruiz had nothing to say to reporters when he arrived in Rome but he did write an optimistic note to Burke. Gasparri had a different angle: he claimed the Mexican Government wanted a settlement only because it needed to float a loan in the United States. Hence the terms brought by Ruiz from the meeting with Calles were quite inadequate, Gasparri looking for stronger guarantees as a kind of act of contrition for what the Mexican Government had done to the Church in Mexico. To anyone who knew Calles, contrition was unimaginable, but the Vatican persisted in demanding firmer guarantees.

chapter 7

The signing
of the
Ruiz-Gil Agreement

The impasse resulting from the Vatican's insistence on firmer guarantees of freedom for the Church continued for long, weary months. It was interrupted by startling news of a totally unexpected development. Elected July 1, 1928, Obregon was scheduled to be sworn in as president in December, according to Mexican law, Calles retaining power until then. Suddenly, on July 17th, Obregon was assassinated, just before he was to have a meeting with Ambassador Morrow. His assassin was José de Leon Toral,[1] a staunch Catholic; a nun, Mother Maria Concepcion Acevedo y de Llata, was accessory before the fact. Calles immediately proclaimed to the press that "clerical action" was directly involved, and Ruiz at Rome further muddied the waters by asserting that it was only natural that the friends of Obregon's victims would eventually get Obregon himself. Ruiz added that Calles would now be more ready than ever to seek peace because he was tired of killings and badly needed money for a hard-pressed impecunious regime, money that would not be available until he had made peace with the Catholics. Archbishop Diaz and Archbishop Hanna, however, deplored the assassination and Burke asked Calles to retract his charge that the Church was involved in the crime. Calles did so, saying that individual priests but not the Church were involved. Then came more trouble for Burke and Morrow from another direction, Rome. *Osservatore Romano*, believed by many to be an official Vatican organ, began a series of articles on Mexico which were viciously vituperative, so much so that Morrow said someone in Rome must have gone mad. Morrow, according to *Osservatore*, was a tool of financial interests and Calles was the actual murderer of Obregon.

At about this time (the date is uncertain), Morrow wrote to Archbishop Diaz asking for information about the true position of the Church on the Mexican question. Who had authority to speak? Apparently Morrow, a Protestant, was bewildered. All along he had taken Burke's word that the Holy See wanted peace but the Liga Nacional, a rebel army, claimed it had the Pope's endorsement, a new subcommittee of Mexican bishops in Mexico was denouncing the negotiations with the Mexican Government, the Knights of Columbus in Mexico had written proudly to the Pope about their resistance, condemning any accord with the Government as surrender.

Archbishop Diaz responded (July 24th) that the apostolic delegate to the United States, Pietro Fumasoni-Biondi, was also the apostolic delegate to Mexico, that Fumasoni-Biondi had appointed Diaz the official liaison between himself and the bishops of Mexico, and that Father Burke was Fumasoni-Biondi's agent. As for the Liga Nacional, Diaz said that the Pope in *Iniquis Afflictisque* (November 18, 1926) had approved the Liga for service in Mexico but only on condition that it operated by legal methods. Later on, said Diaz, the Liga had decided to resort to armed action. The Pope therefore instructed the Mexican bishops (November 16, 1927) "to have no part, physical or moral, direct or indirect, in any action by Catholics under the direction of the League. If the League wants to give up armed action and work under the direction of the bishops, it may do so by changing both its name and its officers." This latter explanation did not entirely satisfy Morrow because the warning was contained in a private communication to the bishops. He asked Burke to secure permission to publicize it, since the endorsement had been widely publicized; in fact, the League had been quoting the original endorsement. It was Morrow's opinion that publicizing the repudiation would set the Church "right" before the Mexican Government, the Mexican people and the American people. Burke pressured the delegate in this matter, the delegate promising he would direct Archbishop Diaz as his liaison to write a letter giving the pertinent quotes from the Pope's repudiation, then authorizing Burke to send this letter to Morrow to use as he saw fit. This apparently did not work out—Morrow weeks afterwards was still asking for authorization of publication of the Pope's repudiation of the League.

On August 3rd the delegate told Burke of a revealing incident involving Archbishop Ruiz as told to him by Gasparri. It seems that Gasparri, his cousin and Monsignor Bernardini were walking the Corso in Rome when Bernardini saw Ruiz and commented favorably about him but Gasparri said, "Ruiz suffers from one great fault. He agrees with the man he talked with last." Then Gasparri explained. Ruiz had agreed with the report he and John Burke had signed (re the Calles Agreement). On the strength of this, Gasparri prepared a summary and informed Ruiz that he and Gasparri would see the Holy Father and plead for a return of the bishops to Mexico. At the audience, the Holy Father said, "But do you not think it would be a scandal to the Catholics of Mexico for the Mexican bishops to return just on *these* assurances?" Ruiz said he thought so!

The American ambassador showed a surprising optimism in spite of the way things were going. On August 9th for instance he visited Calles for a five-hour talk. Calles was angry at Ruiz's remarks about him and said it would hurt the country to bring the bishops back in the light of Ruiz's unfair charges against their President. Toward the end of the interview, Calles said, "The religious situation is a closed incident." But Morrow told Burke, "Sit tight on this. Don't get discouraged. In another week or two we may be able to go on. It is essential to make a settlement with Calles as it would be harder for his successor to make it."

Fumasoni-Biondi, the apostolic delegate, saw little hope. When Burke visited him the next day, he asked the delegate if any permission to publish the Pope's repudiation of the League had come through. The delegate snapped, "Why should that favor be given to Calles at this time?" He seemed to be brooding in a mood of self-pity, complaining about what he considered a gross lack of cooperation from the Vatican and from the Mexican bishops. Except for Ruiz and Diaz, he said, they had never recognized him as the official apostolic delegate to Mexico and he felt sure that the Roman authorities opposed him (e.g. the *Osservatore* articles). He thought the Holy See was being badly advised by the Jesuits who were and had been directing the Liga Nacional. In fact, Marella told James Ryan, Burke's assistant, that the delegate's position was insecure, that the Holy See might "call him down" for his stand on Mexico, charging him with being the tool of Burke, the real power in the negotiations. Burke then talked to Marella who told him that the delegate would send no more communications in the Mexican matter to Rome. Having sent all they should have sent, why send anything else when the word of others rather than theirs was accepted at Rome?

Undoubtedly Fumasoni-Biondi was disturbed also by the reports of undue influence on the Vatican by other than Jesuits. Burke, for example, heard from Morrow in Mexico City (August 17th) that a Mexican friend of the Pope was duping the Vatican and that women, for the most part, were conducting the anti-government propaganda, many men having been driven out of the Church by the *Osservatore* articles. Hysteria was in the air in Mexico. Arthur Lane, chief of the State Department's Mexico desk, asked Burke if Bishop de la Mora could be recalled to the US since he was exploiting the hysterics of women. To which Burke responded that he would be more dangerous in the US than in Mexico because he would enjoy more freedom here. A week later, Morrow reported to Burke that the *Osservatore* articles proved to be less damaging than expected, too ridiculous to convince anyone, and Morrow's mood was on the upbeat. He also mentioned that Avila (connected with certain forgeries) was thought by the Government in Mexico to have instigated the *Osservatore*'s attacks. All this was reassuring to Morrow as he had been one of the chief targets of the *Osservatore* blasts.

Another example of the prevailing hysteria was occasioned by the chief of police's statement (August 22nd) regarding a woman suspect in the killing of Obregon. Burke writes in a memo of that date:

Moreover, his charge that this woman was to inject poison into the arms of Obregon and Calles as she danced with either of them seemed to me rather ridiculous on the face of it. It would be particularly hard for her to do this in the case of Obregon as he had only one arm. This talk of injecting poison through hypodermic needles was typical of a widely evident mentality in Mexico at the present time.

The Vatican continued to delay its decision through September and October and Calles paid scant attention to the church-state problem, giving priority to domestic problems such as the presidential succession now that the Cristero rebellion seemed to have collapsed. The Vatican contributed to the lull by continuing to delay its decision. There had been a rumor that Calles might publish the Calles-Burke letters, which would mean the demise of negotiations entirely, but Morrow secured from Calles a promise (November 8th) that he would not publish the letters, "not out of regard for the Mexican bishops or the Vatican but out of personal regard for Father Burke, for whom he had the highest respect. He would not do anything to embarrass Father Burke." Morrow told Reuben Clarke, who had succeeded Olds as Undersecretary of State, that Calles trusted Father Burke and "was willing to follow his advice on the negotiations. If Father Burke said the publication of the letters might injure the negotiations, he, Calles, would not permit them." Calles also said that he would honor a note written by Father Burke and would respond to it that "any dignitary or official the Church might wish to appoint might come and live in freedom in Mexico and carry on the work of his office." But he insisted that the letter be written by Burke and that Calles' answer be sent to Burke; he was willing to carry on further negotiations through Burke and Morrow. Moreover, he said he would even accept Ruiz as a cooperating negotiator.

Calles' admiration for Father Burke was one of the curious features of the negotiations. He hated the Church yet showed almost filial reverence for Burke. At this time he felt sure that Burke had been shabbily treated by his superiors, that he had made a sincere effort to defend the Church in Mexico but Church officials had not been willing for him to have the credit of bringing to a conclusion the negotiations he had so successfully begun. Calles considered himself and Morrow as allies in an attempt to get from the Holy See "a square deal for Father Burke." (William Montavon, head of the NCWC legal department, in a memo of November 8, 1928, to Burke, said that Calles' admiration for Burke showed that "he has in his makeup a strong element of honor and fairness." One wonders if Montavon's esteem for Burke brushed off on Calles whose record as a rabid anticlerical in the 1930s was hardly an example of fairness.)

On November 20, 1928, Morrow informed Burke that Calles was now ready to authorize the return of the bishops. Calles had announced ten days earlier that unless the bishops returned "in the spirit which Father Burke showed at Vera Cruz he did not wish them to come back"; now he was ready to take them back in a spirit of conciliation ready for amicable discussion. But Morrow felt that this return should be negotiated before November 30th when Gil would take over as President, the assumption being that Gil would not be inclined to promote the return. Fumasoni-Biondi threw cold water on the hopes for peaceful return, insisting the promise be made over the signature of the Mexican Government. One week later, Cardinal Hayes of New York urged the delegate to settle the question before Calles left office. Burke in a memo wrote that the delegate had made it clear to him that the Holy See was disinclined to work through Morrow or enable him to get any credit for settling the question. The delegate however also made it clear

NEVER LOOK BACK

to Burke that he should so inform the cardinal *privately*.

So, the situation as Burke described it to the administrative committee meeting on November 12th was that the authorities of the Church (though who the determining authorities are would be difficult to say) were determined to conclude no agreement with Calles. But "now that Calles is to retire, we have word to be prepared to get busy again on the negotiations." Burke, however, was well aware that the Holy See still continued its demands for more favorable guarantees than those expressed in the Calles-Burke document.

A surprising new development now entered the tangled skein of events. A former Chilean ambassador to the US, Michael Cruchaga, visited Morrow in Mexico City on November 22nd, apprising him that Edmund Walsh, SJ, head of Georgetown University School of Foreign Service, had been authorized the previous June by Pope Pius XI to settle the Mexican problem. Cruchaga said that Walsh had requested his help in presenting to the Mexican Government terms and conditions under which the bishops would return. Two days later, Morrow interviewed Calles who told him that individuals claiming to represent the Church had paid him a visit but warned him not to mention it to Father Burke. When Morrow disclosed Cruchaga's name, Calles laughed and identified him as one of the callers. (Presumably Walsh had waited since June before calling on Morrow through an intermediary, hopeful that Calles' successor would be more amenable than he, as the Vatican seemed to think.) Although Morrow wanted to finish his task before Calles left office, Calles said that the time was too short for that but suggested that Burke and Ruiz might come down from the US to negotiate with Gil a few weeks after he assumed the presidency.

After the assassination of President-elect Obregon, Congress elected Portes Gil provisional president. He took office on November 30, 1928. While adjusting to the new role, he could not immediately tackle the church-state affair. At about this time, certain Mexican bishops issued a pastoral of a decidedly political nature, aligning themselves with the political movement of armed rebellion. It was a problem that Fumasoni-Biondi should have tackled, but in his insecurity he wanted to stay out of the affair, claiming the Mexican bishops had no regard for his word or his authority and that except for Diaz, "all the bishops are in favor of armed revolution." Bernardini finally persuaded the delegate that he had an obligation to Mexico as well as to the United States to suppress the pastoral, or if already published, to withdraw it from circulation. The delegate's last gambit was to say he had no *official* knowledge of the pastoral: he knew only the excerpts shown him. But Bernardini asserted, "You know *de facto* and whether the bishops pay any attention to you or not, it is your duty to telephone at once and order withdrawal of the pastoral. The Holy See will ask you what you did and you ought to be in a position to show you did at once the right thing." Burke supported this, as did Diaz, Marella and Leech who were present. So, on December 4th, the telephone message went out to Ruiz at Los Angeles: "I have just read extracts from pastoral in *La Prensa*. Before publishing it, send me full official text of pastoral and await my answer. Fumasoni-Biondi." Burke, concluding his memo on the episode, wrote: "Thus ended the evening at the delegation: I to my house where I composed a so-called poem to Our Lady of the Cenacle."

Morrow and Burke were not particularly sanguine about their mission of peace and religious liberty as Gil began his term as provisional President. The Vatican had notified Fumasoni-Biondi in November that it would not permit resumption of worship until the government offered "more favorable conditions than those expressed in the letter of President Calles to Father Burke," a rather inept way of saying the Vatican was not disposed to approve a proposal made by Father Burke. After all their work, Morrow and Burke found the Vatican still dissatisfied with their efforts. Burke began to wonder if he had been eased out of his official role as negotiator. Father Edmund Walsh in New York (November 29th) had phoned Morrow who was also in New York at the time, asking for an appointment to discuss the Mexican situation. Morrow, uncertain about Walsh's status in the negotiations, told him he should see the apostolic delegate, his superior (as Morrow phrased it), to find out who had authority to speak for the Holy See in the Mexican matter. Morrow was beginning to wonder himself. Walsh visited the delegate immediately. Next morning, Burke asked the delegate about Walsh's visit but he merely shrugged his shoulders, uncommunicative, and proceeded to remark that he considered Morrow long-winded. This episode troubled Burke because he had felt he was the official agent and properly accredited representative of the delegate. The conversation then shifted to Morrow's suggestion that since the Mexican Government would receive Fumasoni-Biondi as apostolic delegate, he should go down there to settle the controversy. But the delegate said that if the invitation came, he would forward it to the Holy See. If the Holy See empowered him to act, he would do so but he suspected the Holy See would take a long time to think it over. What Fumasoni-Biondi seemed to be saying was that he suspected the Vatican no longer listened to him but bypassed and ignored him.

With his passion for definiteness, Burke must have been exasperated by this incomprehensible muddle. The Vatican wanted to have nothing to do with Calles or Morrow (Marella on December 30th said the Holy See was cold to anything coming from Morrow.) Ruiz was considered unreliable, agreeing with whomever he spoke to last, as Gasparri said of him; the Mexican bishops were at loggerheads, some favoring an early return, others an armed insurrection (like that bishop who said he would follow his own conscience, not the Pope's). Then there were certain American bishops who wanted armed intervention by the United States; Fumasoni-Biondi was nervous, insecure, wondering if he was on the shelf; Father Walsh claimed to be an official Vatican negotiator but was said to be on the side of the rebels. The Paulist who had worked hard to bring about some kind of unity among the 15,000 Catholic societies during World War I was now knee deep in an incomprehensible complexity of official assignments and unofficial opinions. The more complicated the situation became, the more Morrow seemed to rely on Burke. Several times during December 1928 Morrow asked Burke if he would go down to Mexico City if Gil so agreed. On at least one occasion (December 15th) Burke agreed to go, if ordered by the delegate, and the delegate said he himself would go if ordered to do so by the Holy See but that Burke must also go along with him. Morrow had been reading up on Mexican history and told Burke he had come to the conclusion that churchmen in Mexico had almost invariably "bet on the wrong horse" due to lack of foresight and of real knowledge of Mexico and its people. Obviously Morrow had reservations about drawing the Mexican bishops into the negotiations but he was also aware of Mexican Catholics' national pride.

The new year arrived without any dramatic developments. On January 1, 1929, Burke visited the delegate in regard to a draft letter to be submitted to President Gil, hopefully for his signature. The delegate felt it was too lengthy, preferring the type of letter Calles signed at Vera Cruz, but Morrow preferred to send no letter at all. On January 26th, Morrow on vacation asked Burke to come over to the State Department in Washington. He was pessimistic, saying that influential old-regime Catholic families had persuaded the Holy See against concluding any agreement. "The Holy See is not willing to make peace with the present Government under any circumstances." Burke insisted his conclusion was wrong, that the Holy See would have settled even with the Calles Government had it offered sufficient guarantees. Morrow was not convinced; the old-regime Mexicans had succeeded in talking down any proposed agreement with a revolutionary Government. Morrow was also pessimistic about the future cooperation to be expected from the American State Department. He had just come from an interview with President Hoover at Miami and formed the impression that "in a short time the freedom that has been extended to us by officials of the State Department will be chilled and curtailed."

On February 13th Morrow called Undersecretary of State Clark, who relayed his message to Burke. Morrow had gone to visit President Gil to congratulate him on escaping a train-wreck planned to assassinate him. To Morrow's surprise, Gil asked if Father Burke would come down to Mexico to see him at once. Gil was without the anti-Catholic hatred felt by Calles, according to Morrow, and was ready to go along with the negotiations. Burke graciously declined the invitation because he was scheduled to go on a trip to Europe with Fumasoni-Biondi which would include a visit to Rome. There he would talk with Gasparri.

In a private memo (undated—about February 17th or 18th) Burke jotted down what he entitled "Some Thoughts." He was critical of the war-mindedness of the Mexican Catholics, asserting quite emphatically that the policy of priests, bishops, organized laity has been to overthrow the government. "They have entertained no thought of accepting it, even of accepting it with conditions that would permit the Church to return with dignity and resume the public cult." He then goes on to say that "no word of public regret or condemnation has ever been sent forth by Mexican bishop or bishops, or Mexican priest or priests, or Catholic Mexican organizations on the atrocities perpetrated against officials of the Government or the Government itself." Burke claimed that in the struggles to secure a decent living and recognition of the rights of the masses, the churchmen had not been willing to consider how they could help in unifying Mexico on some common, tenable grounds:

No: they identified themselves with a political movement that had in view the restoration of the Church's rights but also the overthrow of all the aspirations of the revolutionary movement in Mexico. A national movement which might have unified Mexico has been neglected; left unconsidered, indeed opposed —not only because in part it was altogether opposed to the Church and the teachings of the Church but also because it was opposed to the political, the traditionally political views of the Catholic leaders . . . either a Government politically favorable to what Catholic leaders ask in Mexico will reign or no Government at all. Rather they would let souls starve and go unshepherded—until the Church's ministers go back in political triumph.

The common opinion of the Mexican bishops, according to Burke, "is that American intervention is the only hope. Only last night Archbishop Ruiz said this to me very explicitly." Which means, Burke continued, that historically these bishops will be put down in the history of their country as they who betrayed it to a foreigner.

But with the United States in Mexico, we will deal with a power that has no sympathy nor understanding of the traditional views and beliefs of the Mexican people. We are not liked in Mexico: we will be loved less after we go in. We have no more right to go in than England had to go into and dominate Ireland. And the Mexican patriotic songs for generations will be against the invader and will hymn maledictions on all who aided him to come.

A stern castigation of the bishops—yet it seems to be an accurate reflection of their mind. Just a few months earlier, Fumasoni-Biondi had said that except for Diaz, all the Mexican bishops were in favor of armed revolution. Had this attitude reached Rome? Months later, after these musings of Burke on the Mexican bishops, Walter Lippmann had an interview with Cardinal Gasparri, papal secretary of state. Gasparri denounced the American Government for its embargo on arms, making it clear to Lippmann that he had hoped to see the armed rebels overthrow the Government.

As February wore on, the State Department learned that an armed rebellion was brewing in Mexico, led by three top generals who wanted to oust Calles from any position of influence. Undersecretary of State Clark thought American intervention inevitable, and deplored it. On March 13th the insurrection erupted, a major revolution. One of the first acts of these rebels was a manifesto of complete religious liberty to all denominations in the territory. In the following weeks the well-armed rebels gathered more and more civilian support in their conflict with the Calles-controlled Gil Government. The Catholic rebels kept up their rebellion independently but interpreted the manifesto of religious liberty as a mere bid for Catholic support, containing "no real commitment to change in the constitution if the rebel generals won." The "political insurrection" gradually petered out but if the Catholic rebels had united with the "political insurrection" the combined forces would have created a serious predicament for the government troops, led by Calles. The refusal of the Cristeros to join up with the "political insurrection" was welcomed by Morrow: it tended to discredit rumors that the Cristeros were involved in the February train-wreck attempt on Gil's life. Gil himself had told Morrow that persons connected with the Liga Nacional had dynamited the train.

The Catholic rebels still continued their rebellion, even though it was a losing cause, as is evident in the following appeal to Mexican citizens dated April 18, 1929 and marked "Los Angeles, California":

The day for which we have longed has at last arrived. It is the will of Christ the King for the glory of all his holy martyrs. Well, then, blessed be the hour in which we live! What are we to do? Certainly we cannot complain if we fail to take advantage of the opportunity given us. Therefore, if you are true Catholic citizens of Mexico, you should with all devotion place at the disposal of the holy cause, all your money and all your blood.

The message ends: "Down with the heretical government of the Revolution! Long live Christ the King!" The heretical revolution cited is, of course, not the 1929 rebellion but the continuing anti-Catholic revolution that began in 1910.

In April, Burke in Rome wired Montavon to say that Augustin Legoretta, president of the Banco Nacional in Mexico City, would be acceptable to the Vatican as negotiator. Gasparri had announced he would "warmly welcome" a Mexican representative to discuss the religious controversy. Since the Holy See now seemed ready to resume the discussions, Morrow informed the Mexican Government he was ready to resume the discussions inaugurated by Calles and Burke. His aim was not to strive for changes in the constitution, desirable as that would be, but merely for a *modus vivendi* to permit the bishops to resume worship. He knew that Calles, the power behind Gil, would never for a moment consent to a change in the constitution. Morrow's efforts however met with considerable immediate opposition due to rumors circulated by defeated rebels that Morrow was responsible for the continuation of the arms embargo. Rumors of a plot to assassinate Morrow were rife, and the State Department felt that Mexican Catholic authorities should repudiate the threats against his life. Bernardini proved to be angrily anti-Morrow in this matter. He engaged in a tirade against him, asserting that he had made himself the agent of Calles in the persecution of Catholics and that it was only natural that someone should seek to kill him, so "there is nothing for the Church authorities to do."

Burke differed from Bernardini, agreeing with the State Department that the bland, non-committal statements from Diaz and Ruiz were not a sufficient repudiation of the threats from Mexican Catholics. In a conversation with Marella at the apostolic delegation, Montavon advocated an emphatic repudiation. His report of the incident is graphic: "I tried to discuss the subject but Msgr. Marella grew excited and spoke at such a high pitch that he could be heard a block away." Obviously Marella suspected Morrow had a hand in maintaining the arms embargo. When Montavon asked Archbishop Ruiz to make a strong statement condemning these threats from Mexican Catholics, he declined, saying that anti-Morrow feeling was so strong among Mexican Catholics that if any bishop denounced a plot to assassinate Morrow, he would lose standing and only irritate his people. Finally, the whole "plot" to kill Morrow was discovered to be a false alarm and the issue died.

Encouraged by evidences of the Vatican's new interest in negotiations, Morrow worked on plans for basing a *modus vivendi* on the Burke-Calles letters (March 29, 1928 and April 4, 1928). Then on May 3rd he received some startling news from Miguel Cruchaga, the Chilean diplomat who had told Morrow several months earlier that Pius XI had appointed Father Edmund Walsh to negotiate the Mexican question. Cruchaga informed Morrow that he had recently held two long conversations with the Pope and that Walsh was now in Mexico purportedly as a representative of Georgetown University but actually to report on the religious situation. On May 4th Walsh visited Morrow to let him know that the Pope favored a settlement as soon as possible. Walsh's role was an enigma to Morrow; in fact, he confided to Morrow that he did not want Burke or Archbishop Diaz to know he was in Mexico yet he did seem to possess some authority to negotiate while disclaiming any power to make a final settlement. (A search of the Edmund Walsh papers at Georgetown University failed to turn up any evidence of a Vatican appointment of Father Walsh as a negotiator.) Another puzzling figure who appeared on the scene about this time was a Britisher named Dupernex who muddied the waters by claiming that Morrow should have promoted the rebels' cause and that the Mexican Catholics he had met considered Burke a dupe of Calles. According to Montavon, what information Dupernex possessed in regard to Mexico he acquired from reading *The Wall Street Journal*.

Ruiz, on the other hand, sounded a helpful note. Interviewed by the press on May 2, 1929, he praised President Gil's recent remarks about the possibilities of religious peace and said that Gil was right in stating that the conflict could be solved by men of good will. "The Catholic citizens of my country" said Ruiz, "whose faith and patriotism can never be doubted, will accept sincerely any agreement reached between the Church and the Government." When Gil heard about Ruiz's interview, he commended him (probably at the instance of Morrow) and stated that it would be possible to conduct discussions between the Mexican bishops' representatives and government officials, and that he himself would gladly confer with Ruiz. Even though the constitution forbade official relations between Mexico and the Vatican, said Gil, this would not prevent informal discussions and "if Archbishop Ruiz should desire to discuss with me the method of securing the cooperation in the moral effort for the betterment of the Mexican people, I shall have no objection to conferring with him on the subject." Burke was happy about this mutual expression of good will but perplexed by two minor concerns. He had informed the State Department of the appointment of Ruiz as apostolic delegate to Mexico but the Vatican would not allow him to publish the news. Secondly, Father Walsh was on the scene in Mexico allegedly as an appointee of the Holy See but Walsh was trying to conceal from Burke any knowledge of his presence in Mexico.

Father Walsh was very much on the scene. On May 8th he informed Morrow that Bishop Miguel de la Mora, a supporter of the rebellion launched by the Cristeros, was so enthusiastic about the Ruiz-Gil exchange that he had urged the Holy See to push a quick settlement. Cruchaga, according to Walsh, had wired Rome asking that, since an adjustment was imminent, Walsh be instructed to settle the differences. When Morrow queried Walsh as to terms he would consider acceptable to the Mexican bishops, he produced a formidable list of maximum and minimum demands, which Morrow explained were inapplicable; Gil had promised only a discussion of the scope and interpretation of the anti-clerical laws, not a change in the laws. Then Walsh fell back on the identical terms proposed by Father Burke a year earlier.

On May 11th, Morrow forwarded to Ruiz via the American State Department a draft of a proposed letter Ruiz might send directly to Gil asking for resumption of the discussions: it represented basically the terms Burke and Calles had agreed upon in their exchange in 1928. It focused on suggested promises that Gil would entertain no desire to destroy the identity of the Church, that registration of priests would not mean that the Government would register a priest not named by the bishops, that religious instructions might be given in a church, that the Government would confer occasionally with the head of the Church in Mexico to prevent unreasonable application of the laws and constitution, and that the clergy would have a right to apply for modifications of the law. The only substantial departure from the substance of the Burke-Calles Agreement was the proposed stipulation that the Government be willing to confer with the head of the Church in Mexico to avoid unreasonable application of the laws. This, Montavon pointed out, was clearer and more forceful than the Burke-Calles correspondence. The point about religious instruction in the churches had been discussed verbally by Burke and Calles.

The next step was to make sure (1) that the Vatican would approve the sending of such a draft letter to President Gil and (2) that Gil would accept in terms of the letter. While waiting for the Holy See to reply, Montavon became involved in a curious bit of cloak-and-dagger theatrics. In his May 15th "confidential memorandum" he reported that Ruiz asked him to accompany him to meet a person who had called on Ruiz and had informed him about an important long-distance phone call to be held that evening between an important person in Mexico City and a distinguished person in Washington, both of whom had requested that Ruiz be present during the phone conversation. The caller turned out to be a Mr. Healey of the Georgetown School of Social Service. To set the stage for the approaching telephonic drama, Montavon provided some background material in his confidential memo. It seems that Father Walsh of Georgetown had been in Mexico City ostensibly to visit the rector of the National University of Mexico but actually to busy himself with the church-state problem "and had been received with open arms by the most radical and fanatical Catholic elements in Mexico City." Father Walsh's collaborator, Cruchaga, had contacted Morrow in Mexico City to inform him that he, Cruchaga, and Father Walsh were working under instructions from the Vatican, and to ask Morrow if he would like to meet Father Walsh. Rather strange, commented Montavon, that an official of an American university would employ a Chilean agent to help him meet an American ambassador in Mexico City. At any rate, Morrow agreed to have Walsh as a luncheon guest on this very day, May 15th. Morrow did not let on what he knew about Walsh's role but Montavon mentioned in the memo that Augustin Legoretta, president of the Bank of Mexico, puzzled by the presence of Walsh in Mexico City, had cabled papal Secretary of State Gasparri, to be informed by Gasparri that Walsh had been asked to report on conditions affecting the Church in Mexico but "had no instructions nor any authority to negotiate any settlement or on his own initiative to do anything whatever toward the settlement of the controversy." Gasparri said that Ruiz, as apostolic delegate to Mexico, was the only person authorized by the Holy See to do anything in the matter.

During the lunch, according to the Montavon memo, Walsh informed Morrow he was in Mexico to report on "the situation" but gave the impression to Morrow that while Ruiz was the official negotiator, Walsh was to conduct the actual negotiations. Morrow of course said nothing more than that Ruiz had authority to act and that he (Morrow) felt obliged to do only what the delegate in Washington and Ruiz approved.

So, Ruiz, Montavon and Healey met at the Georgetown School of Social Service on May 15th with Mr. Cohen, an interpreter: Walsh phoning from Mexico City, talking to Cohen, Ruiz and Healey, who was on an extension line listening in. Walsh asked Ruiz if he had been instructed to act as representative of the Church, to which Ruiz answered, "No." Walsh then told Ruiz he was making a mistake in sounding out his fellow bishops about the meetings with the Government, his argument apparently being that this had alarmed the Catholics, and the government officials would be resentful of the notion that the archbishop would need the consent of his colleagues before proceeding. Then he scolded Ruiz for imprudence in selecting Manuel Echevarria as his agent and instructed him to publicly repudiate Echevarria. (Montavon noted that the selection of Echevarria was only a rumor.) Then Walsh claimed he was in good standing with the American Embassy and felt he could transmit his report on conditions through the diplomatic pouch of the State Department to Ruiz.

Montavon relished the weirdness of the phone call. In his memo he stressed the incongruity of inviting an archbishop to an unknown place for a conference with persons of whom he knew nothing and without advising him as to what would be discussed. Walsh later conferred with Morrow without letting him know he had talked with Ruiz. Morrow told Walsh that the most important service he could perform at this time would be to pacify the Catholic fanatics in Mexico, most of whom were members of the Liga Nacional and devoted to the Jesuits.

The Vatican had been insisting all along that Mexico should send a representative to Rome to discuss the church-state problem but Morrow had been skeptical about this because of the absence of diplomatic relations. On May 16th the good news came from Cardinal Gasparri (through British diplomats at Rome and in Mexico City) that the Holy See had dropped its insistence on a Mexican emissary to the Vatican but had decided that a conference between Vatican and Mexican representatives would be necessary, preferably in a neutral country. The good news was also bad news in the sense that it appeared to be a snub to Morrow and the State Department since it came through British officials. Montavon comments:

The attitude assumed by the Holy See has had only one result, namely to prevent Ambassador Morrow and the Government of the United States from rendering effectively their unofficial assistance to the Church in this trying situation. The apparent snub, which is now given to Ambassador Morrow by the Holy See by employing the British channels for making known its reversal of attitude can easily be interpreted as notice served on the American ambassador and the State Department that their services are neither desired nor appreciated.

The time was propitious for a meeting between Ruiz and the President. The archbishop asked for an appointment with Gil (via Morrow) and June 12th was fixed as the long-awaited day. On May 28th Burke was confined to his home with illness, but Ruiz, Morrow, Lane, Montavon and Burke gathered in Burke's library for a two-hour conference to discuss Ruiz's forthcoming trip. Morrow felt moderately optimistic—the great majority of the Mexican bishops now favored an agreement. But Ruiz dropped a bombshell that shook Morrow. Ruiz said he planned to ask Gil for an explicit promise that the constitution and laws would be changed, that without this, the Vatican would not consent to the bishops' return. This was an unwitting but preposterous rejection of Morrow's policy which consisted of persistent efforts to get the Church back in operation, leaving change in laws to a later time. Such a demand, said Morrow, would be a disaster because Mexico was at that moment on the verge of a political campaign and a demand for change in the constitution would throw the religious issue into the political arena and thereby kill any possible chance of settlement. Morrow spoke with great feeling, stating that he was well aware how Catholics felt about him and his motives. Burke wrote in his memo for that day, "In most solemn, even tragic tones, he (Morrow) assured Ruiz that he was a friend of the Catholic Church; that he deplored the lack of Catholic ministration for the last three years to the Mexican people. . . ." He offered to give up his vacation, to go back if it would serve the Church but he told Ruiz that if he insisted on this demand for a change in the constitution, it would be better that he never went down to Mexico, that a good spirit now exists but he could kill it and put back the settlement of the question for two or three years. Ruiz thereupon backtracked and said he would only ask for a promise that some consideration be given to change in the laws and the constitution. During the exchange, Morrow hinted several times that he would gladly go down to help Ruiz but not once did Ruiz accept.

The next day, May 29th, Morrow heard from Cohen, the man who took part in the telephone call at Georgetown School of Social Service, stating that Ruiz would head up the negotiations with Gil, but that Father Walsh would be his one and only assistant, sending out communications through the Jesuit provincial in Washington. Morrow deplored this turn of events, saying repeatedly to Montavon that Ruiz and Walsh were heading "straight for the rocks." He did concede however that Walsh might help Ruiz because of the influence Walsh exerted over the Catholic extremists.

With June 12th set as the day for the meeting with Gil, Archbishop Ruiz left for Mexico City, accompanied by Archbishop Diaz. Father Burke was willing to go with Ruiz but the archbishop preferred to have the agreement made by Mexican citizens. On June 10th Father Walsh visited Morrow in Mexico City and told him that Ruiz and Diaz had arrived without any specific plan and decided to rely on the terms of the Burke-Calles Agreement. The first session was cordial all around, Gil and the bishops agreeing to accept the terms of the Burke-Calles Agreement. Walsh was not present at the meetings, but apparently spread rumors that the atmosphere at the first meeting was uncongenial. Morrow then submitted to Ruiz a draft decree, embodying the basic principles accepted by Calles and Burke in 1928. The draft was accepted by the Vatican and the meetings had a happy ending. Fumasoni-Biondi expressed his gratitude for Morrow's role but curiously, Ruiz's cable announcing the results of the meeting thanked Burke, the NCWC and Fumasoni-Biondi but not a word of thanks to Morrow. The agreement was comprised of two statements (June 21, 1929), one made by Gil, the other by Ruiz. Gil's statement said that it was not the purpose of the constitution, the laws or the Government of Mexico "to destroy the identity of the Catholic Church or of any other, or to interfere in any way with its spiritual functions." As to certain provisions of the law "which have been misunderstood" he declared that registration of priests did not mean the Government could register priests not named by proper ecclesiastical authority, that religious instruction could be given in the churches, and that all residents of the country enjoy the right of petition regarding the amendment, repeal or passage of any law. The statement by Ruiz said that, as a result of the statement made by the President, "the Mexican clergy will resume religious services pursuant to the laws in force."

Typical of the tributes that poured into Burke after the *modus vivendi* was accepted was a letter from Undersecretary of State Olds, who wrote:

The reestablishment of public worship in a country of fifteen million inhabitants is, indeed, an historic accomplishment and I can well understand your own deep satisfaction. No doubt you consider the result itself as reward enough for all that you have been through, but I shall never feel quite right about it all until I learn that the great institution which you serve with so much ability and devotion has given adequate and substantial recognition of the splendid thing which you have contributed so largely to bring about. Perhaps nobody can appreciate as I do that the result would have been quite impossible without your understanding personality and tireless effort. Your superiors owe you more than they will ever realize or ever can repay. . . . I only hope that the whole situation from now on will have your guidance. With you and our friend below the border standing on guard, we can all of us feel confident that everything humanly possible to work out the problem with an eventual definite concordat in mind will be done. (June 24, 1929)

chapter 8

Burke, Roosevelt and the fragile peace

After the Gil-Ruiz meetings, Father Walsh invited Morrow to attend a diplomatic Mass to be offered in thanksgiving for the successful work of Father Walsh and Cruchaga. Morrow thought he ought to attend and so he consulted Diaz and Ruiz: both prelates said they would not attend and that Morrow should not go. Morrow then consulted the minister of government of Mexico who asserted that the proposed Mass was not pleasing to the Government. The minister of foreign affairs registered a protest with Morrow over the Mass, most of the diplomatic corps attending nevertheless (Burke memo, October 1, 1929).

The course of the church-state conflict had been so clouded by twists and turns of fortune that one might find it hard to obtain a right perspective on the cast of characters. It is crystal clear, however, that Morrow and Burke played the main roles, initiating the negotiations, sustaining them in spite of opposition and composing the documents of April-May 1928 that became the *modus vivendi* of June 1929, terminating the negotiations. Burke's authority as duly accredited agent of the apostolic delegate to the United States was unquestionable: Morrow affirmed that the letter from Bishop Diaz attesting to that authority was on file in the American embassy in Mexico City and had been shown to Calles. In fact, Calles had advised Gil that he should insist on dealing with the priest who had been authorized to engage in the negotiations, Father Burke, and that other claimants be asked to communicate through Burke.

A piquant sequel to the termination of negotiations was a petition composed by Fumasoni-Biondi, the apostolic delegate, requesting Knighthood of St. Gregory for Montavon. The delegate and Marella (June 5, 1929) went to Burke's home with the petition, asking for Burke's approval, which he gave gladly. In this petition to Gasparri, the delegate singled out for special praise Montavon's work in connection with the Mexican question. One main reason for asking for the honor, according to the delegate's letter, was that "some (particularly Father Walsh) were seeking to give the impression that the adjustment made was the result of the labors of the Society of Jesus. As a matter of fact, it was made only after three years of patient labor, and by those who so labored in that time: that what had been obtained could have been obtained two years ago. . . . the NCWC had worked intelligently and courageously from the beginning." The delegate asked no letter of approval for the work of NCWC because the Holy Father had given that approval years ago but he did ask for Knighthood for Montavon. "The studied publicity sought for himself by Father Walsh was injuring the cause of the Near East with the American bishops; was injuring the name of the Church; and injuring also the prestige of the great religious society of which Father Walsh is a member."

The end of the negotiations, unfortunately, did not terminate the persecution. Gil had promised that rebels who would surrender their weapons would be granted amnesty but hundreds who did surrender were put to death. In view of the past turbulent history of church-state relations in Mexico, a sudden cessation of hostilities could not have been reasonably expected. Moreover, Calles was still a power behind the throne, and the constitution was still unchanged and might be brutally applied at any time. The general situation however had improved, especially because of the bishops' rigorous observance of the terms of the *modus vivendi*, Ruiz having ordered the Liga Nacional to change its name and work for peaceful purposes.

In December 1929, Burke discovered that President-elect Rubio was about to visit the United States. With Morrow,

Montavon, Lane and Rublee (of the US embassy in Mexico), Burke met Rubio on December 28th at the Carlton. He pointed out to Rubio that the *modus vivendi* was not at all conclusive or final: it was only an adjustment, though an adjustment the Church welcomed in order to serve the people. But the Church wanted a change in the laws and constitution in order to enjoy the liberty to which it was entitled. The Church did not take part in partisan politics nor use illegal means of enforcing its rights, said Burke, but it did seek an improvement in the conditions of its life and work. He urged Rubio to use his good offices to bring about a change in laws and constitution for the sake of justice but also to give Mexico more stability as a nation. Rubio responded that there were extremists on both sides (and he said he was not on the side of Calles who was hostile to the Church). He stated very strongly that he believed the laws ought to be changed but that an attempt to change now would be a disaster; his own party would not stand by him. "If the Catholics will for the time being be patient and wait quietly, I will be able, after two years, to secure such changes. I think they ought to be made." Morrow, well pleased with the interview, said he had never heard Rubio express himself so definitely.

Rubio took over in February 1930 and Burke reported to the administrative committee that the *modus vivendi* seemed to be working. Ruiz however was deluged with complaints from both sides and had asked Burke to come down to Mexico, presumably as a trouble-shooter, but Burke's ill health prevented the trip. He sent Montavon instead, and Montavon found that one of Ruiz's problems was a Bishop Manriquez of Huejutila, living in Los Angeles in exile but agitating against the 1929 agreement. Another trouble-maker was the Jesuit, Bernardo Portas, who told Montavon, "Kill Calles and a few such and things will be all right in Mexico." Contending that Ruiz had been trapped, Portas claimed that it was a moral obligation for Catholics to war against Calles. Ruiz himself told Montavon that the Vatican was disgruntled over the Government's failure to radically improve the situation but that the Vatican made the mistake of thinking the Mexican Government was one of institutions, whereas it was only a political party shot through with political rivalries.

In December 1931 there was a flareup over the celebration of the fourth centenary of the apparition at the shrine of Our Lady of Guadalupe. Federal employees who took part in the celebration were punished, and the quota of priests in Mexico reduced. Tabasco, with a population of 200,000, was allowed only one priest. Archbishop Ruiz was exiled. Burke arranged for him to enter the US but his grim conclusion was: "From information given me by the State Department, it is beyond doubt that the Mexican Government has repudiated the acceptance of the *modus vivendi* of 1929."

Calles, the grey eminence and political boss of presidents, went about stirring up anti-Catholic feeling and claiming that the Church was incapable of keeping its members in line through obedience. When Calles made these observations to Undersecretary Clark, Burke sent Clark (March 15, 1932) a copy of the Pope's recent letter in which he fully supported the *modus vivendi* and condemned armed rebellion. As to Calles' allegation that the Church could not keep its sheep in line, Burke adroitly responded that Calles would be the first to complain if the Church did command the political activities of Catholics. Burke went on to say that in failing to live up to the *modus vivendi*, the Government was giving a handle to those militant Catholics who had asserted the Government would be more intolerant after than before the agreement.

As the months went by in 1932, it became progressively more obvious that Plutarco Calles was not mellowing with age but hardening in his policy of hostility to the Catholics, especially the clergy. Burke believed that many of Calles' anti-Church moves were political gambits to retain political clout in his party and to show he had not sold out to the enemy. What disturbed Burke even more however was a change that he felt was taking place in the American State Department, verging on a repudiation of Morrow's attitude to the Church. He wrote in a memo (October 16, 1932) that Lane gave him the impression that "he had lost trust in the good faith of any and all the Catholic Church leaders in Mexico, and could no longer positively assure himself of whom he might trust or depend upon."

The attitude of American liberals disturbed and disappointed Burke. In a resolution submitted to the administrative committee for their approval, he called to the attention of American liberals their inconsistency in condemning suppression of liberty in Russia while tolerating it in Mexico: "Those right-minded men and women who fear the rise of absolutism in the name of Communism cannot fail to note the close connection between the avowed purpose of Russia to stamp out all religion within its borders and the excuses which fail to explain or extenuate the same excesses and disregard for human rights in Mexico."

When Franklin D. Roosevelt became President in March 1933 American Catholics expected big things from him in the form of radical changes in our policy on Mexico. They considered him a friend, unlike Herbert Hoover who was generally unpopular in Catholic circles, and they counted on FDR to relax the persecution of their Mexican confreres. The NCWC news service seemed to find ground for hope in the selection of Josephus Daniels as Ambassador to Mexico, saying that, "FDR would have a personal representative in this extra sensitive post." (Dwight Morrow had relinquished the ambassadorship and had become senator from New Jersey in 1930, to be succeeded by Reuben Clark as ambassador; Morrow died on October 5, 1931. Josephus Daniels therefore had succeeded Clark.) Burke and Daniels had worked together during the European war when Burke was chairman of the Committee of Six, Daniels, Secretary of the Navy. On April 3, 1933, Burke called on him and found him anxious to help but quite uninformed on the Mexican controversy, juvenile in his religious concepts, tending to see religion as a matter of good works rather than faith and worship, with no driving aspiration to solve the Mexican problem, a condition of temperament due more to lack of initiative than to lack of courage. Burke laid a heavy emphasis on the theme that the American Government should display a policy of favoring religious liberty in Mexico, his aim being to counteract Roosevelt's theme that religious liberty was Mexico's domestic affair and therefore not an American concern. After the visit, Burke wrote Daniels a letter explaining just why the controversy was full of potential dynamite.

The administrative committee had issued a reasonable statement in January 1933 asking American citizens to help restore religious liberty in Mexico but other statements by Catholics, notably prelates, contained more heat than light. Francis C. Kelley, Bishop of Oklahoma City, addressed a letter (May 30, 1934) to "Your Excellency" (presumably the apostolic delegate) advising him how badly the Mexican question was being handled and suggesting his own master plan. He called Morrow's way of dealing with it a blunder that played into the hands of the revolutionary Government. "Everything ended as I fully expected, in disaster." So American Catholics were really voiceless at this time, in Kelley's opinion. The solution? Follow the strategy Bishop Kelley employed when he handled the Mexican persecution in 1914: bring Catholic pressure to bear on the Government through Senate and House, "practically ignoring the State Department," accept the NCWC's contribution and stir up "a revival by Catholics of the agitation that I stirred up beginning with 1914."

Then on July 26th Josephus Daniels gave a talk. It was a monumental blunder, infuriating Catholics so deeply that many demanded his recall. The occasion was a seminar on education held at Mexico City. He extolled Calles' views on education, his realization of the significance of education for the future of Mexico and his resolve, "We must enter and take possession of the mind of childhood, the mind of youth." The latter statement probably reminded some Catholics of the scriptural verse about the seven devils entering into a man and leaving him in a bad way. The Calles type of education was considered atheistic and socialistic by American Catholics who, already excited about Soviet Communism, became furious over Daniels' remarks. He tried to explain himself, claiming he had the American public school type of education in mind, and the NCWC news service published his explanation in an attempt to quell the excitement, but it was futile. *America, Commonweal, The Catholic World* and other Catholic magazines excoriated him, then the diocesan papers joined in, followed by Catholic societies. Father Charles Coughlin went beyond the ambassador to the President as his target and said that American presidents for the last two decades had aided and abetted the rape of Mexico.

Father Burke found himself right in the middle of the scuffle once again. The new apostolic delegate, Amleto Cicognani, had asked him to work directly for the Holy See in the Mexican affair. Burke reported to the meeting of the administrative board on February 25, 1936, that he had asked the delegate to be excused from taking on this responsibility, "but the next day the apostolic delegate told me that a cable had come from the Holy Father explicitly asking that Father Burke be asked to take up this representation. Feeling that it would be the mind of the administrative committee that I should, I said that I would. This is a little difficult for me to report but I think you should know the fact." Burke did not specify the precise day of his acceptance of this new responsibility to the Holy See: he merely said the episode occurred about a year before. His regular duties as general secretary of the administrative committee, of course, had kept him close to the Mexican controversy.

He visited President Roosevelt on October 22, 1934, and, as was expected, the matter of Daniels' speech came up for discussion. Burke led up to it by informing FDR about Calles' speech at Guadalajara and about an amendment to the Mexican constitution that had passed the Mexican Senate, both of which reflected a trend to ban any education in Mexico except that which was atheistic. Then Burke asserted that, whether he intended it or not, Ambassador Daniels had given the impression that the US Government supported the atheistic education program outlined by Calles in his Guadalajara talk. Roosevelt said he thought that Daniels, as a religious man, would be the last man in the world to favor atheism. Burke conceded this, but said Daniels had given the impression of supporting the atheistic program. "Moreover, Daniels' speech was one that indirectly helped promote the communistic and atheistic program in a neighboring country, and this in itself was harmful to the well-being of our own country."

Roosevelt then said he thought something should be done. What did Father Burke suggest? Burke asked that the US authorities state that the US Government favored extension of education to all peoples but never did nor would encourage a program of education serving atheism and anti-religious influences. FDR thought a while, saying that certain forces in the US were seeking to exclude religion, then added, "I think such a statement ought to be made. I think it should be issued from Mexico City." This apparently satisfied Burke. Roosevelt, however, seemed to feel that the Catholic Church was opposing the spread of popular education in Mexico while the National Revolutionary Party was determined to promote it, so he asked Burke for proof that the Mexican Government was persecuting religion and working to destroy it. FDR was probably overwhelmed by Burke's citation of chapter and verse from the Six-Year Plan, the proposed amendment to the constitution, the reduction in the number of priests permitted to function, etc.— all of which Burke promised to send to the President. Then he requested of FDR his approval of Burke's discussing these matters with Secretary Hull and Mr. Phillips. The President said he would be glad to have Father Burke do so.

Then, according to Burke's memo, the President said,

Father Burke, I think we can go farther than this. I think I should informally send a message to Calles (for Calles, the President said, is the one power in Mexico) saying that I think if the Mexican Government proceeds with a program of exiling the bishops and priests and introducing an atheistic program,

Mexico would make of itself a spectacle before the civilized world." "Would you do that, Mr. President?" "Yes, I will do it informally." I then spoke of my thought that an approach might be made informally here by me to the ambassador from Mexico. But I would like to have the good will of my own Government. The President assured me that I had it and would have it in my plans with the State Department for such an approach and possible conference to be held.

After the meeting with Father Burke on October 22nd, the President expressed his mind informally but vigorously to the Mexican ambassador, bidding him convey to his Government the message that Mexico, as a civilized nation, should allow full liberty of worship to all citizens, and that it should stop persecuting Catholics. Not long afterwards, the ambassador informed Burke and the administrative board that his Government would accept an apostolic delegate if native-born, and would take steps to allow priests to minister in states where they had been forbidden as well as increase the number in other states. The Mexican Government, however, was unwilling to have it made known that it had been influenced by the US Government or by the Holy See and Burke felt obligated to respect this confidence so long as negotiations were pending.

Again, on November 12, 1934, Burke visited President Roosevelt, this time to report that the persecution was worse than ever, that the exodus of exiles to the US was creating a real problem that could only be effectively solved by a discussion between the Mexican and American Governments. Burke left with Roosevelt a memo which he proceeded to read immediately. In the memo Burke reminded Roosevelt that Mexico was exiling hundreds of Catholics including bishops, priests, nuns, laity without due process. The US had been offering them hospitality but this policy would soon be sowing seeds of resentment in the US, for the Bureau of Immigration, the State Department, and the Labor Department would soon be overwhelmed and embarrassed. Therefore, Burke pleaded that the federal Government use its good offices in approaching the Mexican Government to speak somewhat in this fashion: "The exiling of these your citizens is due to certain laws which your country has seen fit to enact of religious struggle and controversy. . . . We respectfully ask if it is not possible for the controversy to be settled and the cause of our own present and possibly future embarrassment be removed." The memo concluded with the suggestion that Roosevelt ask that the Mexican Government confer with representatives of the religious body in question.

Having read it, F.D.R.'s comment was: "I think this might well be done but I think this is putting it in too mild and gentlemanly a way. If I were ambassador to Mexico, I would speak very plainly to the Mexican Government." Roosevelt then promised he would speak about the matter to Secretary of State Hull.

In January 1935 Senator William Borah of Idaho introduced a resolution calling on the Senate Foreign Relations Committee to investigate the persecution in Mexico. Why Borah became identified with such a resolution is somewhat mysterious; he was an isolationist and he soon lost interest in the resolution. The Catholic press, however, and the K of C as well as certain bishops retained their enthusiasm for the resolution and campaigned hard for it, while the US Government considered it a colossal mistake, adhering strictly to the policy that the US should not intervene in the domestic affairs of another nation. In December 1933 the US had voted at Montevideo against any interference on the part of one nation in the affairs of another, thus setting up the basis for a good-neighbor policy. The Knights of Columbus persisted in their attempts to pressure President Roosevelt into positive action, declaring at a meeting with FDR in June that they spoke for 500,000 Knights of Columbus and for all American Catholics. The various Catholic protesters were quite imprecise in defining what they demanded but it does seem that they hoped for American armed intervention.

One of the loudest voices of protest was that of Archbishop Curley of Baltimore, bestowing some choice rhetoric on the administrative committee and Burke. In a talk at Washington, March 26th, he implied that twenty million American Catholics were fed up with Roosevelt's policy. He was even more bellicose in a talk at Baltimore, hitting at Burke in a reference to a mild-mannered priest taken in by Calles. "Let our gentle, sacerdotal diplomats in this country stay at home." As for the good-neighbor policy, he described Mexico as a father who comes home drunk, beats his wife and children, starves them and leaves them in rags. When he asked the administrative committee's support for the Borah resolution, he was most unhappy when every member of the committee voted against any public support of the resolution. He informed Archbishop Hanna, chairman, that if this decision ever became public, he would announce that the administrative committee had no right to speak for him or for any other bishop. Curley wrote to Hanna in such fashion as to give the impression that the administrative committee tolerated the persecution in Mexico. He apparently was unaware of Father Burke's back-breaking schedule and his efforts to rouse American Catholics to rational protest—the meetings with President Roosevelt, the steady push to publicize the bishops' statements on Mexico, the organizing of meetings to inform Catholics of the facts, the sending of hundreds of thousands of petitions and protests to the President, the answering of every false statement made by prominent Mexicans, the constant encouragement to the NCCM and the NCCW to activate their countless affiliate organizations—all the while keeping in touch with the apostolic delegate, the Mexican bishops, the secular and religious press and of course the American bishops.

Supreme Knight Martin Carmody (of the K of C) had conveyed to many American Catholics a clear impression that he favored American armed intervention but eventually claimed that he had never favored it, and that it was a dodge brought up by Roosevelt to confuse the issue. The noted pulpit orator, Father Charles Coughlin, was not at all hesitant about helping along a shooting war. In a letter (February 1, 1935) he suggested to Bishop Noll that he look into the possibility of raising funds to assist the needs of the Mexicans. "To put it bluntly, their chief need is relation to a few good machine guns." The letter was forwarded by Noll to Burke with the note, "Directed him to confer with you, Father Burke, lest his independent action might cross with what the Vatican and bishops may prefer. Arrange for a conference with Borah to post him. J.F.N." Later, in the 1936 election campaign, Coughlin announced he would not hesitate to use bullets, if he did not succeed with ballots, for the preservation of the constitution and liberty of conscience.

Bishop Noll himself on May 13th undertook to write a letter to Roosevelt. The Bishop of Fort Wayne was also a member of the administrative committee, NCWC; he indited a somewhat heavy-handed but impressive letter, urging the President to make a general statement on the right of religious liberty. "You are aware that you are often accused of having a little sympathy for Communism and a statement such as I have suggested would be calculated to end the criticism." Roosevelt sought Burke's advice. In a memo to his secretary, FDR wrote: "Memo for Mac. Will you take this up with Father Burke and ask him how I should answer this?" Mac (Marvin McIntyre) passed it along to Burke who submitted confidentially a proposed answer. Roosevelt drafted a reply that was practically verbatim with the Burke text, professing his reverence for religious liberty and promising that Noll's letter would continue to receive his earnest, thoughtful attention.

That Roosevelt did not lose votes in the 1936 election because of his Mexican policy may have been due at least in part to Burke's advice regarding Catholic opinion and to remarks on religious liberty made by FDR at Notre Dame University when he received an honorary degree (December 9, 1935). Cardinal Mundelein of Chicago, an enthusiastic supporter of FDR also helped by bestowing extravagant praise on the President, the constant target of criticism by the K of C, Archbishop Curley and Father Coughlin.

George Flynn in his *American Catholics and the Roosevelt Presidency* comments on the great importance of Father Burke during Roosevelt's terms of office:

Burke was respected at the White House: Roosevelt often called upon him to interpret and even answer letters from the hierarchy. Throughout the Mexican crisis this priest was sympathetic to both Roosevelt and Daniels. One typical example of his help came when Cardinal Hayes of New York, in mid-1935, expressed his disappointment that the President had not asserted himself in favor of religious freedom in Mexico. Burke immediately set the record straight, telling Hayes all that Roosevelt had done and was attempting to do within the bounds of diplomatic protocol. The cardinal must have been impressed, for he wrote to Burke apologizing for his ignorance and expressing appreciation for Roosevelt's efforts. Although Burke seems to have had little control over the Knights of Columbus, he continually criticized their actions toward the President (p. 180).

The President followed up his conversation with the Mexican ambassador by appointing Sumner Welles, Assistant Secretary of State, as his own personal representative in these matters. Now, even though the Mexican Government refused to hold conversations with the Vatican, Burke (or Montavon) under this new informal arrangement could meet with Welles, "the unrepresentative representative," unofficially. Through these contacts with Welles, Burke came to know and like him, finding him well-informed and alert to all the twists and turns of the controversy. Burke's main aim at the moment was to secure the Mexican Government's permission to allow an apostolic delegate into Mexico; although the Government had already consented to this, it consented only to the entrance of a native Mexican as delegate whereas the Vatican felt that Mexican bishops would not offer full obedience "to one of their own." Welles warned Burke that in his meetings with Roosevelt, any publicity released in regard to them would probably result in a breakdown of discussions. Wishing to help Welles reply to Catholic protests against Roosevelt on the score of his Mexican policy, Burke furnished him with a model reply tactful enough to turn away wrath and ending with the assurance that Roosevelt has championed and will continue to champion the principle of freedom of worship and of education for all nationals in every country of the world. On one occasion (July 15, 1935) Welles asked Burke if the President should make a public pronouncement, to which Burke responded that the Mexican Government could justly charge him with breach of faith if he did so, since the President had promised secrecy about the discussions. Welles said he would so inform FDR.

On August 31st, the Mexican Government issued a decree on nationalization of property which Burke felt was evidence of a purpose to destroy the Church in Mexico. Welles conveyed to the Mexican Government Burke's reaction to this and the Government responded that it would be willing to consider holding a conference with an apostolic delegate in regard to the decree. Happily, Calles was now out of the picture, having been ousted by President Lazaro Cardenas. The exile took up residence in San Diego, California. The big question was of course, the appointment of an apostolic delegate to Mexico. Welles told Burke that he had urged the Mexican ambassador to suggest the appointment of a non-Mexican but the Mexican Government insisted on a Mexican. The Vatican cabled that it would not appoint an apostolic delegate unless the Mexican Government gave guarantees that he would be allowed to carry on his functions without being exiled. So the controversy dragged on.

On January 6, 1936, Burke received a visit from Monsignor Egidio Vagnozzi of the apostolic delegate's staff. He showed Burke a letter from the Holy See relating to the Vatican's position on the troubles in Mexico and outlining its attitude toward armed rebellion. Burke wrote in his memo for January 6th that the letter was addressed to the apostolic delegate in response to the delegate's inquiry about armed rebellion by Catholics in Mexico. It said that the attitude of the Church must be plainly stated—that the Church sought peace and would be against armed rebellion. But with regard to the action of the citizens of a country, the Church would insist upon obedience to constituted authority. When such authority became tyrannical, the Church could not see its way to condemn citizens who, by armed rebellion, sought to destroy such tyranny provided the results of the rebellion did not bring worse consequences in the way of tyranny than had existed before. The letter contained a long quotation from the "Summa." Burke's memo continued:

After reading the letter, Monsignor Vagnozzi turned to me and said, "You see the situation is now in the hands of the Jesuits. They have shown their power. The Holy Father is not really informed of the situation or the facts."
I said I felt like giving up all part in the work. Monsignor Vagnozzi at once said that I must keep on. . . . The impression, I felt, was being given that the Church (the Holy Father) was engaged in jockeying for position over small matters; warding off this or that or asking for this lesser thing; showing an absence of knowledge or judgment on the larger questions involved. I said I had tried faithfully to report and to act as the delegate had instructed me. I had ever sought to place the position of the Holy See in the highest light, the worthiest way. It might be my fault, I said. But I couldn't help reporting the impression made on me that the United States Government was in turn being impressed by the vacillating, wavering, unforceful and indefinite character of our conversations. . . . Monsignor Vagnozzi not only agreed with me but went far further in his adverse criticism of the present Vatican secretariate than I had done.

On January 9, 1936 the apostolic delegate, Cicognani, became excited about the incorporation of a bishops' committee relating to a certain seminary for the training of Mexican "seminarians" in the US. He was emphatic in his denunciation of Archbishop Curley and Bishop Kelley. "The former was not honest; the latter had no brains." He said he would not break with Curley "as his predecessor had done" but that when a new rector was appointed, "he would leave the university alone."
In his memo for the day, Burke added, "And here, at the

end, I may say that the atmosphere in which I must think and work is not Christian, and there is a vagueness as to why I was brought into this work—though I've been in it a long time and by now, should, I suppose, know better."

On January 14, the delegate showed Burke a long report he was sending to Rome, citing the good work of President Roosevelt, the unlikelihood of a Mexican revolution, and asking for instructions, especially as to the status of Father Burke. Then in February as the Mexican Government was framing guarantees, the Mexican bishops released a pastoral letter on education which the Government interpreted as an attack and this slowed down any improvement in the situation. President Cardenas insisted that his really big problems were the agrarian, the industrial and foreign capital but that many Mexicans felt the churchmen were deliberately trying to make the religious question dominant. Frank Tannenbaum, the American historian from Columbia University, wrote a friendly letter to Burke, saying: "I still wish—as I said to you—that the Mexican Church openly and heartily accepted the social and economic program of the Mexican revolution and of this administration —that it cleared itself of the charges of being against the agrarian movement and against the labor movement."

At this time Daniels had been helpful with his talks with Cardenas and the religious situation was improving. Sumner Welles was invaluable in his efforts, the delegate expressing his gratitude to him on June 10th, while Welles also expressed "the complete confidence of the US Government" in Father Burke. In the meantime Cardenas was attempting to persuade state governors to open the churches and allow more priests to officiate, denying at the same time that he was either Socialist or Communist or opposed to the teaching of religion.

Father Burke's last meeting with the administrative committee took place on September 21, 1936, a very brief meeting that adjourned early so that committee members might attend his investiture as monsignor. He reported to the visiting committee of the administrative committee on his recent meetings with representatives of President Roosevelt, with the American ambassador to Mexico and also on messages received through the Mexican ambassador. Through an appeal from Ambassador Daniels, a public funeral from the Cathedral in Mexico had been granted for the late Archbishop Diaz. Many more churches were opening, many more states permitting more priests to function, but the efforts to have an apostolic delegate to Mexico appointed had failed. The Holy See, said Burke, was unwilling to appoint unless the Government gave guarantees. "One day it says it will, the next day it says it will not." The conditions governing actual exercise of religion, according to Burke, had improved but the attitude of the Government was hostile, the law nationalizing property was working great injustice in the ruthless confiscation of Church property, and at least eight bishops were not allowed to go to their see city. The most sinister factor of all was the government system of education, indoctrinating young minds against religion. "This is not a hopeful report but it is the best I can give."

It was not until February 5, 1937 that Archbishop Ruiz, by decree, was allowed to return as apostolic delegate to Mexico. The return of Ruiz, to a country whose government was profoundly Marxist in official orientation, did not terminate the persecution. A *modus vivendi* is as fragile as the infidelity of those pledged to support the agreement and unfortunately there were Mexican Catholics who deplored the compromise and Mexican officials who refused to adjust to it. Blessed are the peacemakers such as Dwight Morrow and Father Burke but the uncompromising still rely on violence as the only sure way to settle an argument.

chapter 9
The Depression and the New Deal

When the Democrats nominated the Catholic Alfred E. Smith for the presidency in June 1928 they unwittingly set in motion a wave of intolerance more massive in sheer volume, if not in actual bloodshed, than any event in American history. Other factors besides religion helped to defeat Smith, but these others served to tranquillize the uneasy consciences of respectable citizens who felt ashamed of their bigotry. In their platform, the Republicans promised "a continuation of this great public peace of mind now existing which makes for national well-being." This appeared to many as a justification for voting against Smith, for 1928 was a time of economic prosperity. Then too remnants of "the red scare" of the early 1920s still survived in 1928 to remind citizens to vote cautiously and prudently for a true-blue, white, Anglo-Saxon Protestant candidate. Al Smith was anything but that, with his fractured grammar, his informality, his raspy New York accent, his Tammany connections, his opposition to Prohibition, and his radical ideas on farm relief and hydroelectric power that smacked dangerously of socialism. Native Americans in white robes, on the other hand, were proud of their anti-Catholicism and their fiery crosses; they were said to number five million.

This outbreak of bigotry was a crushing blow to Father Burke's dream of seeing the country he loved wedded in faith and worship to the Christ he loved. The hopes he based on the thousands of Catholic lives sacrificed for America in World War I, the steadily growing Americanization of Catholic immigrants, the progressive demolition of old stereotypes of

172   NEVER LOOK BACK

Catholicism—all these hopes were dashed when the vultures of bigotry came back like a dark cloud to plague the nation. In his report to the November 1928 meeting of the administrative committee (after the elections) he discussed this bigotry and the possibility of counteracting it for the future. One major proposal was that a conference of learned Catholics be held, probably under the supervision of Catholic University, and Burke said that plans for it were already in hand. The National Council of Catholic Men during the coming convention at Cincinnati would obtain suggestions from laymen for the preparation of an apologetic, inviting to the conference representatives of publishers of defense pamphlets. Burke also reported that Michael Williams, editor of *Commonweal*, had visited him asking support for a non-political Catholic defense committee he had organized. The NCCM eventually formed a Bureau of Catholic Defense and Apologetics, headed by Grattan Kerans, to coordinate the work nationally, and a conference on apologetics was held at Catholic University on February 13, 1929, with Archbishop McNicholas as chairman. For long months the theme of a new apologetic was mulled over but even the Catholic University meeting seemed to have been no great success. Archbishop McNicholas saw an imperative need for developing a higher, scientific apologetic but Burke undoubtedly felt that a scientific apologetic would hardly succeed where the sacrifice of young men's lives had failed to impress. Historian Richard Hofstadter said in 1955 that American Catholics never really recovered from the "trauma" induced by the 1928 campaign.

During his first months in office, President Herbert Hoover basked in the sunlight of continuing prosperity. New railroads were constructed, innumerable new skyscrapers loomed up on the skyline, millions of automobiles rolled off the assembly lines. Business was booming, workers investing in stocks that bore promise of phenomenal profits, real estate get-rich-quick schemes were proliferating everywhere. Then came the day of stark tragedy, October 28, 1929, in some respects the saddest day in all American history. The great depression was on, grim, sullen, inexorable. Unemployed walked the streets looking for jobs, the breadlines grew longer every day, five million men were out of work by 1930, fifteen million by 1933. Meanwhile President Hoover, who had fed millions in post-war Europe, was able to feed his own people only pious hopes and an occasional cheery prediction that America was at long last turning a corner. He finally came up with a promising project, the Reconstruction Finance Corporation, but crippled it by barring federal spending, insisting that the states and local charities should take care of the unemployed.

Father Burke soon saw that the depression would affect every level of Catholic life and compel the NCWC to focus its main attention on the problem of unemployment for years to come. His statement on unemployment, adopted by the administrative committee on November 10, 1930, was not abstract speculation. He could not walk the streets without seeing visible proof that the old American traditions of "rugged individualism" and "unplanned economy" were not opening up new frontiers, securing employment for men at their old jobs or creating emergency projects to feed families on the verge of starvation. The depression had hit home to the NCWC itself, forcing Burke to reduce his own budget radically, especially salaries. At the same time, he feared a planned economy would invest the federal Government with excessive control of the lives of citizens. In the November 1929 meeting of the administrative committee he said he suspected that Hoover was veering toward a federal Department of Education; therefore in his first conference with Hoover, he asked him to name Dr. Pace and Dr. Johnson of NCWC to a proposed advisory committee on education, which Hoover did. Burke felt a federal education department was un-American but inevitable, and he recommended that Catholics be trained to enter those areas which would have a secular or even anti-religious cast. Whether Hoover ever contemplated a federal Department of Education, the fact was that the great depression barred the way to the vast expenditures necessary for such a department. Burke's opposition to creeping federal control was evident in a letter he wrote to the Interstate Commerce Commission declaring that the NCWC opposed a certain bill because "its gross paternalism is particularly injurious in that it moves farther and farther away from the individual citizen that civic responsibility which rests upon him and of which he should be actively conscious."

In spite of the depression, with its inevitable layoffs in personnel and reduction of agenda, the NCWC struggled along. A bright spot for Burke was Notre Dame's conferral of an LL.D. upon him in 1930 but a sad note was his announcement at the November 1930 meeting of the administrative committee that Justin McGrath, head of NCWC News Service, was a victim of a heart disability following his work at the International Congress of the Catholic Press at Brussels. McGrath, an intense person, evoked strong personal reactions pro and con but he aligned himself with Burke on large issues such as the need of Americanizing Catholicism and gave him moral support at crucial moments. Cantankerous to some he might have seemed but he was invaluable to Burke as a prodigious worker, as well as a skilled journalist trained in the secular press.

President Hoover incurred the antipathy of many Catholics for not having renounced more vigorously the support he received from bigots in the 1928 campaign. His image in Catholic opinion was further impaired by a note bearing his signature, sent to the *American Lutheran* magazine in October 1930 on the occasion of the 400th anniversary of the Augsburg confession, and implying that the Lutherans had always supported the idea of separation of church and state. After publication of the note, the White House was deluged with Catholic protests. In the name of the administrative committee, Burke protested Hoover's assumption that Luther had fathered the separation of church and state that is the American tradition. An editorial in the *New York World* said that Hoover had not meant to insult Catholics, that under the pressure of his duties of office he may have signed the letter without reading it carefully, which was correct. One of Hoover's aids had written and sent the message.[1] Burke feared that his protest might estrange the President from American Catholic contacts but there is no evidence of such a result. At an administrative committee meeting he announced he had been invited to the White House (February 6th) for a conference of civic, religious and financial leaders to construct a plan to stop hoarding of currency and encourage the return of money to the banks in order to avert a national disaster. Burke being ill, his assistant Father William Ready attended. Through Bishop Schrembs, Burke had secured Father Ready, a Cleveland priest, to take over the work of Father James Ryan as assistant general secretary. Ready handled his role well, to the immense satisfaction of Father Burke, who was also pleased to secure the services of Dr. Francis Haas as director of the National Catholic School of Social Service, succeeding Father Karl Alter who was appointed to the see of Toledo.

The work of NCWC received a welcome stimulant and encouragement with the publication of Pope Pius XI's *Quadragesimo Anno* in May 1931 on the occasion of the fortieth anniversary of Pope Leo's *Rerum Novarum*. Pius XI called for a just wage, advocated workers' sharing in the ownership, management or profits of a business, endorsed labor unions, and proposed that vocational groups—one for each trade—should join forces in order to become self-governing bodies with the right to set prices, wage scales and conditions of work. His endorsement of unions was acclaimed by unions as vigorously as it was regretted by management. *Quadragesimo Anno* became authoritative for social actionists. One item seemed to present a difficulty for Father Burke, the Pope's concern for the common good, a principle he had to balance carefully against the special attention his role as general secretary of NCWC required him to give to the interests of the American Catholic minority.

Franklin Delano Roosevelt was elected to the presidency in 1932 largely because of the domestic discontent generated by the shuffling timidity of the Hoover Administration. Roosevelt surrounded himself with top economists as "braintrusters," welcomed new ideas and assured the people through intimate "fireside chats" over radio that he was personally concerned about the plight of the unemployed and anxious to offer the nation a "new deal." In general, FDR attempted to adjust production to consumption, distribute wealth more equally, adapt existing economic organizations to the service of the people and make doubly sure that purchasing power was distributed through every group in the nation. This involved colossal expenditures of federal moneys for the job-providing construction of public works.

FDR had been helped to the presidency by means of a massive Catholic vote. He himself was professedly a low church Episcopalian but politically friendly with many Catholics such as Al Smith (who later turned against him). During the 1932 campaign FDR attracted a strong Catholic following by quoting from *Quadragesimo Anno*, calling it "one of the greatest documents of modern times." The main factor however in his winning popular support was the people's impatience for a change from the inertia of the Hoover regime. One fairly common impression among Catholics was that FDR borrowed from Monsignor John A. Ryan's reconstruction program of 1919 (often called The Bishops' Program) many items of the New Deal but there is no real evidence to show that Roosevelt studied the Bishops' Program or *Quadragesimo Anno*. George Q. Flynn, in his *American Catholics and the Roosevelt Presidency: 1932-1936* examined this question carefully and concluded that much of this Catholic identification of New Deal and Catholic texts was wishful thinking on the part of Catholics. "Perhaps the most judicious conclusion that can be drawn from all this evidence is that while FDR and his advisers knew of the papal program, their knowledge was in the context of general American reform ideas" (p. 49). Whatever the explanation, the fact was that eleven proposals in the 1919 Bishops' Program eventually became federal law, under the New Deal.

When Roosevelt was elected, Burke looked for a change in

his personal relationship with the President of the United States just as the people expected a change in domestic policy. Burke's many meetings with Hoover had been proper, polite and cordial, nothing more. For example, he wrote a memo (July 3, 1929) of his visit that day to the White House, accompanied by Pietro Fumasoni-Biondi, the apostolic delegate. In the memo he hinted at his weariness in listening to the bromides and commonplaces exchanged in the conversation, his last paragraph summing up the whole frosty affair: "At times brief silences reigned. Then Hoover said he was glad the delegate called and was happy to see him. The delegate took this as ending the interview, rose and said, 'Mr. President, I am ready to serve you in any way I can.' 'Beautifully said' replied the President—and then as if to check further enthusiasm, added: 'Father Burke and I often hold conferences together.' We said good morning." Father Burke looked for a little more warmth than this in FDR and he was not disappointed.

The new President was inaugurated on March 4, 1933, but Burke could not arrange to see him at that time because he was in Rome, having been delegated by the administrative committee to act as their representative at the elevation of the apostolig delegate, Fumasoni-Biondi, to the cardinalate. Burke did visit the new President on April 13th. His memo of the visit began: "Entering the executive offices again—and I had not done so since the publication of my letter against the Lutheran salutation of President Hoover—memories crowded in. Though I had visited here in Wilson's time, I had never seen Wilson here, nor had asked to see him. But there were Harding and Coolidge and Hoover, and now Roosevelt." Burke recorded that FDR greeted him with "warmth and energy" but "one questions whether the energy is sustained by serious thought or not. Indeed, I fear Roosevelt may grow tired of thinking, or believe he has thought enough when he has thought too little. He proposes large questions, but one fears he hardly knows the depth of their roots." Roosevelt at first asked Burke to tell him about his trip to Rome but Burke thought it would be a waste of time and passed up the opportunity. So Roosevelt plunged into a consideration of two large issues in which the Catholic Church might be of help: the dole to the needy and the back-to-the-land movement. He inveighed against the dole, saying that federal aid should be in the form of work else the individual would lose his dignity. Burke then told him the administrative committee had always taken the position that federal aid should be given through the states, with the local community, the city, the state encouraged to promote a sense of responsibility and personal dignity. FDR said he agreed and that his own experience (as state governor?) showed that where aid came directly from the federal Government, the local community grew careless and indifferent. The second item was that people should be urged to go back to the land, small churches be built in rural areas, country parishes honored, etc. Burke then described to FDR the work of the Rural Life Bureau, NCWC. The visit ended with Roosevelt's farewell assurance that he would be pleased to see Father Burke at any time.

The National Industrial Recovery Act, passed in June 1933, came to grips with the industrial recession in a series of codes to govern each industrial and trade association. It was designed to encourage national industrial recovery and combat unemployment: it called for self-regulation of industry through codes of fair competition, the National Recovery Administration (NRA) being empowered to fix wages, prices and conditions of work. Cardinal O'Connell of Boston declared that NRA "merits the unqualified and wholehearted support of every American." Like many other Catholic leaders, Father Burke agreed with the cardinal in this instance. In his "Spiritual Significance of the NRA," an undated article in the Paulist archives, Burke pleaded for the exercise of those virtues needed for the success of NRA. One paragraph stated:

The NRA seeks to make justice and honesty superior to business, cleverness and money manipulation. Greater still, the NRA demands for its success the spiritual gift of brotherly love. We use this word here in no sentimental way. The NRA not only presupposes but exacts an actual, constant, living consideration by every one for all of his fellows. It asks the cooperation of all the main factors in industry and agriculture—the manufacturer, the producer, the laborer and the consumer—the purchasing public.

He called for truthfulness, "the truthfulness that will tell in the business records fully and honestly how that business is conducted." He pleaded for fair dealing, for bond issues and mortgages carried out without manipulation at the expense of the unsuspecting, for loans that do not bring on foreclosure and bankruptcy. "The owner, the manufacturer, the employer has a conscience: he must not impoverish fellow human beings in order to enrich himself. For labor is a spiritual commodity as well as physical; only the spiritual can measure labor adequately as only the spiritual can adequately guide the just use and stewardship of property." Finally, he asked for hope in that hopeless time, praising the NRA as a cooperative effort built on the hopefulness of the American people, and affirming that this hope will "save us from the chaos of Communism."

The New Deal, as Roosevelt described his recovery program, gave rise to a multiplicity of new legislative proposals. This caused Burke to advise the administrative committee (April 1933) that this situation should be watched else federal legislation inimical to the interests of the Church would be framed, perhaps with no malice whatsoever on the part of the legislators but simply out of ignorance of the impact the bills would have on Catholic concerns. Here Burke walked a tightrope between concern for the common good and concern for the Catholic minority, anxious to insure that "in the changed world, the Church and her institutions enjoy, at least in great part, the liberty that is hers." He had in mind bills relating to banking, education, the Reconstruction Finance Corporation, the federal banking system, mortgages, farm relief, hospitalization of veterans, public health, immigration and birth control.

Bishop Turner of Buffalo, for instance, wrote Burke (March

7, 1933) voicing his apprehension that if the federal Government were to take over the banks, it would be harder to deal with government officials than with friendly local bank presidents and directors. Turner wanted Burke to declare that the NCWC was opposed morally, spiritually and patriotically to any radicalism in the crisis.

On June 12, 1933, Father Burke visited the President to present the new apostolic delegate, Amleto Cicognani. As prelude to his memo for that date, Burke described certain courtesies shown by the President out of respect for the delegate, marks of recognition reserved for the special representatives of other governments. The President greeted the delegate by saying, "Of course, I wouldn't say this publicly, but I hope the day will come when I will be able to welcome you as an ambassador." Shortly he was launched on a discussion of the economic and social condition of the country, interjecting praise for the papal encyclicals as having great impact on the social and economic thinking of the people and recalling that he had quoted *Quadragesimo Anno* in a campaign speech. He said the US would do everything possible to prevent a European war, commenting that Mussolini held in his hands the balance of power.

The Ku Klux Klan's anti-Catholic agitation, according to FDR, was ninety percent ignorance, and he cited as an example an incident at Warm Springs, Georgia. Roosevelt told the apostolic delegate that there was not a single Catholic in that town when he established there a farm for children afflicted with infantile paralysis, his own handicap. A native said a Catholic nurse would not be welcome "for we've never had a Catholic here." FDR then told the native that his secretary, Miss LeHand, was a Catholic, and in a short time nurse O'Mahoney arrived and soon worked herself into the good will of the people. He regretted that the nearest priest was forty miles away at Columbus, Georgia. Next he spoke of the appointments of Governor Gore of Puerto Rico and Governor Murphy of the Philippines, both Catholics, and FDR was proud of these appointments. Laughingly he said, "I told Governor Gore not to make any speeches favoring birth control." (Burke noted in his memo that the allusion was to former Governor Beverley of Puerto Rico who had used his influence to promote birth control—until Father Burke protested to FDR.) The President saw a back-to-the-land move as cure for Puerto Rico's evils—for instance, gifts of land by the vast sugar centrals to householders so the families could have an acre of their own. The President then bade the delegate farewell, expressing the hope that His Excellency would do them the honor of taking tea with himself and Mrs. Roosevelt when she returned in the fall.

As the months wore on, the New Deal presented other problem areas for Burke, e.g., the implications of social and health insurance for Catholic charitable institutions, the problem of rural rehabilitation and "sheltered workshops." The latter were Catholic correctional institutions, such as houses of the Good Shepherd, where inmates did some gainful work. Manufacturers claimed these institutions competed with them and therefore should observe the NRA codes but NRA exempted them, classifying them as remunerative or therapeutic institutions for physically, mentally or socially handicapped persons. Friction developed when the houses of the Good Shepherd failed to use the NRA labels on their products, problems that often landed up on Father Burke's desk.

Some of the problems occasioned by the NRA had no precedent in Catholic history. One day a Mr. Rosenblatt, divisional code authority of the NRA and code administrator for the motion picture industry, arrived at Burke's office, sent by FDR, to report that the American Federation of Labor had appealed to President Roosevelt to help persuade Cardinal Dougherty to lift a boycott he had imposed on many movie theaters in Philadelphia. The producers were ready to accept Dougherty's terms but he refused to hold any conferences with them. Rosenblatt said that Philadelphia had over 500 theaters, that the decline in patronage had forced a reduction in wages or dismissal of employees, and that 52 percent of these employees were Catholics. Burke felt he had no authority in the matter and relayed the problem to Archbishop McNicholas. Unfortunately, the NCWC archives did not yield any hints as to the outcome of the case.

Before FDR's inauguration, the country was in a state of shock and on the verge of revolution and collapse, according to one NRA official. One of the earliest projects designed to save the nation from collapse was the Civilian Conservation Corps. On September 12, 1933, Father Burke wrote to all the bishops stating that any priest, with his bishop's consent, could apply for a chaplaincy in the corps. Unlike other major nations, we had seemingly infinite natural resources but the US never had a real national policy for the development of its land and water resources. Roosevelt, as a first step toward such a policy, decided to send jobless men into the forests to work on reforestation, and on the conservation and development of our natural resources. William Green, head of the AF of L, said the plan was fascistic, while a Communist claimed it amounted to forced labor. But before long the Conservation Corps was an unqualified success, recruiting young men between 18 and 25 who were unmarried members of families on relief. Roosevelt felt it was probably the most successful of all his projects, facilitating the planting of two hundred million trees as a barrier against eruption of a new dust bowl. At its peak the corps numbered 500,000 men in over 2,600 camps.

No priest applicant for a chaplaincy could be assured of an appointment to a camp in his own diocese; this meant that some bishops were reluctant to release their priests for service in the camps. On August 14, 1933, the apostolic delegate announced in a letter to all bishops that he had appointed Father Burke to take charge of all information and data coming from the bishops relating to the spiritual work done by Catholic chaplains for the men in the camps. This created an immense amount of paper work for Burke and his small staff because many of the letters had to be checked with the War Department, which directed the work along with the Forestry Service. The delegate was anxious to make sure that a record of Mass attendance, etc., would be kept to send to the pastors of the young men. Thus Burke's office became a central clearing house for all this information. (By April 1935 Burke had arranged for the assignment of 189 priests as civilian chaplains. The War Department estimated that 33 percent of the men in the camps were Catholics.)

On December 19, 1933, Father Burke paid a visit to President Roosevelt in regard to civilian chaplains at the camps. FDR accepted his suggestion that a committee of religious leaders be formed to work out a better contractual arrangement. The committee was formed but came up with a plan for only 57 additional reserve chaplains; after continued discussions a satisfactory agreement was reached, including an acceptable salary and expense schedule. Some weeks earlier, Burke was happy to inform the administrative committee that the President had appointed Father Francis Haas, director of the National Catholic School for Social Service, as a member of the influential National Labor Board, the board which enjoyed final authority in all disputes between labor and capital.

On April 30, 1934, Burke had another meeting with the President, this time for an hour. He began by saying that the bishops of the administrative committee had authorized him to inform the President that they were "unanimously and emphatically opposed" to the seventy-five-million-dollar proposal for aid to the schools through the states. While they opposed such a federal grant, they would not come out against it publicly because they felt this would be interpreted as episcopal opposition to public education in general. "The bishops were not opposed to such public education," Burke told the President. "Indeed, they wished to promote it." Then he started to give reasons for the bishops' stand but FDR interrupted, "Father Burke, you know that I am opposed to all and every kind of centralization of education and all federal financial aid to education. I learned my lesson from my experience in New York State." He had vigorously approved an eight-million-dollar appropriation for education to find that, when he became governor, the appropriation had grown to ninety million, which was 45 percent of the yearly budget of the state.

After commenting on various other matters, the President "changed his attitude from a pleasant and light-hearted one to one very serious and expressive of worry. He began immediately by saying that Father Coughlin was a man of good impulses, and, the President said, 'in my judgment absolutely sincere'." But FDR felt he had overstepped the bounds the previous Saturday night. He had tied himself closely with the "Committee of the Nation" and this committee, according to Roosevelt, "is made up of such men as Vanderlip, who is a gambler, and Mr. Harris, who is a gambler, and Mr. Rand." It seems that the Committee for the Nation had been urging that more silver be purchased in order to raise the price of silver but Roosevelt did not consider this expedient and in fact had rejected attempts to force him to buy silver or artificially raise its value. Then the Treasury Department compiled a list of holders of silver "and to my surprise, it named Father Coughlin as a holder of silver."

FDR then pointed to a statement by a Miss Collins in the Sunday *Herald-Tribune*. She had authority to invest the moneys of the Radio League of the Little Flower and had speculated in silver with twenty thousand dollars of this church fund, actually speculating on a 10% margin (not investing) but claiming she made the investment on Mr. Roosevelt's word. "Father Burke," said the President, "I never gave any word to anybody. I did the best I could and I was told that if I bought silver it would go up. I did buy silver, but when it went up only two points, I didn't feel justified in buying any more." His concern was that he felt his word had been cited for all this speculation and that Father Coughlin had taken advantage of this. He then praised Coughlin's sincerity but deplored his stirring up religious bigotry and his attacks against Jews, Treasury Secretary Morgenthau in particular.

Finally, FDR asked Burke his opinion of a vast insurance scheme he had in mind, including every kind of insurance. "We ought to make provision whereby there would never be the disaster of 1929." FDR asked Burke to think it over and Burke responded with the suggestion that perhaps private religious organizations, owing as they do a debt to society, could be asked to donate 1 percent or one half of 1 percent of their collections to this great fund.

May 27, 1935, was a sad day for President Roosevelt, for Father Burke and for liberal Catholics generally. The US Supreme Court declared the National Recovery Act unconstitutional. Public opinion, favorable to NRA and the New Deal generally during the depression, had come to regard it as a reform that had served its purpose now that a few signs of economic recovery were beginning to appear. Big business propagandists insisted that the New Deal was destroying American freedom and that it was a communistic, totalitarian project run by power-mad bureaucrats. Herbert Hoover decried its restraints, claiming that "the maximum possible economic freedom is the most nearly universal field for release of the creative spirit of man." Burke, however, remained loyal to the New Deal concept even after the Supreme Court struck it down. His confreres, Monsignor John A. Ryan and Father Raymond McGowan of the social action department, NCWC, drew up a statement of Catholic social principles called "Organized Social Justice" and published it as a pamphlet, signed by 131 noted Catholics. It was a ringing protest against the high court decision and called for a new constitutional amendment that would permit the enactment of a new NRA. In Monsignor Ryan's tribute to Burke in *Catholic Action*, he treats at length Burke's willing and eager role in getting "Organized Social Justice" officially approved and published by NCWC.[2]

One of Roosevelt's most highly publicized enemies was Father Charles Coughlin, whom FDR had criticized in his April 30th interview with Father Burke. The most widely known priest in the 1930s, Coughlin had become a celebrity largely through his radio sermons on the papal social encyclicals, publicizing them more extensively than any other Catholic commentator. His interpretation of them however was out of line with most Catholic commentary, not only because of his personal invective in the pulpit but also because he gave far less attention to employer-employee relations than to international bankers, "the money changers in the Temple." Having supported Roosevelt effusively in 1932 ("Roosevelt or ruin"), he turned violently against him in 1934, abusing him scathingly. He enjoyed a tremendous popularity among ordinary citizens, non-Catholic and Catholic, until he lambasted Cardinal O'Connell and later drifted into anti-semitism, his Waterloo.

Ryan had admired Coughlin at first, stating he was on the side of the angels at least insofar as he was stirring up interest in social justice. But by 1936 he found it difficult to hold himself in, convinced that Coughlin was doing a great disservice to social justice because he misunderstood the papal encyclicals. On August 10, 1936, Father Burke visited FDR and very shortly, the President brought up the question of Father Coughlin, saying nervously, "Father Burke, don't you worry about Father Coughlin, for I am not worrying." Burke said he regretted an indignity offered the President at Cleveland, to which FDR responded that he did not mind Father Coughlin calling him a liar, but he did mind Father Coughlin's reference to FDR's father. "However I will say nothing until November 3rd" (the coming election day). He explained to Father Burke that Coughlin had stated in a public speech that the President's father had such little trust in his son Franklin that he excluded him by will from the management of the father's estate. In fact, the President was a minor when his father died and could not take charge of his father's estate till he was twenty-one, but his father's will named him executor and he did take and fulfill that office when he became twenty-one.

Burke's memo on the visit is most interesting. It was the President who had asked to see him, not vice versa, and Burke wondered why. At the end of the memo, he wrote: "To me at the end and now afterwards, it seems to me that President Roosevelt's soul was suffering, and in his suffering he had asked me to come. That is why I wrote above that I hope I had met the situation worthily. President Roosevelt seemed hurt; wounded. There is a dignity, even a glory to suffering, and man appears noblest when in most need of help. One wished that he had more strength within himself that he might give more. Much may have caused this suffering; the major part of that much seemed to be the words of Father Coughlin. It is the more striking that, while it was a priest who hurt him, he sends for a priest who may give him some measure of healing."

As the August days brought the presidential elections nearer, Ryan began to be concerned about the outcome, fearing Coughlin might control enough anti-Roosevelt votes to defeat the President in his bid for reelection. Says Francis L. Broderick in his *Right Reverend New Dealer: John A. Ryan*, "Father Coughlin and Monsignor Ryan had been building up to a clash for a long time. Neither wanted the public spectacle of two Catholic priests at each other's throat, yet neither was willing to let the other's statements stand unchallenged as the teaching of the Catholic Church, and polite argument finally gave way to public brawl" (p. 222). On October 8th Ryan went on the air under the auspices of the Democratic National Committee and denounced Coughlin. He denied that the President or any of his advisers were Communists and then went on to say that Father Coughlin's monetary theories and proposals found no support in the encyclicals of Leo XIII or Pius XI.

In March, Father Burke had sent notice to all members of the NCWC headquarters staff (including John A. Ryan) that no member should express political opinions or participate in political activity. He wanted to keep NCWC completely out of the political hassle building up in preparation for the 1936 elections. Al Smith, Father Gillis and other Catholic leaders denounced the New Deal while Cardinals Hayes, O'Connell and Mundelein criticized Coughlin's barbs against FDR. After Ryan had unleashed his attack on Coughlin, Archbishop Mooney, chairman of the administrative committee, phoned Burke from Rochester immediately to say there would be protests from American bishops against Ryan's delivery of a political speech under the auspices of the Democratic Committee.

Burke thought the NCWC was on safe ground because it had forbidden such speeches by staff members, but Mooney contended that Ryan should resign, then he would be free to make all the political speeches he wanted, Mooney being "quite angry and emphatic" about Ryan's failure to consider how his speech embarrassed the NCWC. Burke then told Mooney he thought it would be a grave mistake to force Ryan to resign at this time, that the consequences would be worse than the disobedience, the punishment too heavy for the crime. Ryan's resignation, according to Burke, would surely be interpreted to mean that the bishops had sided with Father Coughlin and had put themselves publicly in opposition to President Roosevelt's candidacy. This argument failed to impress Mooney but he asked Burke to speak to Ryan as a friend. On October 12th Burke met with Ryan who said he had explicitly stated on radio that he was not speaking on behalf of NCWC but on his own personal authority, and that he had felt obliged to publicly remove the impression that Coughlin was speaking in the name of the Church. Now that he had delivered the talk, he felt even more certain that he had done a service to the Church that needed to be done by somebody. He would gladly resign from NCWC if that would help NCWC but he said he agreed with Burke that resignation at this time would be a disaster. Then Burke told Ryan he had promised Mooney he would phone him, which was satisfactory to Ryan, and thus the interview ended. John A. Ryan remained at NCWC.

In a letter to Archbishop Mitty, September 23rd, Father Burke mentioned that Bishop Gallagher, Coughlin's bishop, reported that in his recent visit to Pope Pius XI, the Pope had said nothing to him about Father Coughlin, which he interpreted as an indirect approval of the radio preacher. "But the facts are as stated in the *Osservatore*" wrote Burke, "the Holy See does not fully approve Father Coughlin's activities; that this was made known to Bishop Gallagher by the Holy Father himself in the audience he granted to Bishop Gallagher; that the Holy Father, while eager to respect every liberty of speech, deplores, and informed Bishop Gallagher he deplored, the offensive language against the Chief Executive in public by Father Coughlin." Burke did not want to call Bishop Gallagher a liar: he said that what probably happened was that the Holy Father told Gallagher not to state publicly what the Pope had told him to do but to do it in his own name. The Pope will not interfere in American politics, said Burke, but has told Gallagher what is on his mind and feels that Gallagher ought to take the proper measures.

Burke went on to say to Mitty that the Holy See has wondered for two or three years, and even queried why the American bishops had not taken action. They know the country best and yet they permitted the situation to grow and grow. The Holy See however will not interfere. "I for one earnestly hope the word will not have to be said by the Holy See. For then in the light of the present political campaign, it will be said that influences back of Roosevelt or influences back of Landon have succeeded in getting to the Holy Father."

Again, on September 29th, Burke wrote Mitty, praising a public statement Archbishop Schrembs and Archbishop McNicholas had made on the Coughlin affair. The ordinaries should act, wrote Burke, but he did not think they should act corporately, as this would look as though the bishops sat in conference and pronounced against one of their fellow bishops. "But if a number of bishops publicly state their own mind and direction for their own diocese, the effect will be orderly, and I think, fruitful." He added confidentially that this opinion was also the opinion of Archbishop Mooney. On election day, Coughlin's candidate, Lemke, suffered a disastrous defeat; Roosevelt swept 46 of the 48 states. *The New York Times* commented, "As for Father Coughlin, it will not now be necessary for his ecclesiastical superiors to quench his political ardors or subdue his boasts. Time and the event have seen to that" (Nov. 6, 1936). Archbishop Mooney eventually however forbade him to deliver political speeches.

chapter 10
Birth control and immigration laws- black Catholics-red Russia- Hitler and anti-Semitism

If national political issues, especially those deriving from the New Deal, were the central focus of Father Burke's concern during his years as general secretary, this is understandable in the light of his role. The administrative committee and its secretary considered themselves protectors and defenders of the Catholic minority, confronted by a hostile Protestant majority whose legislative representatives aimed to protect the interests of the Protestant majority, the Protestant ethic and way of life. In view of these circumstances, the American Catholic Church a half-century ago was not motivated by the overriding anxiety for the common good that can be found in the documents of Vatican II. The bishops reflected the social defensiveness of American Catholics as well as the uncompromising pertinacity of the Roman theologians.

Yet as a Paulist, Burke had imbibed Hecker's fellow-feeling toward Protestants and at times felt unhappy about the inflexibility of a mentality that regarded Protestants as "heretics." At the November 12, 1928, meeting of the administrative committee, the bishops on the committee discussed the question of Catholic financial aid toward the building of a chapel at the federal prison for women at Alderson, West Virginia. Should the National Council of Catholic Women secure the permission of the ordinary of every diocese where a Catholic woman wanted to contribute money toward the building of the chapel? Archbishop Dowling questioned the wisdom of endorsing a project to build a chapel where "heretical" as well as Catholic services would be held—unless Bishop Swint of West Virginia obtained from proper canonical authorities assurances that such a chapel arrangement would not be a violation of canon law. Schrembs put thumbs down on any *participatio in sacris* such as was represented by this chapel proposal and Lillis thought it might be licit only if the Catholic chapel were secluded in an alcove in the auditorium.

Father Burke then consulted authoritative decisions. One Holy Office decision had it that Mass could be offered in "heretical temples" for a grave reason (conversion of Protestants being cited as a grave reason). A sacred penitentiary decision said simply, "It is permissible for grave reasons to contribute money for the building of "heretical temples." Thus, the NCCW convention had approved the fund-raising project for the chapel, and Bishop Swint, ordinary of the diocese had sanctioned it; but the administrative committee, more Roman than Rome, rejected this project as an illicit instance of Catholic cooperation in the erection of an "heretical temple." Father Burke probably considered this an unreasonable judgment but he was only the general secretary.

In solving particular problems relating to interfaith contacts, Burke seems to have looked for what he called "the mind of the Church." This was a traditional phrase but imprecise, somewhat nebulous for a man who admired definiteness of expression. He felt quite certain, for instance, that the mind of the Church discountenanced the notion that "one religion is as good as another." When Father J. Hynes, president of Loyola University, New Orleans, asked him about the propriety of going on a radio chain that highlighted Protestant and Jewish preachers, Burke strongly opposed such participation. In the theology of the time, "the common pulpit" was anathema to Catholics as it lent credence to the notion that "one religion is as good as another." In that pre-Vatican II era, seminarians were instructed sedulously to avoid anything that smacked of indifferentism or any actions seeming to imply that other churches enjoyed a parity with the Roman Catholic. Diocesan chanceries refused permission to priests to speak on a public platform with a rabbi or minister for fear that Catholics might think the priest believed that "one religion was as good as another."

In the area of social justice, however, Burke had no reluctance about mixing with non-Catholics. In 1926, leaders of French Catholic social work organizations tried to have the Holy See forbid all Catholic organizations from maintaining any contacts whatsoever with organizations not explicitly Catholic. Burke considered this a very short-sighted approach in view of the fact that social action was quite unrelated to the Catholic Church's claim to uniqueness. He encouraged NCWC employees to keep abreast of the latest developments in social action by participating in social work conventions and seminars, regardless of sectarian labels. In 1928 he sent Father C. H. LeBlond and Sarah Weadick of the NCWC bureau of immigration, and Mary Carey of the National Council of Catholic Women, to the International Conference of Social Work at Paris. These contacts with non-Catholic organizations in the area of social work continued under Father Burke's direction until his death. He did not consider them, even if they involved joint efforts with other religious leaders, as participation in "inter-faith relations."

There was very little cameraderie between Burke and Federal Council of Church leaders, however, although the Federal Council had a broad social action program. At its very first meeting, the Federal Council had emphasized social justice by accepting a report on "The Church and Modern Industry." This stress on the Church's obligation to reform the social order continued through the years and roused the ire of conservative Protestants. The NCWC and the Federal Council seemed to have kindred goals, at least in the field of social action, but the Federal Council's emphasis on theological ecumenism probably alienated Father Burke, an emphasis frequently publicized through indignant protests from conservative evangelicals in the Federal Council. On April 13, 1932, Burke presented to the administrative committee a statement of the Federal Council on the intermarriage of members of different Christian communities. His comment was acid. "The statement is in many ways so child-like, so hopeless and even so pitiable that I do not think any answer should be made." Actually it was more the inconsistency in Federal Council positions rather than the statement itself that annoyed Burke. The statement supported Catholic teaching basically, advising Protestants contemplating marriage to agree with their partners, if possible, on one church and one religious belief, before marriage, as well as an agreement to bring the children up in one faith. Burke's objection was that the Federal Council itself strenuously objected when the Catholic Church made suggestions of this kind. (The Federal Council of Churches was the predecessor of the present National Council of Churches.)

In the nineteenth century, the reading of the Bible in the public schools had been a prolific source of Catholic-Protestant tension. On April 29, 1930, Burke presented to the administrative committee an interesting proposal from the American Civil Liberties Union. Roger Baldwin, via John A. Ryan, promised that the ACLU would finance a suit to ban Bible reading from public schools if Catholics would inaugurate the suit. The committee rejected the offer, asserting that it was not opposed to the reading of the Bible in the public schools from an approved text with explanatory notes. The commitee, moreover, felt that it should not institute any action in collaboration with the ACLU.

Indicted in 1915 for sending birth-control literature through the mails, Margaret Sanger formed the National Committee on Federal Legislation for Birth Control in 1923. As general secretary of NCWC, Father Burke entered into the NCWC's fight against birth control in the late 1920s, publishing pamphlets and opposing bills designed to relax federal laws forbidding the sending of contraceptives and birth control literature through the mails. It was to be expected that he would meet with zealous opposition from Margaret Sanger; but he also encountered stiff criticism from certain priests who contended that NCWC should stay out of "the work of trying to keep federal legislation Christian." They viewed his efforts as meddling in politics; he saw their surrender as defeatist: "To stand off from public life is to allow Christian standards to be taken out of public life." Revulsed by any Church involvement in partisan politics, or by any form of clerical behind-the-scenes chicanery, he nevertheless stood fast for "keeping our laws as Christian as possible."

The federal laws put birth control devices and literature in the category of "obscenity." Burke asked the administrative committee if it would consent to the transfer of birth control to a category other than "obscenity," saying that a number of medical associations with powerful influence might give support to the birth control laws under a different category. The committee however would not budge from its traditional policy of opposing any change whatever in the penal code relating to birth control.

The general secretary decried the nationwide trend toward birth control that was beginning to reach even to our relations with Latin America. In April 1931 he said that the American Medical Association and the AF of L resisted the recent birth control bill but he deplored the support given it by Protestants and Jews. It thus became a largely "Catholic" issue rather than a concern for the common welfare. In November 1932 Burke warned the administrative committee that the isolation of Catholics in their opposition to birth control gives the impression that Catholic disagreement with birth controllers is mere Catholic polemic, not a defense of basic morality, and he urged enlisting the help of the laity. He noted that Margaret Sanger was present and active at many of the hearings on birth control bills, anxious to promote more hearings—not necessarily to help passage of the bills but to promote and publicize the cause. In 1933 Burke came into conflict with the Health Committee of the League of Nations on Maternal Welfare and Hygiene of Infants which had recommended birth control in a report. The Irish, Italian and Polish delegations protested and Burke successfully proposed that the report be rescinded.

During that year, 1933, clinic after clinic for birth control purposes opened in one state after another. Even in Puerto Rico a bill was introduced to permit birth control clinics to operate. Beverley, the governor, endorsed the bill in ambiguous language and the bishops of Puerto Rico were up in arms. Burke protested to the Secretary of War (who had jurisdiction) that the governor had exceeded his powers of office and violated his duty to oppose laws contrary to the laws of the United States and the mind of Congress.

A new Catholic organization began to form in New York City in order to help the battle against birth control. Burke heard about it and wrote his friend, Judge Alfred Talley, on January 4, 1933, about this "Catholic Committee in New York" with which Talley was associated. He informed Talley that the NCCM and the NCCW had been doing the work to which the Committee was about to address its efforts but had been deputing non-Catholic doctors and other non-Catholics for individual tasks in connection with the fight against birth control; these non-Catholics would not care to appear in the name of a Catholic organization. This was an adroit way of informing these well-intentioned activists that they had more zeal than expertise. Cardinal Hayes wrote Burke praising him for his handling of the group and commenting, "I have found it difficult as Archbishop to convince some of our fine, zealous men and women of the value of strategy. On various occasions they are strong for an open fight which is not always the wisest course."

The promoters of birth control, on the other hand, were long on strategy. Taking advantage of the economic crisis, they began 1934 (one of the worst years of the depression) with a conference on birth control and national recovery, at the Mayflower Hotel in Washington, following the convening of

Congress: several hundred delegates attended. The next day the delegates attended a hearing on the Pierce Bill, Montavon of the NCWC legal department appearing in opposition to the bill. A Dr. Mundell, professor of obstetrics at Georgetown Medical School, also opposed the bill, contending that legislation permitting dissemination of birth control devices, etc., was uncalled for since pregnancy could now be regulated by the theory laid down in a book called *The Rhythm*, published by the Latz Foundation. Margaret Sanger immediately came back with a rebuttal to the effect that this book, advocating a form of birth control, was being sent through the mails in violation of federal law. The obvious and highly damaging implication was that Catholics were practicing what they opposed publicly: Catholic publishers were sending *The Rhythm* through the mails. At a similar hearing on a birth control bill in the House of Representatives, the president of the District of Columbia Medical Society favored relaxing the existing laws, asserting that publishers of *The Rhythm* were violating the laws. At these hearings, there were references to pamphlets on *The Rhythm* circulated by Our Sunday Visitor Press, much to the embarrassment of Bishop Noll, head of that press. The existing law specifically forbade mailing of pamphlets explaining "by what means conception may be prevented."

In a hearing on a later bill, much was said about a change in Catholic thinking on birth control, as revealed by the *Rhythm* book. Burke was uneasy about the future of federal laws on birth control materials, one of his worries being that the depression had compelled him to eliminate the NCWC bureau of publicity, thus rendering a strong defense of the laws almost impossible. In a meeting in November 1934 he told the administrative committee that customs officials were considering what to do about the *Rhythm* book, "a copy of which was taken from the baggage of an American birth control advocate returning from Europe." (Perhaps a stratagem for provoking a test case.) He told the committee that the most recent birth control bill died with the adjournment of the Senate but this was accomplished largely through the work of one man, Senator McCarren.

Burke met with opposition to his stand on birth control from within as well as outside the Church, the problem that also confronted John A. Ryan, one Catholic moral theologian who enjoyed the respect of liberal thinkers. Francis Broderick, Ryan's biographer, said that Ryan talked a language alien or irrelevant to his liberal friends in his opposition to birth control while some of his Catholic friends disagreed with his reasons for condemning it. Not all Catholics agreed with, or understood the "perverted faculty" argument: many preferred to accept the teaching on the authority of the Church without looking for reasons. But to Burke and Ryan, the "perverted faculty" argument, while not a revealed truth, was so close to being self-evident that it needed no proof. In dealing with his liberal friends, Ryan usually had to contend with the objection that birth control was a purely private affair but Burke's NCWC role required him to cope with the *legal* difficulty of upholding the federal laws banning dissemination of birth control materials via the mails. This was hard to sell to Americans who prized the right of free speech and a free press, guaranteed by the Constitution.

One of the first organized efforts undertaken by the administrative committee of NCWC after its own establishment was the creation of a bureau of immigration (1920). Its aim was to care for the spiritual and material needs of the Catholic immigrant and to become a clearing house for information relating to Catholic immigrants of all nationalities. Branch offices were established at various ports but Ellis Island, New York, got special attention not only because nationality groups had been allocated to fifteen different Protestant groups with no protest from authorities but also because 6,000 immigrants daily passed through Ellis Island. Father Burke took an extraordinary personal interest in this bureau because he considered immigration the implementation of the Declaration of Independence. That document listed among the grievances against the King his deliberate obstruction of laws for the naturalization of foreigners and his refusal to pass other laws "encouraging their migration hither."

In a talk at Utica (1920) Burke said that America "claims not only to be the home of democracy. It claims to have such vitality that it can welcome to its home the children of all the nations of the world, and give them the privileges, the rights, the duties of that democracy." Later on in that talk, he discussed America as an experiment, "We are an experiment because we are constantly bringing into our own body, men and women from other nations." In another address found in the Paulist archives in New York, Burke points out that the unity of the states has belied the prophets of doom who predicted the nation's early demise. Against all the probabilities of history, these states invited here millions from every other country. "To them they gave the full right of citizenship, making them equal to their own children, making common the land which they themselves had come to possess and to enjoy." America was based on the premise that all men are created equal and founded on "a determination to do justice to all, and to unite as one and keep united as one in doing justice. That sense of doing a common justice, of being determined to do it as one people—is the sense of America."

This explains somewhat Father Burke's personal interest in the immigrants. He wanted to do his part toward a program of equal justice under law so that the immigrants could become the mature personalities God intended them to be. The routine work of the bureau was vast: some 800,000 immigrants entered the country in the twelve months after July 1, 1920. Burke had to keep a cool eye on Congress; labor was beginning to flex its muscles to clamp down on "cheap labor" from Europe; nationalism had intensified after World War I and many native-born citizens decried the notion that America was a haven for "foreign rabble."

Until 1921 no restrictions had been placed on immigration

but that year saw the beginnings of the quota system, limiting immigration to 3 percent of each nationality in the population according to the 1910 census. Then in 1924 the National Origins Act (effective in 1929) changed the quotas to 2 percent of the 1890 census of each nationality. In 1931 Congress was quite ready and willing to restrict further immigration because of the depression. In the lively debates that went on at this time, Burke refrained from criticism of the reductions even though he was aware that the goal was to reduce immigration from Southern and Eastern Europe, from which so many Catholic immigrants came. The nativists here in America were alarmed, or claimed to be alarmed, over the steadily increasing Catholic Church membership due to immigration, but Burke pleaded for reunion of families divided by the quota laws, insisting that the break-up of families causes social unrest and violates our common humanity.

Bruce Mohler headed the bureau of immigration from its very beginning, and remained with it after Burke's death. As Justin McGrath saw eye-to-eye with Burke on major press issues, so too Burke's choice of Bruce Mohler was felicitous. They became very close friends and each helped the other. Bruce told his wife that in the early days of the bureau, he used to have hard sledding with senators who manifested no love for immigrants. Burke undoubtedly buoyed up his spirits after a discouraging Senate Committee hearing. As the years went on, and NCWC attained more prestige, Bruce Mohler's troubles became fewer and fewer, at least in regard to senatorial civilities.

It has been said quite correctly that the influx of millions of Europeans into the United States between 1865 and 1915 was a phenomenon comparable to the gigantic migrations which overwhelmed the Roman Empire in the fifth and sixth centuries. But the Americanizing of the immigrant was a task of enormous magnitude, one that was made difficult in the period of World War I by nativists who wanted to coerce immigrants into learning English and eliminating from their way of life all that seemed foreign to these hysterical Americanizers. Father Burke's approach was to give them a more positive program of civic education, and from the funds of the National Catholic War Council he provided for immigrants liberal support for the dissemination of suitable materials. In his article on "Father Burke and Civic Education" in *Catholic Action*, December 15, 1936, John A. Lapp mentions that more than five million copies of the "Civics Catechism on the Rights and Duties of American Citizens," in various languages in booklet form or newspaper publication, were produced under Burke's direction with War Council funds. Lapp, director of the civics program, said that this booklet "became the most widely distributed document on civics education ever produced in the United States." The nationwide series of courses in civics education embraced entertainment features in which were interspersed brief lessons in civics along with "inspirational addresses by immigrants as well as Americans."[1] The civics lessons were given first in a foreign language, then repeated in English.

Federal child labor laws have had a precarious existence in American history. The first two were ruled unconstitutional by the US Supreme Court in 1918 and 1922. To keep the issue out of the hands of the Supreme Court, a groundswell of support for a child labor amendment to the Constitution developed but it failed to be ratified, only 27 states having ratified by 1937. While the amendment was being evaluated by the public, John A. Ryan, Raymond McGowan and other Catholic leaders backed it but many bishops opposed it, Cardinal O'Connell of Boston going so far as to urge (unsuccessfully) Archbishop Curley of Baltimore to fire Father Ryan from Catholic University for his advocacy of this "nefarious and bolshevik amendment." At the height of the amendment controversy, in April 1934, Father Burke observed to the administrative committee that there was a general impression that NCWC favored the amendment but that this was untrue. In fact, the committee had agreed to continue the policy, established back in 1923, of refusing to approve federal child labor legislation, leaving the question to the individual states. What Burke's own position was cannot be ascertained. The opposition of many of the bishops on the committee was premised on the notion that federal power to regulate child labor would reach right into the home, subjecting parents to federal power and perhaps even lead to federal control of education. Montavon usually reflected Burke's mind: in 1936 he contended that the American experience did not justify fear of federal power, but Burke unquestionably felt nervous about concentration of federal power. The National Industrial Recovery Act of 1933 banned child labor but this New Deal act was declared unconstitutional in 1935. At long last, in 1941, the US Supreme Court reversed the first early decision invalidating a child labor law and a constitutional amendment became unnecessary.

Was Burke a pacifist? In the sense of total pacifism amounting to a rejection of all wars, no. There is nevertheless a vigorous antiwar theme running through many of his discussions of violence, nationalism and power politics. It was not entirely the product of his disenchantment with war after World War I but had its roots deeper in his dedication to the motto, "The peace of Christ in the kingdom of Christ." This was the motto of Pius XI's pontificate and it reflected Burke's emphasis on the idea that no nation is in a strict sense sovereign, only God being sovereign, all persons and governments being therefore subject to the overarching moral law enunciated by Jesus Christ. This emerges from a reading of an article he wrote for the *Catholic Historical Review* (April 1928) entitled "Attitude of the Church Toward Nationalism." Here he cited Decatur's toast, "My country may she ever be right but right or wrong, my country," as an example of a deplorable nationalism that exalts nation above God's law. Mexico he also saw as an example of ugly modern nationalism, its rulers contemptuous of moral law.

On Armistice Day, 1929, Father Burke was called upon to deliver the address at the laying of a wreath on the tomb of the

Unknown Soldier in Arlington, Virginia, an annual ceremony attended by representatives of the seven welfare organizations that served the fighting men during the First World War. The theme of patriotism or the glories of victory were conspicuously absent from his remarks. Like the psalmist, his thoughts were of peace, not of affliction, and he concluded his short address by speaking of the thousands of civilian workers who "are here through us in spirit" and who go back "renewed in devotion to consecrate themselves to that for which this man died—the peace of the nation, the peace of the world." (The civilian workers referred to were the civilians who worked in the welfare organizations during the war.)

In view of the hardline Catholic theology of the time in regard to the ecumenical movement, the administrative committee thought thoughts of peace but not of Christian unity. On April 9, 1929, John A. Ryan read Father Burke's report to the committee (in his absence). In the report Burke called attention to a forthcoming International Catholic Week to be held at Geneva that summer. The purpose of the Week was to put before the world, at approximately the same time as the next assembly of the League of Nations the Catholic viewpoint on international questions, peace being an obvious focus of attention. The idea of the Catholic Week had been inspired by a Universal Religious Peace Conference to be held at Geneva in 1930. The mention of the Universal Religious Peace Conference raised some hackles in the administrative committee, which decided that it would have nothing to do with that 1930 conference; it feared the aim of the conference was to bring about a confederation of religions. Father Francis Haas, however, attended an international meeting of this group in Germany some months later and reported back to the administrative committee that the group had changed its name to The World Conference for International Peace Through Religion, "thus explicitly repudiating any intention of seeking to promote Church Unity." In the light of Vatican II, this fear of ecumenical meetings seems incredible.

In 1929 the National Broadcasting Company offered free national broadcast time to the National Council of Catholic Men. Father John B. Harney, superior general of the Paulists, appeared before the administrative committee to protest that this "Catholic Hour" program would harm the already financially harassed WLWL station of the Paulists, said to be the first Catholic station in the country. The committee however approved the NBC gift of broadcast time, provided NCCM would extend its apologetic program to WLWL. In 1930 the NCCM assumed responsibility for producing the Catholic Hour, the bishops being reluctant to identify with views expressed on the program. The Catholic Hour was inaugurated on Sunday, March 2, 1930: a one hour program once a week on twenty-two stations. The administrative committee entrusted Archbishop Schrembs and Father Burke with the direction of the program. Schrembs and Burke formed an executive committee with Karl J. Alter as director of the speakers' program: the noted Paulist Choristers under Father William Finn furnished the music. Mr. Dolle, executive secretary of the NCCM, was a member of the executive committee. Burke sent out a formula of general directions for speakers with the reminder, ". . . even though the director of the speakers' program shall have seen the manuscript, the NCWC does not make its own the particular personal views that may be expressed by the speaker. In these matters, the NCWC considers it should allow the widest liberty possible, commensurate with Catholic faith and teaching and practice." The Catholic Hour was an outstanding success, accoladed by non-Catholics as well as by Catholics for the high quality of its music and preaching. As to subject matter, Burke held strongly to the position that the Hour's purpose was not mainly cultural or social but to propose and explain Catholic teaching.

A radio committee of the White House Conference in 1930 suggested that a certain joint report on religious broadcasting be signed by a Catholic, Protestant and Jew but Father Burke objected to the wording of the statement. He told Mr. Dolle not to present to the conference a statement he had prepared,

"They are determined to have us agree to a common denominator of religion . . . there can be no common denominator between truth and falsehood, between Christ and error." He insisted on absolute honesty in affirming that the Catholic Hour's aim was to explain the Catholic religion. In his statement, Dolle had said that Catholic institutions always employ radio "for the promotion of education and to promote a better religious and cultural life in America." This, said Burke, was simply untrue: the Paulists at WLWL had the avowed purpose of explaining Catholic doctrine. This must be asserted of the Catholic Hour, according to Burke, and there must be no weakening of this policy by implying that the Catholic Hour had agreed to sink religious differences.

Probably the most controversial talk given over the Catholic Hour was one delivered on a Sunday in November 1932 on "The Catholic Church and the Black Man." Father James Gillis, a Paulist, was the speaker. The talk was a message of sympathy for the oppressed blacks in America, an act of contrition for the sin of kidnapping and enslaving thousands of innocents. It caused an uproar in the South. Station after station of the coast-to-coast network was reported to have cut the speaker off that Sunday afternoon. "The black man must suffer incessantly . . . if he were to rise in rebellion he would be shot down like a dog and I fear that vast numbers of 'liberty-loving' Americans would say that it served him right." Advocating desegregation in the schools and the end of laws banning the marriage of whites and blacks, Gillis stirred up the letter writers and an avalanche of letters poured in.

Father Burke had some old friends who were furious. How did he handle their personal protests to him? With charity and finesse. Yes, he understood the depth of emotions generated by the race question in the South: yes, the NCCM and NCWC would accept the complaints graciously but the proper procedure was to write to the speaker himself, for the NCCM In its contract with the speakers promises the widest liberty possible, commensurate with Catholic faith. There are bound to be differences of opinion: Catholic Hour speakers had differed in their interpretations of Pius XI's *Quadragesimo Anno* (thus putting Gillis in a class with Pius XI). Yes, there can be honest differences but a national Catholic Hour should not be expected to deny freedom of speech to a speaker! A soft answer turneth away wrath.

Should the NCCM and the NCCW go "color blind"? Specifically, should societies of black Catholics be permitted to affiliate with NCCM and NCCW? This was the question Father Burke proposed for discussion at the November 12, 1928, meeting of the administrative committee. The answer that seems so obvious today was not quite so obvious in 1928. At that time, restaurants, theaters, hotels, even parochial schools were still segregated in Washington, and as late as 1939 the Daughters of the American Revolution refused to allow Marian Anderson to give a concert at Constitution Hall even though she had been acclaimed all over Europe and in the Soviet Union. In fact, at a meeting of representatives of the Federated Colored Catholics society and NCCW, the blacks felt they as well as the whites would suffer embarrassment if the former were invited to general meetings in certain hotels in Washington. At this administrative committee meeting, Burke requested "some expressions of encouragement from the committee to the colored groups" without inviting technical affiliation, and a resolution was approved "to give encouragement and assistance to Catholic societies of colored people."

Again, on November 10, 1930, the question of affiliation came up but no agreement was reached as to a course of action. Bishop Lillis thought the problem was "too delicate for discussion in view of the attitude of the bishops in the South." (One can imagine Father Gillis' reaction to such "delicacy.") In November 1932 Burke brought the question up again.

Two months earlier (September 3-5, 1932), The Federated Colored Catholics of the United States held their eighth annual meeting. According to the invitation announcement, the organization aimed to unite colored Catholics with "right-thinking white friends" into a great national Catholic interracial movement "so necessary for the permanent evangelization of the American Negro." It was a sad index of the times that conversion, rather than the material and spiritual uplift of the blacks, should get the emphasis. Burke wrote to Dr. Thomas W. Turner of Hampton Institute, Hampton, Virginia, saying he admired the work of the Federation. "I would favor and I know the bishops would favor, conference with yourself and other leaders on these matters." He added that the question of the establishment of a national Catholic interracial movement, being a national issue, should be submitted first to the bishops. Then he received a letter from Bishop Emmet Walsh of Charleston, South Carolina, saying: "Personally I feel that the plan of Dr. Turner is a wild dream but I feel he should be given a hearing." Walsh asked if Burke would arrange to meet Dr. Turner and he enclosed "the wild dream" to which he had referred, a rather prosaic statement entitled "Letter Proposed for the Hierarchy." This text listed a litany of matters colored Catholics would like to see done in order to win non-Catholic colored people to Christ: every bishop should remove any rulings which deny to blacks the same practices of religion accorded to whites; where civil law forbids this, bishops should work for the repeal of statutes so limiting the free exercise of religion and should enlist influential white laymen to work for repeal; every bishop should order all Catholic institutions in his diocese opened to blacks; every bishop should indoctrinate the faithful in the true Catholic attitude toward colored people and encourage the religious vocations of blacks; finally, no colored Catholic should be excluded from Catholic University and institutions such as NCWC, and that in cases of lynching, etc., NCWC news service articles should condemn such outrages.

Father Burke set November 14, 1932, an administrative committee meeting date, as the date for meeting with Dr. Turner; if convenient, at the NCWC office, with the whole committee or a subcommittee. As it turned out, Archbishop

McNicholas and Bishop Walsh were delegated to meet Dr. Turner and his associates. On the day of the meeting, Bishop Walsh was apprehensive that Dr. Turner might try aggressively to force matters but Burke thought it would be best to assume the best of intentions in the colored group. McNicholas and Walsh returned from the meeting with Turner to report that they found these colored Catholics had "a thoroughly proper attitude and were satisfied to do what the bishops wished." The committee then decided that a survey of the entire problem be made during the coming year and that a liaison official be appointed for the NCWC and the black organization.

A pencilled note on Burke's report for this meeting mentions that Miss Bresette of the staff of *Social Action* attended a board meeting of the Federated Catholics and reported that "discussion on the subject of discrimination was aimed generally at Catholic universities and at the Catholic churches, but primarily at the Catholic University of America and Catholic churches in Washington which will not allow Negroes admission." One man at the meeting said that he was educating his son at Harvard because Catholic University would not admit him, that the son had become interested in Communism and Fascism and the father therefore wanted to take his son out of Harvard for a Christian education, "but where am I to send him?"

A split in the ranks of the Federated Colored Catholics led eventually to establishment of the Catholic Interracial Council in New York under Father John La Farge, the Jesuit. One may be tempted to regret the leisurely pace at which Father Burke and the committee handled this long-neglected cause but the division among the blacks may have suggested caution. Francis Broderick in his biography of John A. Ryan says that Ryan tried, unsuccessfully, to get a Negro settlement house started in Washington in the mid-1930s but this was followed by "a long, surprisingly indifferent silence punctuated only by gingerly mediation between rival factions of Negro Catholics."[2]

In a memo (January 9, 1936) Burke referred to a report the

apostolic delegation was preparing to submit to the Holy See on the Negro question but which he found quite unsatisfactory. Burke's comment was that the blacks are "a worthy race" and that the best way to build them up, to convert them to the faith, is to give them a sense of their responsibility as individuals and as a race, not by telling them that they are a people among whom we must do missionary work. Whether any of his suggestions for the report were accepted, he knew not.

By 1920 the Caribbean had become an American lake. The Yankee grip tightened on republic after republic and Latin Americans quipped, "There is no god but the dollar and the Yankee is his prophet." President Hoover conformed to the established pattern when he attended the International Conference of American States at Havana in 1928, arriving in a formidable battleship, with American marines still in Nicaragua. In 1929 fortunately he declared "a retreat from imperialism in Latin America" and Franklin Delano Roosevelt continued the good neighbor policy in his term of office beginning in 1933. The new benevolence under Hoover and Roosevelt brought the Catholic Church in Latin America into closer contact with American Catholics. In certain ways, however, the American Occupation was not quite as benevolent as the official policy, thus creating special church-state problems which the native bishops referred to Father Burke, whom they had come to know through his work in Mexico.

Haiti had a disjointed religious history. From 1804 to 1860 it was in schism from Rome, many of the clergy being defrocked religious, the people uninstructed, with voodoo flourishing due to misery and disease. Many of the problems facing Burke in regard to Haiti arose from the American Occupation, which he had witnessed at first hand in 1925. In a letter to Burke in 1928, three Haitian bishops thanked him for his constant interest but complained that almost all the measures the Haitian Government proposed for the development of religious works had met with hostility from the American Occupation which tried to block them. The Occupation Administration had opposed the appointment of bishops to certain areas as well as the improvement of schools, all of which was in violation of the Concordat between Haiti and the Holy See.

In December 1929 Father Burke spoke to President Hoover and this meeting led to the appointment of two Catholics to the Haitian commission. Burke then sent Montavon to Haiti to investigate the situation and make clear to this commission the bishops' situation: they could not fraternize with the Occupation which was cordially hated by the natives, and they had publicly agreed with the political aspirations of the people for independence. It was largely due to Montavon that the commission reported that the Catholic schools were the foundation of the educational system in Haiti and "deserve more generous support." At about this time, the administrative committee allowed Burke to become the American representative of the Haitian bishops.

As an aftermath of what Teddy Roosevelt called "the splendid little war with Spain," the United States found itself with several new possessions at the end of the century. Promoted by the Hearst press and endorsed by investors and soldiers of fortune, the war left us with the Philippines and Puerto Rico. As Thomas A. Bailey says in *A Diplomatic History of the American People*, "In the closing days of the war American troops hastily occupied the island of Puerto Rico lest the shooting stop before all the imperial plums were picked." As in Haiti, so too in Puerto Rico, the bishops had troubles with the Occupation officials.

Father Burke became involved in a Puerto Rican birth control episode in 1936. Bishop Byrne of San Juan wrote him on January 25th alerting him to the fact that Mrs. Dorothy Bourne would be a house guest at the White House on January 27th; she was endeavoring to have herself appointed head of a new department of social welfare in Puerto Rico. Bishop Byrne asked Burke to do what he could to have someone appointed who had respect for the Catholic people and the Catholic principles on the island. Obviously the bishop had in mind someone who would not advocate birth control. Burke wrote President Roosevelt on February 6th quoting Byrne's letter and urging him to follow the bishop's suggestions. Roosevelt replied on the 17th, assuring Burke he would give the bishop's recommendations full consideration but that in all fairness he must say, "I know of her and her fine service in the relief of the needy and the improvement of social conditions. She is, as you know, high-minded and conscientious and an indefatigable worker." Burke wrote the President once again but without success. Bishop Byrne, in a letter to Father Burke on August 27th announced: "The Puerto Rican Recovery Administration has just started birth control clinics here with federal money. . . . I have lost confidence in the present Washington administration."

This was an exasperating disappointment to Father Burke. In 1935 he had taken the matter of the Puerto Rican Emergency Relief Association to the President. Certain officials of this organization had been circulating birth control propaganda in violation of the laws of the United States by which they were supposed to function. As a result of the protest, Bishop Byrne of San Juan was asked by the President to offer constructive suggestions about a rehabilitation program for Puerto Rico, and Father R. A. McGowan was sent by the NCWC social action department to Puerto Rico to conduct a survey and draw up recommendations for a program. McGowan spent two months in Puerto Rico at this task that had now proved to be futile and unappreciated.

Burke also kept in touch with the situation in the Philippines to help protect Catholic interests. He favored independence at an early date despite the opposition of certain bishops in the Philippines but in accord with the aspirations of most of the native clergy. Burke became a close friend of Frank Murphy, appointed by Roosevelt as American high commissioner of the Philippines in 1933. Actual independence however did not come to the Philippines until 1946.

In the early 1930s, the recognition of Soviet Russia was an explosive issue. Woodrow Wilson had broken off diplomatic relations with Russia when the Kerensky regime was toppled in 1917 by the Communists. When Roosevelt took over he began to inquire into a change of policy, possibly to help lift the US out of the depression by promoting trade with the vast Russian market (the assumption being that the depression was an international problem) or, more probably, to improve the climate of international relations. A large part of Burke's time in 1932 and 1933 was devoted to this question of recognizing "red Russia." Father Edmund Walsh was at first the most vocal Catholic critic of recognition (but later muted his criticism in a curious fashion). In early 1933 Burke wrote to the members of the administrative committee asking their opinion. Archbishop Murray of St. Paul responded, February 3rd, recommending that the committee take no official position but employ every means available to defeat recognition, denying any stability in the Soviet Government and citing the impropriety of admitting conspirators to the family of nations (like inviting Al Capone and his gang into your home, according to Murray).

Lillis opposed recognition; Boyle wanted to know what the Holy See felt about it; Schrembs was dead set against recognition but did not explicitly urge a battle against it. Noll was inclined to take a neutral stand. McNicholas felt that if labor had united against it because of bad working conditions in Russia, why should not the bishops speak out in protest against the religious persecution? Hanna, the chairman, felt the committee should not take a stand at this time.

Burke wrote in the name of the committee to the Undersecretary of State, William Phillips, saying that the administrative committee was convinced that recognition of Soviet Russia "would be a grave mistake and would do unwarranted injuries to the institutions of our country." He alleged denial of religious liberty and the undermining of accepted standards of private, family and public morals, explaining however that the committee did not want to make a public protest as this might be considered interference in a purely political affair, of which they were not sure they knew all the facets. The committee's concern, according to Burke's letter, was moral and religious but they reposed trust in the wisdom of our Government. The undersecretary promised he would forward the statement to the President.

Finally, on November 16, 1933, Roosevelt exchanged notes with Litvinov, Russia's commissar for foreign affairs, in which Russia promised to stop subversive activity in the US, allow religious liberty to Americans in Russia and bind itself to a settlement of financial claims. The exchange constituted recognition of Russia. American Catholics, largely because of their trust in FDR, assented to the recognition. The Soviets of course welched on their promises and Americans generally had to take comfort in the idea that diplomatic recognition does not mean approval.

The shadow of Hitler hovered over the International conference on Social Work held in London in July 1936. As the delegate of NCWC, Father Walter Foery of Rochester, New York, attended this meeting and reported to Burke. He described the meeting as veering toward two lines of thought: one emphasized the essential dignity of the individual person, the other stressed the utility of the individual in his service to the state. This latter group, contending that usefulness to the state was the only criterion of value, was largely an enthusiastic and very articulate Nazi representation. In every German address, said Foery, the totalitarian state was the central theme, the Conference thus providing a marvelous forum for Nazi propaganda. The German refugee priests, however, kept silent (obviously from fear).

Foery's report to Burke stated that the Conference demonstrated that the US was still far behind other nations in legislation affecting human welfare but he said that the Conference laid too heavy an emphasis on case records, not enough on the value of the individuals described in the case records. Aside from Catholic delegates, the prevailing opinion was that the Church was disintegrating but personal religion increasing; this was strongly stressed in order to convince the delegates that the totalitarian states' quarrel was with the institutional Church, not with religion itself. The Catholic Church was not openly attacked but there was severe criticism of its teaching on individual rights, many speakers insisting that the morality of an act depends on its benefit or harm to the state.

In the United States, at this time, certain conservative Catholics claimed to find an impressive parallel between the structure of the totalitarian state and the structure of the Catholic Church: a pyramid of power centered in a leader endowed with tremendous authority, exercising his power in a political apparatus demanding corporate unity, absolute obedience, rigid discipline, unquestioning acceptance of a saving body of doctrine. It was a superficial but dangerously deceptive parallel, especially when these same Catholics dismissed democracy, with its stress on personal liberty, as a Protestant concept. Burke, like his friend John A. Ryan, repudiated "rugged individualism" but supported "sane individualism" in political affairs. His stance was based on the importance of the individual in the scheme of salvation.

In the period of Hitler's ascendancy, Father Burke wrote an article entitled "Christ and the Individual Soul" for the March 1934 issue of the *American Ecclesiastical Review*. Burke emphasized not only that Christ redeemed every individual person but also that every person redeemed must anchor his hopes in the faith that Christ is his personal savior. Not in a cozy privatism unconcerned about the neighbor but in a personal encounter, especially in the sacraments, that reaches out to the neighbor. "In Christ the individual is redeemed. In Christ the individual redeemed finds life and life more abundantly. His personal perfection and the subject matter thereof are not limited to self; they reach to the farthest horizon of human need and of human love, of human consecration." Between the lines of this article, the reader could find Burke's distaste for big federal Government and for any collective system that would repress personal liberties.

In 1936 fortunately most American Catholics looked with skepticism on the continuing rise of Adolf Hitler even though the Vatican had signed a concordat with the Fuehrer. They realized that the German leader was slowly undermining Roman Catholicism. Rumors of Nazi terror and reports of Hitler's anti-semitic crusade made Burke curious about the actual status of his fellow Catholics in Germany. In 1936 Dr. Edgar Schmiedeler, NCWC, visited Germany and on his return reported to Burke the various important conversations he had held with German Catholic leaders. A certain unspoken reluctance to criticize the Fuehrer was evident in the items quoted in Schmiedeler's accounts of the conversations. Cardinal Bertram of Breslau, for instance, said: "We must fight the pagan movement but we must not speak against our Government or against individual leaders in the Government. After all, it is God's will that for the time being the present rulers should have authority over us." From these conversations, as reported by Schmiedeler, Burke could derive a sense of the danger to peace represented by Hitler, and from the muted tones of these Catholic leaders a sense of the atmosphere of terror freezing the hearts and minds of Germans, causing them to close their ears lest they hear too much.

The problem of Hitler's anti-semitism was soon brought to Burke's doorstep. The Nazi "final solution" was designed to annihilate all who had Jewish blood: it reached therefore to Catholics of Jewish ancestry, especially those in influential positions such as writers and journalists, doctors and lawyers. Archbishop Rummel of New Orleans wrote Burke on June 26, 1936, suggesting that Catholics should follow the example of what American Jews were doing for their co-religionists. Burke responded that he had recently brought the apostolic delegate a petition from a priest asking that American bishops make a joint protest against the Nazi Government. The delegate said he would send it to the Holy See but Burke thus far had received no indication of a response. He believed that the Holy See was presenting the matter to the German hierarchy, the Holy See's guiding principle being that the bishops of one country should decide whether bishops of another country should act in regard to a project such as this one. There was a real danger, as Burke saw it, that a US relief committee might at once undertake propaganda embarrassing to the country whose refugees they wanted to help.

Father H. A. Reinhold, a German priest then in the US, made contact with Father Burke through Archbishop Rummel of New Orleans, asking to present to the bishops' meeting the plight of the German Catholics suspected in Germany of being of Jewish descent. Burke was impressed by the stature of pro-moters of this "American Christian Committee for German Refugees, Catholic Group," which included Carlton Hayes, the historian; George Shuster, managing editor of *Commonweal*; Father James Gillis, editor of *The Catholic World*; and ap-parently Michael Williams and Father Raymond McGowan of NCWC. The administrative committee agreed to submit the matter to the general meeting of the bishops in the coming November but Burke warned Reinhold that launching the proj-ect before the bishops met in November would be a great mis-take. Reinhold promised nothing would be done without the authorization of the bishops. The bishops approved the com-mittee for the German refugees in November but Father Burke's untimely death on October 30th prevented him from hearing of the bishops' decision. Called "The Catholic Com-mittee for Refugees," it aided 7,000 refugees in its first ten years.

Father Burke had developed a fairly close friendship with ap-ostolic delegate Amleto Cicognani as he had done with Fuma-soni-Biondi. Cicognani personally requested the Holy Father to make the general secretary a monsignor, a domestic prelate. Pope Pius responded that he was always glad to hear good sug-gestions and the conferral of an honor on "the well-deserving Father Burke" was a good suggestion. So the general secretary became Monsignor Burke on September 21, 1936, at the Shrine of the Immaculate Conception, Washington, D.C. His superior, Father John B. Harney, wrote Burke that the Paulist reaction was far from enthusiastic. No one considered the recognition adequate. "To be frank, while I am officially satisfied, and realize the sincerity and good will of the apostolic delegate, yet personally and privately I feel that he did not fully achieve his kindly intentions."

Father Burke responded that Harney's was the only unhappy note he had heard but he was encouraged to know that his superior and fellow Paulists felt he deserved a higher honor. He was however not interested in honors, he told Harney; in 1927 he had refused an honorary Roman doctorate in theology until a previous superior general had forced him to accept it. "It would not be exact to say that I have refused a bishopric. It would be exact to say that if I had wished it, I might have had it by expressing the wish. It is also true that I have been asked by those in authority if I would accept a bishopric—even without jurisdiction—and I have positively answered "no, not under any circumstances." His reasons for not accepting? First, he wanted to consecrate himself to a religious life where he would be just "one among many" and secondly, he felt that a general secretary should never be "elevated," that he could do his work better as general secretary if he remained a priest, and he contended that the tradition should be established at NCWC that the man do the work for the sake of the work itself.

On October 26, 1936, Burke presented Archbishop Mooney with a little problem that might seem large from the standpoint of protocol. When news came that the Vatican Secretary of State, Cardinal Pacelli, was to visit the United States, the apostolic delegate discussed with Burke the protocol for the future Pope's meeting with President Roosevelt. (Press rumors had it that the cardinal was being sent over to silence Father Coughlin.) Cicognani and Burke agreed that the delegate should make arrangements through NCWC, that the general secretary should accompany Pacelli on the visit to the White

House and that the delegate should so inform the cardinal. But the morning of the 26th, the delegate sent for Burke to inform him that the Cardinal had decided to visit the President at Hyde Park, New York, and would not come to Washington. The delegate was convinced that all this had been prearranged, the invitation to Hyde Park being solicited by Bishop Spellman. As general secretary, Burke protested to Mooney that this was a painful snub to the delegate who, though not recognized by the American Government, has a position of dignity and responsibility here. It was also a snub to the NCWC. "For one particular bishop to assume all this responsibility and to be abetted in it by the Cardinal Secretary of State is to show oneself indifferent—to say the least—to a representative organization which the bishops have officially established and with generous sacrifice supported." Whether Burke ever received a reply is uncertain. He died on October 30th. Before his death, however, he had greeted Cardinal Pacelli in Washington along with the delegate, the cardinal deferring his trip to Hyde Park until November 4th, the day after the reelection of Franklin D. Roosevelt.

chapter 11

Friends and associates

Eighteen years old, with more exuberance than experience, Helen Lynch looked for employment in New York City. At the beginning of the century, New York City was a bustlingly different world from the quiet South Pacific islands of her native New Zealand but she dropped into the office of *The Catholic World* one day in 1905 and asked for a job. That she was impressed by the young editor would be an understatement: she was awed. Bubbly and extrovert, full of ambition, idealism and spontaneity and with a remarkable capacity for sustained, painstaking work, she was eventually hired and soon became one of Father Burke's assistants.

One of her favorite recollections was of the day when he asked her to purchase some Easter cards. She returned with a handful of sweetish bluebird cards which needed only one look from the editor before he threw them unceremoniously to the floor. Her revenge was to send him one of the cards by mail that Easter, then another and another each Easter until he himself laughed heartily over the episode. Before long, she was one of many under his spiritual direction. When he was away travelling, he would write her letters of advice—newsy, humorous, affectionate, always with a nugget of spirituality and always addressed to "My dear child." These messages were usually occasioned by important anniversaries in her life or festive days prompting words of celebration. The content was generally encouragement to cultivate a deeper and more sensitive awareness of the Holy Spirit dwelling within her as well as a solid devotion to the Blessed Mother. Helen Lynch kept most of the letters she received from Father Burke over a period of thirty years. After eight years at *The Catholic World*, she continued to hear from him even though she entered the order of Religious of the Cenacle in 1913. These letters spanning the years from 1905 until his death in 1936 are now in the Paulist archives and constitute an invaluable manifestation of the mind and heart of a great man.

Early in his priesthood, Father Burke had developed a deep interest in the art of spiritual direction. His forte was not preaching; he was at his best in pastoral work that required a very personal rapport. In 1905 he wrote to Helen, "To know that I have even interpreted God and his beloved Son more clearly, more effectively to a soul, is the keenest joy to me; and outside of my own personal, happy communion with God, the greatest joy that the priesthood has for me." Spiritual guidance as an art is in eclipse today, overshadowed by psychiatry and psychology, but it was in the not too distant past a highly esteemed and devoutly cherished tradition (though in some rare instances sicklied over with an air of elitishness). What was said of one of its adepts in the last century could be said of Father Burke: "The direction of souls was, in his eyes, the work par excellence: he himself regarded it as the indispensable ransom of his external and beneficent but manifold and overwhelming occupations; it was the really priestly part, the corner held in reserve of a life devoted to the rush of business."

It is amusing to read *Testem Benevolentiae*, the 1899 condemnation of Americanism (the Paulists were said to be the targets of the condemnation) and find that Americanists were said to minimize the value of spiritual direction. The Paulists were widely known for their spiritual direction, witness Father Burke, who considered it an invaluable spiritual aid. Burke's spiritual guidance was not some sort of psychomechanical technique but a personal encounter designed to achieve an intersubjective unity with the person directed; no stilted whispering of pious texts or ponderous sentiments but an encounter with someone he really wanted to help, a coexperience achieved not by asking questions but by trying to become quietly present at the center of that person's soul, assuring him or her that the problem was as uniquely personal as this person's own individuality. The solution was not a pat answer from a textbook but one that would emerge only after honest self-revelation by the person under direction and after benevolent listening on the part of the director. Self-discovery would disclose the need for God who is the way, the truth and the life. This intimacy could be found in the letters of spiritual direction of St. Bernard to Ermengarde of Brittany, of St. Francis de Sales to St. Jane Frances de Chantal and in countless other letters of direction that have been at times interpreted by the prurient as titillating excursions into sexuality. In the mystical literature of the Church, however, allusions to the bride of Christ and the nuptial union of the soul with God are a long and venerable tradition. Personal love of Christ cannot be adequately expressed in purely intellectual concepts.

No one can doubt the warmth and depth of the friendship of Father Burke and Helen Lynch in Christ and in each other. "I have missed you here—which goes without saying. In the work and the questions that come up I feel that you have grown so close to me that you take a place here which no one else ever can" (April 8, 1909). This was probably written to Helen when she was away on vacation. Four months later, writing from Canada, he says: "Keep well and happy. On your healthy looks when I return depends my trip." At Christmas 1920 he writes, "And the blessings that you brought to 60th Street (*The Catholic World* office) long ago still endure with me and with you. Often does the street itself speak of it—its flags may be useless but you have sanctified them; the old stairs are gone but the door through which you entered is still there, and the stairs still lead to the same room where the editor sat. . . . but what is there and what you put there is of heaven, enduring, reminiscent, loving." He wrote this letter seven years after Helen's entrance into Cenacle and on January 28, 1921, he noted, "I haven't celebrated a Mass in the last 15 years without mentioning your name at the canon . . ."

In his letters he put a heavy and insistent emphasis on individuality, warning her repeatedly against following stereotypes.

"God would have his glory fulfilled on earth in an infinite number of ways—in a way that no one else can fulfill it." He encouraged her to be herself, and to do that little work, "that little which unless we do it will never be done" (August 14, 1906). After she entered the novitiate, he wrote her that she must shake off any sense of martyrdom since the world does not grow old to those who love God" (July 9, 1915). Those who love Him are not soured, ". . . no raucous note sounds in their appeals or warnings as sounds in the editorials of some of our Catholic journals. . . . They make merry with God." Yet he urged her to firm up her dedication, making sure she was holding nothing back. "I am reminded of those words which I often spoke to you: 'Let no man who has put his hands to the plough turn back.' " This theme is found, in Latin, in a stained-glass window of the old chapel of St. Paul's College, Washington, D.C. (the Paulist seminary). Under the figure of a farmer ploughing, eyes straight ahead, are the words, *Nemo mittens manum suam ad aratrum et respiciens retro aptus est regno Dei.* ("No man who puts his hand to the plough and looks back is worthy of the kingdom of God.") His fondness for this text reveals the firmness of his own dedication to the religious life. In Padua, in 1929, he wrote an interesting comment in his diary, "I have visited many churches. They are historic memories—for the most part they are of the past. Christ is of the living. Let no man who puts his hand to the plough look back." It was an appropriate motto for a priest whose social action kept him oriented to the future, not the past, whose dedication would not permit him "to keep his options open," and it is not at all improbable that Father Burke himself suggested this text for the St. Paul's College stained-glass window when the chapel was being built in 1913.

His strategy was to encourage and approve, not to scold. In a 1909 letter he said, "I have told you there is nothing in the way of perfection that your soul cannot reach to. God has blessed it naturally; God has led it through natural channels of reading." He managed to work his favorite word "definite" into a letter: "Be your best, most zealous self; be the most emphatic pronouncement you can be of the intimate, personal, definite love of God" (April 8, 1909). He did not hesitate to give her supreme praise. On retreat at St. Paul's College in May 1916 he wrote her, "From here I went with my dreams that have not all been fulfilled. You are one of the dreams come true."

Burke's letters to Helen disclose the wretchedly bad health he suffered in his later years, attributable in large measure to his back-breaking schedule. From 1917 to 1922 he shuttled back and forth between New York and Washington, editing *The Catholic World* in New York and working with the War Council and NCWC in Washington. He seldom enjoyed good health in the latter years. Time after time he was felled by a heart spasm, a mysterious fever or some other debilitating ailment that drained all his strength. "The old reserves of energy are not there any more" he wrote on July 9, 1920, saying that recovering his strength will take a year. In October of that year he wrote from St. Vincent's Hospital in New York, and from Miami Beach in November, where he had gone under doctor's orders. On July 9, 1922, he was back at St. Vincent's (but jubilant over the good news of the NCWC triumph at Rome). In March 1924 he confessed that his heart had been acting up but the specialist assured him there was nothing organically wrong; what he needed was a complete rest. Staying in bed must have been a torture for him; he had a compulsion for work. His priest friends who lived with him said that he loved to play bridge but, if he had the dummy hand, he would spend the time writing or translating psalms. He had several spells of sickness and an operation in 1924 and then in October of that year, he wrote her that he had been granted a leave of absence until February 1, 1925. He continued to suffer from one ailment after another including an abscessed ear, defective teeth, a paralyzed right arm (which only meant he had to use his left arm for writing).

Certain phases of his *Catholic World* and NCWC work as

well as doctors' orders to recuperate from illnesses required that he do extensive travelling, a not unwelcome compulsion because he loved the sea. On October 16, 1908, he wrote Helen from England, bewitched by Louise Imogen Guiney "who has not lost her humanity" nor "wrapped a cloak of dignity about her august personage." Miss Guiney was a Catholic writer so presumably he went to England and Ireland in search of articles; good articles by competent American Catholic authors were hard to come by sixty years ago in the United States. Miss Guiney brought him to Oxford to show him the room where the undergraduate Newman had lived, then to Littlemore where Newman preached the "Parting of Friends" sermon ("which if you haven't read, I will read it to you when I get back"). Athletic Imogen climbed over instead of under fences in showing him Newman's old haunts.

On October 21, 1908, he wrote from Downside Abbey, praising the Benedictines for having the best spirit of all the religious orders in England. "Their spirit comes nearer to the Paulists than anything I have seen over here." They could put life into the Catholic Church in England and "the very aim and object of the Benedictines is the conversion of England." Burke saw the Catholic nobility content to remain in their beautiful castles of faith, the rest of the laity reposing under the spell of class and caste, but England would listen if the Benedictines moved out into the streets asserting "the truth we know and the vision we see." At Glastonbury Abbey he muses on "who was to blame for it all" but then reminds himself, "Let me attend to my own heart." But a few lines farther on in this letter to Helen he is back to the conversion of England and to Hecker, "the heroic leader raised up by God." Men do not appreciate him now nor will they for some years to come but "some day the vision will dawn."

October 29, 1908, he wrote Helen to tell her about his visit to his father's birthplace at Trim, near Dublin. At Killiney, near Dublin, he bought a "charming" pajamas suit of light green, then visited Maynooth and stayed with a descendant of

Daniel O'Connell, the liberator, finally catching up with General Butler at Bansha Castle; he rhapsodized over his conversations with this *Catholic World* author. In December 1924 he wrote from Puerto Rico, where he took in hand some problems the local bishops were having with the American Government. In January 1925 he wrote Helen from the USS Woodcock in Guantanamo Bay, Cuba, telling her of his work at Port-au-Prince, Haiti, where the Haitian bishops were running into trouble with the hated American Occupation Administration.

In January 1928 he was back from his trip to Cuba: "I am loaned now by the bishops of NCWC to the Holy See. That makes my work not only difficult but it disorders and breaks up my NCWC work." His fidelity to pledged secrecy was so rigid that he did not tell her why he went to Cuba (to meet with Ambassador Morrow in Havana). He wrote on April 19th that he had to take a journey that included a visit to the apostolic delegate, Fumasoni-Biondi, who was in the Far West, but he did not mention to her that he would see the delegate *after* talking with President Calles in Mexico. Returning from that trip, he had to rest for four days. In February 1929 his schedule took him to Rome on the SS Vulcania with Fumasoni-Biondi, the apostolic delegate. There he met with Cardinal Gasparri, the secretary of state, and with the Holy Father, Pius XI. Monsignor Spellman, the future cardinal, acted as interpreter. The Pope told him he was pleased with his style as general secretary. Then he was off to Jerusalem, back to Paris to meet his niece, Elizabeth Salmon, studying at Louvain, and finally back to the States on May 15th, greeted by a doctor's report that he had overstrained a heart muscle and must rest for a few weeks, but he managed to visit President Hoover on July 19, 1929.

Some of these letters to Helen (now of course, Mother Helen Lynch of Cenacle) reflect his poetic vein. On the SS Minneapolis to Europe he wrote that he had cigars and fruit enough for six months (he had no great love for either) but he was more interested in "the star-studded night" and the freedom of the ocean spaces. He told her of "the pitching of the boat and the huge mast sailing straight into the stars" and he ends, "May the Lord of the wonderful sea and the free air bless thee, Helen." In another letter, he told her of his reverie about a quiet place in the woods where he went for peace, drawing his canoe up on the bank of a nearby stream "as the sunset covers with gold the green of the trees." He was probably daydreaming about Lake George where he had built a church at Huletts in the summer of 1903.

Helen Lynch was not the only recipient of letters from Father Burke. Voltaire's ten thousand letters constituted an undammable torrent of correspondence but Father Burke also piled up an incredible record, dashing off messages in every spare moment. Eighteenth-century letter writers proceeded on the assumption that gossipy letters make for warm friendships but Burke's letters were warm with spirituality. Helen Lynch entered the Cenacle novitiate in early 1913. Grace Murray became Father Burke's secretary at *The Catholic World* on March 17, 1913; she remained for seven years. During that time and until Father Burke's death in 1936 she received hundreds of letters from him. As in the case of Helen Lynch, Grace Murray became Father Burke's "spiritual child" and his letters to her, right up until his death, bear out that relationship. "I brought you faith" he said in one letter. "I haven't always been to you what I ought to be but I've given you the best in me and have trained you carefully, if somewhat harshly —in a very high way. My heart was in the work." As with Helen Lynch, he advised a positive approach to spirituality. On April 28, 1931, he said in a letter, "No saint has been a saint through self-denial but through self-assertion. This may sound heretical but if you look into it, it is not so. Self-denial of itself leads nowhere. Self-denial that puts down the lower self to give the higher self, our self in Christ, its expression, yes; it achieves because it is positive."

Here and there throughout the letters interesting little items appear. On August 24, 1918, he wrote Grace about a meeting with John R. Mott, the outstanding American ecumenical leader of the time, in which Burke upbraided Mott's YMCA for

226   NEVER LOOK BACK

breaking down religious unity. "Yesterday afternoon I met John R. Mott and told him how I regretted the refusal of the YMCA and the way they had blocked the common drive. I told him the YMCA had by this action torn down the religious unity we had sought to build up since the war began, that they had made a cleavage in religious sentiment and that they were solely responsible for it. He didn't like it of course and denied it." Elsewhere in this letter he told how a colonel from the general staff of the army had informed him of the general staff's decision not to let the Catholic nursing sisters (connected with the army) wear their habits at any time. "At this I must say I got mad and used some strong language." The next day Burke saw General Jervey of the general staff and he promised to revise the order, allowing sisters to wear their habits travelling in this country and on the way to France, and to wear a special headdress.

In May of 1935 Father Burke wrote FDR a note of praise for his speech on the bonus bill (the bonus for veterans) and he told Grace in a letter (June 2nd) that he had enclosed in his note to Roosevelt a copy of his *Christ In Us*. FDR's comment on the book was "I am delighted to have it and the finest thing that can be said is that its sincerity and spirituality are like its author." On October 26, 1936, four days before his death, he wrote her that he had gone with Cardinal Pacelli to the press club dinner and the night before that, to dinner with the cardinal, the delegate and others at the delegation: He had arranged for the cardinal's visit to Mount Vernon but did not accompany him, undoubtedly because of Burke's physical condition. He also mentioned in this letter that he had given a conference to Paulist students at their seminary in Washington on October 15th, the fortieth anniversary of his taking the Paulist habit.

Father Burke gathered about him a dazzling variety of friends from all walks and conditions of life. One alluded to his "Gaelic charm," an attraction that would not explain the diversity of personalities he drew into his fellowship. On August 6, 1910, he wrote Helen Lynch that he would like to write reams about his trip to Gettysburg with Father Walter Elliott (who had fought there with the 5th Ohio Regiment). "When we came to where the 5th Ohio—his regiment—stood and fought, he pointed to the monument and then jumped out of the carriage saying, 'Boys, I must make a speech' and he did make it." Elliott told them exactly what had happened and how it happened—forty-seven years after. "So you will be resigned" he notified Helen, "to hearing Gettysburg for some time to come."

Burke's closest friend on the administrative committee was Bishop Muldoon of Rockford, Illinois. Burke's letters to him show clearly that he admired Muldoon as the most capable man on the committee, the man whose balance, care and insight led and guided the committee.

On May 29, 1927, a new and glamorous name appeared in the letters from Burke to Helen Lynch. Maude Adams, star of *Peter Pan*, had donated her estate of 400 acres at Ronkonkoma, New York, to the Cenacle order. Father Burke met her and a friendship developed. Unbaptized, with apparently no formal religious affiliation, she esteemed moral excellence but had her doubts about the formal teachings of the Christian religion. Burke wrote to Helen that he had talked with Maude Adams about religion and presented Christ to her as the supreme example of moral character. "He cannot be simply a picture of our own emotions and aspirations [a Modernist] but a concrete, real, living Christ whom we may know in truth and power." In a letter to Maude Adams herself in May 1928 he again presented Jesus as beauty in its highest form, moral excellence, urging her to read about Jesus in the Epistles of St. Paul. From his letters to her, it appears that he talked with her a number of times, but usually communicated with her by correspondence. In an August 13, 1928, letter he reminded her of a talk they had about immortality, "You felt you were a leaf on the wind of time" and Burke suggested Jesus' words, "I am the vine, you the branches." In a letter to her on October 27, 1928, he assures her that the message he is trying to convey is "the truth that God didn't make me to be a non-me but a real and eternal me with himself." As for her difficulty with the

228   NEVER LOOK BACK

idea of serving God "for a reward," he suggests that she read the thirteenth chapter of St. Paul's Epistle to the Corinthians. In April 1930 Father Burke asked Monsignor Bernardini of the papal delegation about the possibility of administering baptism to a person unwilling to become a formal member of the Church. The answer was of course, no. In April 1931 she tried to visit Father Burke at his office in Washington but the office was closed, and again, on June 11, 1933, she called at his home but he was not there. She left flowers and a note, "With love, dear Father Burke, I was going to say 'from us both' but I'm not sure about Mother." Burke did however have the pleasure of a visit with her the next day.

There were nine children in the Burke family, two dying at a very early age. The others all survived John. Mary, the eldest, endowed with a keen mind and trained to be a teacher, married John R. Salmon, a lawyer. Father Burke enjoyed chatting with her because they shared so many interests, literary and otherwise. Thomas became a Paulist. Ordained in 1896, almost three years before John, he was known for many years as the outstanding Catholic pulpit orator of his time (though Father Sheen and Father Coughlin overshadowed him in popularity in the 1930s). They seldom met in the course of their priestly work but they did get together at home for great holidays like Christmas, and they corresponded regularly. Thomas was proud of his younger brother but there is a certain tone of for- ·mality in his letters to John. John, on the other hand, always felt inferior to Tom in natural abilities. In 1919 Thomas was elected superior general of the Paulist Fathers. 1921 brought a day of sadness; the mother of Tom and John died on May 26, 1921.

Annie was shy. She became Sister Benedict of the Sisters of Mercy but seemed to find convent life rather difficult. Her letters were always pious and proper, replete with clichés and news about the family. James was the pride of John's life, perhaps because he had achieved the highest secular success of any member of the family, becoming one of the top officials of

Guaranty Trust Company in spite of the fact that he never went to college. The noted Thomas Fortune Ryan had supreme respect for his business acumen. Unfortunately James suffered a breakdown in February, 1933, resigned his job and died in 1942. Elizabeth was the kindly spinster, generous and thoughtful, a public school teacher not interested particularly in men. Younger brother Willie lived with his sister Elizabeth in his latter years.

Three ebullient and prankish nieces played a large role in Father Burke's life and affections. They were Mary's children. They figured not only in many of his games on holiday visits but were also the subjects of his post-holiday conversations with his friends. A striking contrast to Father Tom's formality in correspondence was the style of the nieces' letters, their free and easy chatter and offhanded humor. Uncle John was not too adult to play jacks with them, even on the floor of *The Catholic World* and in spite of his six feet four inches. Mary showed an early literary bent and eventually taught creative writing, American and English literature at Georgetown University. Elizabeth graduated from Louvain, the first woman ever to receive a doctorate at this awe-inspiring institution. She had a distinguished career at Fordham as professor of philosophy. Katharine was the breeziest. She began one letter to Father John with the salutation, "Dear Johnnie," expressing her fond hope that he will regain his sanity. Inviting him to her graduation from high school, she told him to cancel all other engagements for that day, even meetings with an archbishop or the president. "The one nearest and dearest to your heart comes first." There was a lively competition among the three nieces as to who stood first in Uncle John's affections.

Iona McNulty was secretary to Father Burke from 1920 until his death in 1936. Her predecessor was a girl considered by other personnel beautiful but remote until she suddenly eloped with a man from the War Council. Not long after, Iona was called from another department to act as secretary for Father Burke. She had come from Philadelphia in 1919 "on her

NEVER LOOK BACK

way to see the world," having no special interest in church affairs and intending the NCWC job only as a stepping-stone to further travel. The day on which Father Burke asked her to do the work, however, became an anniversary in her calendar, and in his. He thought her odd at first: as she later expressed it, "I was just sort of quiet and unfrivolous and self-possessed, or seemed to be." Actually she was shy and inhibited as he was the first man she had ever really known, her own father having died when she was only nine years of age. She grew up with her mother, six sisters and no brothers. One day he told her that her dress was too long and that she looked like an old woman, so she became "a flapper" in appearance; a few years later Father Burke was informing her that her skirt was too short.

Gertrude Delahunt and Grace Murray from *The Catholic World* told Iona on one occasion that she was good for Father Burke because she helped him shed some of his "old fashioned ideas." She smoked cigarettes before nice girls smoked. This however did not bother him as it did Father Kerby who had banned all smoking at the National Catholic School for Social Service under pain of expulsion. (Possibly Burke's lenience was due to the fact that he was a chain smoker.) But he did object to conspicuous lipstick. In the early years, according to Iona, Father Burke was usually calm, sometimes excitable but not unbearable.

Then, in the 1930s, she felt Father Burke was taking her for granted, treating her like "an old shoe," whereas he seemed to be impressed by other girls who had this talent or that virtue. Unable to hold in any longer one day, she blurted out to him while he was eating his lunch that she was doing the work not for the NCWC or for the Church or anyone else, "I'm doing it because of you but what I'd really like to do is to go off wandering and see things." Surprisingly he took it in stride and replied with an amused smile, "I was going to ask you if you didn't have some gypsy blood in you."

Iona remembers that after his heart attack in 1930, he at times became "cross" with her, less and less pleased with her work though she was actually doing better work, getting a firmer grasp on details. In fact, in 1933 or 1934 she felt like resigning "for his benefit" and told him so. It was smack in the middle of the great depression, a very bad time to resign, but she thought that someone fresh and different might prove more acceptable to him. She wrote him, probably from Nantucket, but he responded that she ought to stay on, at least that she ought to finish law school "which she was attending" before making her decision. She decided to stay on and was admitted to the Bar.

On one occasion she complained when he was cross with her and he responded that he had such a hard time that day getting down to the office that he had arrived dead tired, exhausted, too weary for conversation even had he tried to be affable. From that moment on, she knew the reason for his "cross" moods. She could even forgive a strange innovation he began to insist upon after 1930. Previously, she had typed all her memos to him or drafts of letters awaiting his final touches. After 1930, he suddenly declared one day that no one can compose as successfully on a typewriter as in longhand, so from that time on, she had to write her letters in longhand. Certain gossips around the office claimed that Burke was a tyrant but Iona maintained she didn't know any priest or any employer to whom she could express herself as freely as she did to him. "I'm not exactly proud of it but he put up with a lot from me as well as I from him and yet he was willing to forgive, and understand why, and build on what he had rather than try to make me over into somebody else."

Father Burke's working day, according to Iona, was long on man hours, at least in his early years before his first heart attack, which she dated at some time in 1929. Strangely the previous spells of chills and fever seemed to disappear after the heart attack but she believes that he never really recovered from the first attack. In the early period before 1929, he usually came to the office before 9 A.M., had his chicken sandwich about 2:30 P.M., then a brief nap at his desk, and worked until 7:30 P.M., Saturdays until 4 P.M. In those early years at

NCWC, he used to allow his back correspondence to pile up because he wanted time to think over the problems presented in the correspondence. His letters were always carefully worded, according to Iona. He dictated swiftly (probably because he had thought over his points carefully), sometimes pacing the floor as he dictated and leaving to Iona the task of discovering from the contents of the letter the identity and address of the addressee. This made her work more challenging. Though he claimed he could compose better while writing, she found that his thoughts in dictating flowed smoothly, quickly and coherently with none of the hemming and hawing and throat clearing secretaries often expect of executives. He would have nothing to do with bells and buzzers. "He whistled when he wanted me." This used to amuse Bishop Muldoon when he dropped into the office but as time went on, Father Burke succumbed to the use of a little bell he tinkled. When he left the office to visit a government official, diplomat or the President, he was usually accompanied by Mr. Cochran, later by Montavon, the head of the legal department, or perhaps by Bruce Mohler, director of the bureau of immigration.

Burke's assistants, under the title of assistant general secretary, were strikingly different in many ways. His first priestly assistant was Father James Hugh Ryan. Handsome, Rome-educated, he lived with Father Burke and Father McGowan at 2405 20th Street in Northwest Washington. In 1921 he became acting general secretary while Burke was recuperating from an illness. On Burke's return he was made executive secretary and head of the education department, NCWC. It was he who accompanied Archbishop Schrembs, as secretary, to Rome in 1922 and was immensely helpful to him in obtaining the restoration of NCWC after its suppression. He was appointed rector of Catholic University in 1928.

From the time when James Ryan went to Catholic University until 1931, according to Iona, Father Burke had no priest assistant, though Father McGowan or Father John A. Ryan occasionally pinch-hitted for him. He was very fond of Father

McGowan but his acquaintance with Father John A. Ryan was more impersonal and businesslike though they shared many similar interests and ideas. Father Michael J. Ready arrived in 1931 from Cleveland to become Father Burke's assistant general secretary. Iona worked with Father Ready from the time of Father Burke's death until 1942, finding that a rather remarkable change in his work habits took place as soon as he assumed charge; he had not played second fiddle very intently but suddenly confronted with the vastness of his responsibilities, he became a hard-working, dedicated executive as soon as he was on his own.

One of Father Burke's most competent lay assistants was Justin McGrath, head of the NCWC news service. Bishop William Russell of Charleston had been appointed chairman of the department of press and publicity, NCWC, when the various departments were organized in 1920. He intended to hire a certain priest for the news service, paying him $2,000 a year. Burke hit the ceiling, insisting that the job demanded and deserved nothing less than high-level, professional skill and experience. So Burke went to Hearst, Justin McGrath's employer, induced him to release McGrath over Hearst's objections that Burke was taking away the best man in his employ, and Justin McGrath took over with the news service. His salary was $15,000 a year; "He was worth every penny of it" said Iona. Burke gave him a free hand though at times he must have had some difficulties with this high-powered, candidly independent journalist, but he and Burke usually agreed on the big questions. On large issues of public concern as well as on press problems, Burke was happy to consult his new assistant.

Without attempting to probe beneath the surface to discover his tempo, his warmth, the secret springs of his intensity, what was the image that Father Burke presented to his secretary in his NCWC years? According to Iona McNulty, he was big physically as well as spiritually, six feet four inches in height, with thinning brown hair but never bald, large light blue eyes. He suffered from an almost total lack of vision in one eye but wore glasses only for reading. He walked with a very light step and a slight stoop in his posture, but almost always with a warm smile. There was a childlike quality about him: he liked to be liked, to win at cards, to be told he looked neat and yet, according to Iona, he showed a carelessness about his physical appearance. In his younger days, she felt "he could charm the birds off the trees" but later on, he looked anything but charming. She told him one day that he looked "a sight"; "Father, you are a disgrace, inexcusable." He needed someone to keep his hat and coat brushed, remind him to have his hair cut, his shoes shined. Yet in some areas, he had his little proprieties that became fetishes: when Iona obtained cash for him from the bank for his travels, he had to make sure that all the bills were laid on top of each other, "faces up." At Christmas his brother James would present him with a gift certificate for a new hat but Iona would have to make the purchase. The irate clerk would complain, "Why doesn't Father Burke come down himself to try on the hat?"

In the early years, he used to play tennis occasionally but then changed to golf at his doctor's orders (for a while). His most inexplicable friendship was probably that with Gene Sarazen, the top golfer in the country in 1922. Burke had little interest in golf itself and Sarazen even less interest in ecclesiastical affairs but the two men enjoyed a sustained friendship, meeting occasionally and corresponding as well. In his younger days, he was a New York Giants baseball fan but never showed any real interest in the Washington team when he was living in that city. Christy Mathewson was a sort of abiding hero to Father Burke. When the great New York Giant speedballer died, Burke wrote a poem about him (which the *Washington Star* never published even though Iona delivered it to the *Star* office).

His favorite relaxations and diversions were literary, for the most part. In the afternoon, after his brief nap at the desk, he would read *The New York World* (with special interest undoubtedly in those literate columnists, Franklin P. Adams and

Heywood Broun). Next came a perusal of *The Living Church, Christian Century* and *The Christian Science Monitor*. He did most of his reading in his room at his residence: Edward Arlington Robinson, Gerard Manley Hopkins, Francis Thompson, A. E. Housman, T. S. Eliot, the essays and poems of Alice Meynell, the cameo-like verses of Emily Dickinson and Gamaliel Bradford's biographies of Civil War heroes. His favorite spiritual reading was Lallemant, a seventeenth-century French Jesuit who exerted a strong influence on Hecker as well as on Burke in his focus on the interior direction of the Holy Spirit and on prayer as nourishment of apostolic action. Travelling, Burke took along any light reading current in the Gay and Golden Twenties or a paperback from abroad. (He at one time spoke of making Iona his literary executor but she talked him out of it.) Agnes Collins, the NCWC librarian, spent long hours obtaining books from the Library of Congress for him. A clerk at the Congressional Library asked Miss Collins how Father Burke found out about books even before their publishers knew about them. On one occasion, Father Burke asked for *any* of Rilke's books, to be told that they were not only not available but even unknown at the Congressional Library.

One of his less literate diversions was card-playing—gin rummy, cribbage or contract bridge. He was accustomed to playing with the priests residing at his home or with the apostolic delegate or some member of his staff who might drop in. He was not a teetotaler but seldom drank liquor of any kind. He was quoted as saying that priests sitting around drinking might easily launch into gossip about ecclesiastical politics, for which he had a profound aversion. Iona McNulty said that he lacked utterly any trace of ecclesiastical ambition. Bishop Alter once remarked that Burke never socialized at night, not because he disliked meeting people but because he felt that nocturnal conversation might project him into situations in which he would be importuned for information about NCWC affairs. His policy was to avoid any discussion of official matters outside the NCWC office.

236

One of the priests who lived with Father Burke at 2405 20th Street, N.W., Washington, was Father Fulton Sheen. He expressed his appreciation in a letter dated October 23, 1935: "The five years of priestly inspiration you gave me, when it was my happiness to live with you, will always be one of my greatest debts of gratitude."

Father Burke would have regarded as ridiculous the notion that he was an avant-garde feminist but he certainly preferred women to men as coworkers in any organizational effort. As mentioned earlier in this book, he claimed that women's organizations take their work seriously while men's groups tend to become social clubs. Probably women understood him better than did men though one cannot be sure that he was not at times naive in his esteem for women or in his knowledge of their moods and predilections. One day he discussed nuns' dress with Bishop Emmet Walsh: he advocated that they wear secular dress but feared that vanity might tempt them to retain the old garb, the habit being more attractive. As to the laity, he vigorously espoused more elbow room, more opportunity for lay initiative, as well as more pastoral consultation with the laity; during his tenure as general secretary there were usually only four priests on the scene. The laity had a special charism; why delegate priests to do their tasks? When Margaret Sanger was campaigning for birth control in Burke's early days at NCWC, he and Mary Regan went about lecturing against birth control, but suddenly one day he blurted out that the whole idea was ridiculous; a priest and an old maid talking to married women about birth control.

Burke must have entertained certain preferences in regard to candidates for political office but never did he display, according to Iona, any partisan preferences, accepting any president after election without bias or reservation. He showed no enthusiasm over Al Smith such as was evident in 1928 at NCWC, admiring him to a certain degree but anticipating he would bend over backwards not to help the Church if elected. Bishop Gibbons of Albany had found this to be true of Smith's governorship of New York. Many at NCWC were jubilant when Franklin D. Roosevelt was elected president in 1932 but Father Burke wryly observed that "the day will come when they will sing a different tune."

A feature of his life that was immutable, according to Iona McNulty, was Burke's loyalty to and affection for his religious community. In signing his name to a letter or document, he always added CSP to the signature: his stipends went out regularly to the Paulist Treasurer in New York ($3,000 a year from the War Council, $4,000 a year from the Welfare Council—a goodly sum at that time). He visited St. Paul's College frequently, occasionally gave the weekly conference for the students. In later years, Father Cartwright used to come in from the seminary to Father Burke's office once a week: they would hear each other's confession. Iona was quite impressed; she admitted that she preferred complete anonymity in confession. Fathers Mullaly, Elliott, Skinner, John E. Burke, O'Neill, Finn, McSorley and Thomas, his brother, were familiar to her through visits or correspondence. Father Burke made the old 59th Street parish in New York come alive to her as he reminisced about memorable moments with his Paulist confreres. He often spoke about the day when he received a postcard from Father Doyle, his predecessor at *The Catholic World*. It had a tragic memory for him in that Doyle had mailed the card from Denver with the words, "Over the rockies and into the golden West." After writing and mailing it, Father Doyle was taken off the train at San Francisco and rushed to the hospital where he died.

Burke's great friend, Father Kerby, died in the summer of 1936. With an aching heart he wrote a eulogy for this "prophet of the better hope" for the September *Ecclesiastical Review*. On September 21, 1936, he was invested with the robes of a domestic prelate at the Shrine of the Immaculate Conception in Washington, the bishops of the administrative committee purchasing the robes for him. When Cardinal Pacelli visited NCWC headquarters, death was almost visible in Father

Burke's face and general presence.

On October 30th, he went to his office, grimly silent, conversed with a visitor and then left the office after giving Iona his usual priestly blessing, but this time—without a word. She next saw him lying on his bed at home in the afternoon, his coat off and Monsignor Ready saying the prayers after administering the last rites. Frances Boyle, the housekeeper, gave Iona the light green summer blanket Iona had given Father Burke as a birthday present the previous June.

Frances Boyle described the death in a letter to Mother Helen Lynch a few weeks later. She reported with rugged simplicity how she had found Father Burke lying on his bed after she responded to his ringing of a bell. He asked her not to get excited but to call a doctor as he had a pain around the heart. She phoned the doctor, watched Father Burke for a moment as he looked at her silently, then she rushed into the library and phoned Monsignor Ready at the office. Returning, she stood at the head of the bed, her hands under his chin, saying: "Father, you are not leaving; what a sad parting for me!" In the letter to Helen Lynch she went on to comment that the chapel, the library, the bedroom were vacant and that she could not realize he was gone but she had the consolation of knowing she had done all she could for him in those last few minutes. "He never liked any splash, [liked] simple things, to me at times he was like a child" and yet she had looked to him as a father. "Now we have a very lonely house."

Father Burke's sister Mary wrote Helen Lynch (November 9th) that the doctor had identified the cause of death as a clot of blood in the coronary artery. Students from the National Catholic School of Social Service (which he had co-founded with Father William Kerby) took their turns in kneeling by Father Burke's body day and night until Tuesday morning, November 3rd, when Paulist students from St. Paul's College in Washington carried the body to the Shrine crypt of Catholic University for the office of the dead and for Mass at 10 A.M. Fifteen archbishops and bishops, hundreds of priests, nuns and laity were present. Archbishop Amleto Cicognani, the apostolic delegate, celebrated the pontifical Mass and Bishop Boyle of Pittsburgh preached the eulogy. Tuesday night, Burke's Paulist confreres at St. Paul the Apostle Church in New York City sang the office for the dead. Wednesday, November 4th, Father Thomas Burke, John's brother, offered the funeral Mass at the church, Father Edward Mullaly, CSP, preached the sermon and Cardinal Hayes gave the final absolution. Members of his immediate family, relatives, employees of his beloved Paulist Press and hundreds of other friends and admirers attended the Mass for the greatest Paulist of the century. He was buried in the crypt of the church, next to his beloved Father Skinner and close to Hecker, Hewit, Simmons and Searle.

It would be impossible to summarize the hundreds of tributes that came from all over the world, from the Pope, the President, senators, clergy and laity, NCWC staff and religious communities. None was more heartfelt than that from Father Raymond McGowan[1] of the social action department, NCWC, a humble and devoted friend:

Monsignor Burke, or Father Burke as I knew him best, was at once the greatest and kindest man I've had the good fortune to know. . . . to him more than to any one man is due the organization of the National Catholic Welfare Conference. . . . or should I go on to speak of his tremendous capacity for work even in sickness? Or of his appreciation of the beautiful in nature, in poetry, in sculpture, in buildings and bridges, in flowers, of the beauty of the altar? Or of his marvelous spirituality? Or of his sense of the unity of all in Christ? A great man has gone.

chapter 12

The summing up

What were John Burke's most notable achievements? Undoubtedly, his founding of the NCWC was his greatest single accomplishment. The large mural covering the lobby wall in the USCC building in Washington shows Cardinal Gibbons blessing Father Burke. The cardinal had authorized him to convene the meeting of national Catholic leaders at Catholic University in 1917 but it was Burke who actually inspired the idea of the national coordinating organization in the mind of the cardinal, presided over the development of the idea in its early stages and then directed the destinies of NCWC until his death. Justin McGrath, head of the NCWC press department, recognizing what the restoration of NCWC meant to Burke in 1922, said: "The rest of us were only employees but you were the father of the child." Today the existence of NCWC is taken for granted because of its continuing success in unifying the work of the many dioceses of America and broadening the perspective of clergy and laity.

To the American public, the old NCWC was probably best known for its social action department whose progressive social and economic programs radically altered the conservative reputation of the Catholic Church in America. It was the total NCWC, however, that was collectively responsible for bringing the Catholic Church in America to civic maturity. Through the various departments, NCWC helped immigrants up the educational, economic and social ladders so that American Catholics can no longer be written off as second-class citizens. The statue of St. Francis Xavier Cabrini, Patron of Immigrants in the Shrine of the Immaculate Conception in Washington, bears witness to the spiritual influence of NCWC among immigrants. It serves to remind us also of the dream that failed: Burke had hoped to unite American culture and Catholic faith in a new civilization more just and compassionate than any in the tortured history of the past. It was the relentless march of that history that caused him to yield his dream to the reality of a continuing pluralistic world: America would not be converted to Catholicism.

Burke wrote a number of devotional brochures and translated several French religious classics but his impact was more notable in his diplomatic work in Mexico than in his literary work and editorials. At first glance, it may seem that his efforts as peacemaker were futile in Mexico. The agreement signed by Burke and President Calles in 1928 formed the basis of the 1929 *modus vivendi* that was so grossly violated at a later time. This consequence however, was due not to any defect in the 1928 document but to the intransigence of Mexican Government officials and the uncompromising stubbornness of certain Mexican aristocrats. That the *modus vivendi* failed to insist on a change in the constitution was unavoidable: under the circumstances of tension then existing, Burke and Morrow could not have pressed for anything more than resumption of worship. That the spirit of the government leaders did not improve was no fault of the framers of the *modus vivendi*, Burke and Morrow. Many an evenhanded peace treaty has been wrecked by men who misconstrued or rejected the prudence and fairness of the negotiators. Yet it may well be that whatever spells of peace the Mexican Catholics have enjoyed in the last fifty years are due in some measure to the *modus vivendi* of 1928.

To locate Burke's thinking in the ideological spectrum, both in his work at NCWC and in the Mexican affair, is no easy task, but his general orientation seems to have been that of a moderate, with a leaning to the left in the area of social justice. In the Paulist archives, among the Burke papers, there is a page torn from a copybook which probably gives a clue to Burke's middle-of-the-road orientation. It is a quotation from Macaulay's *History of England*:

NEVER LOOK BACK

Everywhere there is a class of men who cling to whatever is ancient, and who even when convinced by overpowering reasons that innovation would be beneficial, consent to it with many misgivings and forebodings. We find also everywhere another class of men, sanguine in hope, bold in speculation, always pressing forward, quick to discern the imperfections of whatever exists, disposed to think lightly of the risks and inconveniences which attend improvements and disposed to give every change credit for being an improvement. In the sentiments of both classes there is something to approve. But of both the best specimens will be found not far from the common frontier. The extreme section of one class consists of bigoted dotards: the extreme section of the other consists of shallow and restless empirics.

While his mental compass kept Burke close to the center in his thinking, there was a dazzling diversity of facets in him that defied simple classification. Our generation stresses the immanence of God but there was in Burke a certain transcendental quality that was not lost on the sensitive. Josephus Daniels remarked one day, after talking to Burke, that he felt he had been in the presence of God and Daniels was not speaking in irony. Some of his friends spoke of his "Gaelic charm" but the more common reaction of his associates was to regard him with a certain sense of awe. From his memos we get the impression that he lived in an almost constant awareness of the presence of God and of the love of Jesus.

In his memo of June 8, 1925, the day before the anniversary of his ordination in 1899, he wrote of his awareness of Jesus' love for him:

Tonight as I look back, that fact is as evident as my own existence. Thy love has chosen, protected, recalled and saved me many times without number. It has its own purpose with regard to me and of its purpose it will not fail. From the earliest years it called me to the priesthood, it provided my education, it called me to the Paulists, it made me thy priest. It guided my work therein and used me as the instrument to promote thy glory. It selected me for the editorship of *The Catholic World* for many, many years; it led me to the War Council work and then to the Welfare Conference. Of myself I failed utterly times without number. Thou hast graciously redeemed my unfaithful self. Thou hast loved me and will not let me go. This realization overpowers me, thy love shames and exalts. I wish to give—to give all and to have the power of giving increased by the Holy Spirit. . . . I am lost in contemplating the splendor of thy love. In wonder, in gratitude, in mystery, I am lost in thee.

This meditation was not the fervorino of a novice resonating words he had just read in a book of devotions: it was the memo of a veteran priest of many years who meant every word as the expression of his conscientious conviction.

Was he a theological conservative? Labels are risky but Burke was theologically conservative in the sense of accepting traditional doctrines. He was determined however not to allow human elements in the Church to block out the light of Christ. At times he wrote and spoke as sternly and frankly about defects of the clergy as did St. Catherine of Siena. At such moments, tempted to disillusionment, he focused his attention on the mystery of the divine dwelling in the Church in spite of human failings of its members. His first testing came with the suppression of NCWC, a disgraceful episode that could shake the cedars of Lebanon. What made this particular affair so offensive for him was that he revered the papacy and the reigning Pope who was duped by the trickery. Some years later, he was again scandalized by what he considered the double-dealing of church officials regarding Vatican policy on Mexico. "Their lips are proclaiming peace" he wrote in a memo. "Their lips exalt the Church as the champion of peace. Yet their sympathies are with those who are either preparing for war or who would not be worried if war would come. . . . I don't see how we can serve two masters—prayer and the sword." He was not conservative in the sense that he would agree with everything said by officials of the institutional Church simply because it was said by officials of the institutional Church.

These memos in which he deplored the words or conduct of church officials might be regarded by some as displays of petulance by a man suffering from a wounded ego harassed by criticism. His illnesses may at times have rendered him overcritical but he seems to have been using the memos to help him locate himself and his conscience in the midst of bewildering situations. On one occasion he told a lie, a "white lie" consisting of a statement that a certain senator was preparing to introduce a bill whereas he knew he was making the statement to prevent another senator, who might give the bill the kiss of death, from introducing the bill. He agonized over this in conscience, writing a record of it in a memo to keep before his eyes the fact that he told a lie.

While he was a liberal in his views on social justice, he was no doctrinaire radical believing with Marx that you must crack eggs in order to have an omelette. His experience in Mexico with the radicals who absolutized the state, running roughshod over liberals, would not permit him to feel at ease with radicals, romantic or otherwise. Had the framers of the Mexican constitution been liberals they would have promoted civil liberties but they recognized and promoted only the liberties of those who agreed with them. Burke was shocked by American liberals like Norman Thomas who encouraged the closed-minded dogmatists south of the border while condemning the closed-minded conservatives in the United States. On the other hand, Burke also reprobated conservative Mexican clergy who were concerned about preserving the social status quo but unconcerned about the misery of the peons.

Bruce Mohler of the immigration department of NCWC used to say that Burke gave leadership to the bishops, meaning leadership in the social and economic areas but not in theology. This was undoubtedly true. The secular press often marvelled that a church so conservative theologically as the Catholic Church could provide so many forward-looking social and economic documents. Some of this leadership was due of course to the papal encyclicals of Pope Leo XIII and Pius XI, and to

William Kerby and John A. Ryan, but much of it was also due to the managerial skill and personal influence of Burke. A comparison of his reports to the administrative committee with the minutes of the same committee's meetings indicate Burke's persuasive influence. The bishops usually went along with his suggestions. Yet there was never any attempt on his part to manipulate the bishops' judgment. In one document, the hierarchy referred to Burke's "almost scrupulous reverence for the word and act of the hierarchy." It was not so much Burke's pressure but the bishops' respect for his judgment that engendered so many progressive statements from NCWC.

He enjoyed the same respect from government officials. Franklin D. Roosevelt, for instance, constantly called upon him for advice, and Newton Baker, secretary of war in World War I, wrote him in 1921: "The great war tested men as well as institutions and that I came to rely on your justice and broadmindedness was due not only to the patriotic spirit of the great Mother Church which you represented but to your qualities as well. It will always be a happiness to recall our work together and to feel that in private as in public life I can remain with admiration and esteem, gratefully your friend, Newton D. Baker."

It is nevertheless true, on the other hand, that Burke did not exert in the intellectual community of his day a leadership commensurate with the leadership shown by Father Hecker in his day. Burke did not create bridges of understanding with the top scholars and literary luminaries of the era. One reason was that Burke gave himself more extensively to social reform than did Hecker, especially to improving the lot of the immigrants. Another reason was that the NCWC administrative work consumed so much of his time. An even more plausible explanation, however, was that he was a loyal and obedient defender of the Catholic theology prevalent in his time and this school, rigidified by the papal condemnations of Americanism and Modernism, did not at all impress American intellectuals enamored of freedom, creativity, flexibility and open-mindedness.

Much as they admired Burke as a person, he was to them the representative of an immobile, unchangeable institution. It was an American tragedy and the Catholic Church's loss that a great man like Burke should have been isolated from contact with American intellectuals by the old school ties of Roman theologians.

It is risky (some would say, pointless) to speculate about Burke's reaction to contemporary developments in the Church and the world today, were he alive at the moment. It seems to me highly probable that he would have willingly entered into the spirit of Vatican II: his respect for ecumenical councils was unquestionable. He was a loyal member of the Church and faithfully reflected its teachings. During life he faithfully reflected the "immobile" stance of Vatican I and would reflect faithfully, were he alive, the Vatican II concept of a church that must change to meet the needs of the times. His special devotion was to the Holy Spirit and he did not believe the Holy Spirit was immobile but actively at work in the Church and in the world in every age. He had no delusions about the Church being locked into the past. "He that puts his hand to the plough and looks back is not worthy of the kingdom of God."

His forte, however, was not "intellectual" theology but social reform and he would probably see the future of the Church in the modern world as pointing in the direction of the socioeconomic improvement of the human condition. Of the sixteen documents of Vatican II, he would have waxed ecstatic over *The Constitution on the Church in the Modern World*. There is an excerpt (see page 24) which I have already quoted from his diary and which seems prophetic: "The worth of the individual man as such—the sense of personal responsibility—the proper decent personal standards of living—education for all—restlessness and determination to improve and progress—these are the moving powers of the world." These, according to Burke, "the Christian cannot neglect."

What would he think of contemporary American culture and its permissive way of life? He would undoubtedly still cherish the American dream of equal justice, recognition of the dignity of every man and equal justice for all, but he would give short shrift to any uncritical accommodation to public or private standards of morality out of line with the Gospel. He had deplored and condemned, for instance, the laissez-faire capitalism built into American society in the 1920s.

As he neared the end of his life, Burke was realistic enough to have reservations about certain persons and a few projects but no reservations whatever about his choice of the priesthood as a vocation or any somber musings about the Christian faith. His only question about his vocation was whether he had measured up to his ministry of service with Christ-like compassion. The American bishops answered that question with affection and admirable conciseness in one of the touching tributes they paid him in their "Appreciation" of his service to God and country: "By his sweet Christian gentility and rugged piety he, almost unknowingly, made thousands debtor unto him, never giving a thought to self when another was to be served."[1]

Notes

Chapter 1

[1] Iona McNulty, Father Burke's secretary at NCWC, said that he told her that he decided at the age of 13 to study for the priesthood.

[2] Richard J. Purcell, "Ireland and the Civil War," *The Catholic World*, April 22, 1922, p. 119.

[3] Burke prepared this 24-page typed response to "Americanism," *Dictionnaire de Spiritualité*, but never published it.

[4] In his *Theodore Roosevelt: an Autobiography* (1913), Roosevelt told how he once pardoned outright a man convicted of murder in the second degree on the recommendation of Father Doyle of the Paulist Fathers. Toughs in the neighborhood had secured the conviction by intimidating community officials.

Chapter 2

[1] James F. Finley, *James Gillis, Paulist*, Hanover House, 1958, p. 114.

Chapter 3

[1] The American Federation of Catholic Societies came into organized existence in 1901 at Long Branch, New Jersey (Cf. Aaron I. Abell, *American Catholics and Social Action: 1865-1950*, Hanover, 1960). It was a loosely organized group of autonomous societies, numbering some very progressive Catholic leaders in its membership but it failed to grip the imagination of the Catholic public or take any very dramatic initiatives, and by 1917 had lost much of its initial momentum.

[2] Letter from Mother Helen Lynch to Rev. Vincent F. Holden, C.S.P., November 3, 1955: "He explained to me that this diagram would ultimately have its fulfillment when the bishops of the United States would meet once or twice a year to pool their information and statistics and to discuss policies affecting the interests and activities of the Church in the United States. . . ."

[3] Williams, *op. cit.*, p. 118-119.

[4] Cf. also letter from Baker to Burke, March 2, 1921, Paulist archives, New York.

[5] The structure was: the fourteen archbishops; the administrative committee of four bishops; the executive committee composed of four

bishops, six members of the committee on special war activities; two committees in operation on war work, the committee on special war activities and the K of C committee on war activities (cf. Williams, *American Catholics and the War*, p. 152).

[6]Elizabeth McKeown, *War and Welfare: a Study of American Catholic Leadership*, Univ. of Chicago Ph.D. dissertation, 1922, p. 135.

[7]*Ibid.*, p. 147.

[8]*Ibid.*, p. 7.

[9]Mary Dineen (later Mrs. Mary D. Coyle) was secretary to Burke with the committee on special war activities but he remained editor of *The Catholic World* until 1922.

[10]Paulist archives, New York.

[11]Thomas T. McAvoy, Univ. of Notre Dame Press, 1969, p. 367.

Chapter 4

[1]James Hennesey, S.J., "The Distinctive Tradition of American Catholicism" in *Catholicism in America*, ed. by Philip Gleason, Harper and Row, p. 33.

[2]Cf. John T. Ellis, *James Cardinal Gibbons: Vol. II*, Bruce, pp. 298-305.

[3]*Ibid.*, p. 299.

[4]*Ibid.*, p. 305.

[5]Iona McNulty, secretary to Burke at NCWC, remembers him telling her about a meeting of the administrative committee in August 1919. At this time Burke felt he had a responsibility to urge establishment of a national headquarters but he also knew that the bishops did not want an NCWC headquarters in addition to the annual meeting. He requested an interview with Bishop Muldoon, chairman of the administrative committee. Muldoon granted the interview with some reluctance. "Father Burke, what is it you want?" Burke replied, "I have something on my conscience that I want to get rid of. . . ." When he had finished, Burke said to Muldoon, "Now, Bishop, that's been on my conscience. It's no longer on mine, it's now on your conscience." Muldoon went back to the committee meeting, supported Burke's position and persuaded the other bishops to do likewise. The matter was then presented to the bishops' meeting in September 1919. They agreed to open a headquarters in Washington.

[6]Quoted by William J. Kenney, CSP, in *The Work of Father John J. Burke: 1917-1922*, an unpublished dissertation, St. Paul's College, Washington, D.C., 1950, p. 87.

[7]For text of petition, cf. Kenney, p. 88.

[8]Bishop Louis Walsh of Portland, Maine wrote Muldoon on May 27th that "our two redmen" and their two associates in Rome tricked the Holy Father as much as they tricked the American bishops. "If in the sequel, the quartet feel the heavy hand, it will be a blessing for the Church in Rome as well as here."

[9]The text of the Instructions can be found in Ellis, *Documents of American Catholic History*, Bruce, pp. 607-609.

[10]In 1966 the National Catholic Welfare Conference and the National Catholic Welfare Conference, Inc. passed out of existence and were succeeded by the National Conference of Catholic Bishops (NCCB) and the United States Catholic Conference (USCC), a civil corporation.

[11]John T. Ellis in *Documents of American Catholic History* (Bruce) says: "De Lai succeeded in convincing Benedict XV that the NCWC was a risky experiment that carried in it dangerous overtones of a national church in the United States" (p. 604).

Chapter 5

[1]In his *Fall of the Russian Empire*, Father Walsh wrote of his twenty months in Russia from March 1922 to November 1923, but did not allude to this visit to Rome.

[2]According to the Japanese consulate at Chicago, this Admiral Yamamoto was not the Yamamoto who masterminded the attack on Pearl Harbor but another Admiral (Gombei) Yamamoto who became prime minister and died in 1937.

[3]Francis L. Broderick, *Right Reverend New Dealer: John A. Ryan*, Macmillan, 1963, p. 167.

Chapter 6

[1]On the K of C million-dollar campaign, cf. M. Elizabeth Ann Rice, *The Diplomatic Relations between the United States and Mexico as Affected by the Struggle for Religious Liberty in Mexico: 1925-1929*, a Catholic University of America doctoral dissertation, C.U. of A. Press, 1959, p. 97.

[2]The Vatican position was puzzling. The pope forbade Catholics in the Liga (National League for Religious Defense) to engage in military action but withheld publication of the ban for many months. Bishop Diaz, returning from an audience with Pope Pius XI on July 14, 1927, said: "The Pope is confident that eventually the Church will win her battle in Mexico. . . . I told him of affairs as I had viewed them and he expressed the opinion that the Calles Government must fall, and that with its fall the Catholic Church will regain her old

standing." Burke, trying to reconcile the ban with implications of the Pope's words to Diaz, reasoned that the Vatican did not favor reprimanding "loyal Catholics who, even though their action might be misguided and detrimental to the real interests of the Church, were fighting for what they considered to be the good of the Church."

[3]Rice, p. 111. In a letter to Kellogg, Morrow said Hayes and Judge O'Brien sent Burke to him.

[4]*Ibid.*, p. 115.

[5]See Rice, pp. 62-69, for an in-depth study of Calles' motivations.

[6]*Ibid.*, p. 63.

[7]*Ibid.*, p. 202, appendix B for the text of this letter.

[8]*Ibid.*, p. 129.

[9]*Ibid.*, p. 133. Morrow, however, said that Burke and Calles "appeared to make an excellent mutual impression on each other" and exchanged letters which if ratified by the Vatican "would have led to a prompt resumption of public worship." (*Catholic News*, New York, May 8, 1943.)

Chapter 7

[1]Rice, p. 141. Calles told Morrow that Toral was a teacher in a Catholic school, "that all of his associates were priests and that he had gone to confession the day prior to the committing of the crime."

Chapter 9

[1]Merlin Gustafson, "President Hoover and the National Religion," *Journal of Church and State*, Winter 1974, p. 88.

[2]Rt. Rev. John A. Ryan, "Monsignor Burke and Social Justice," *Catholic Action*, December 15, 1936, p. 20.

Chapter 10

[1]Cf. Aaron I. Abell, *American Catholics and Social Action: 1865-1950*, p. 196.

[2]Broderick, p. 262.

Chapter 11

[1]Raymond McGowan, "Tribute of a Priest Co-Worker," *Catholic Action*, December 15, 1936, pp. 23-26.

Chapter 12

[1]Cf. *Catholic Action*, December 15, 1936, p. 5.

Further Reading

In contrast to the vast amount of materials at USCC dealing with Burke's NCWC career there is at USCC and in the Paulist archives an almost total lack of papers or documents relating to his youth and seminary days. The papers at USCC pertaining to his later life, however, are so abundant that this biographer must resign himself to handling only the highlights of his career. Researchers will meet with gracious cooperation at USCC but the old NCWC files here are inadequately organized: for that reason I have not attempted to give the location of particular papers by section, cabinet or file.

In writing on the National Catholic War Council, I found indispensable Elizabeth McKeown's *War and Welfare, a Study of American Catholic Leadership*, a University of Chicago doctoral dissertation, September, 1972. The Catholic University archives now contain the collection of the War Council records (215 boxes) as well as minutes of meetings of the bishops of the National Catholic Welfare Council (1919 to 1927) and the William Kerby papers. John Tracy Ellis' *Life of James Cardinal Gibbons*, Vol. II, Bruce, 1952, focuses on the cardinal's life but also gives invaluable information about the origins of the War Council and the Welfare Council. *The Work of Father John J. Burke: 1917-1922* by William J. Kenney, CSP, an unpublished dissertation (St. Paul's College, Washington, D.C.) is especially good in its treatment of the suppression of NCWC.

Aaron I. Abell's *American Catholicism and Social Action: a Search for Social Justice, 1865-1950* provides many items of significant information about movements and events in which Father Burke was involved. In her *Full Circle*, Loretta R. Lawler records the history of the National Catholic School of Social Service from Burke's cofounding of the School in 1918 till 1947: he figured largely in every stage of the School's development until his death in 1936. Archbishop Karl Alter, who lived with Father Burke next to the School, kindly gave me an interview on Burke's life and work.

The documents on the Mexican affair, to be found at USCC, are numerous and exhaustively detailed. I found Robert E. Quirk's *The Mexican Revolution and the Catholic Church: 1910-1929*, Indiana U. Press, 1973, very helpful in giving a panoramic view of the whole revolutionary movement that began in 1910. Sister M. Elizabeth Ann Rice's *Diplomatic Relations Between the United States and Mex-*

ico. . . . 1925-1929, a Catholic University of America doctoral dissertation, 1959, is a painstakingly researched account of four troubled years. A brief but good study of the Mexican affair is *John J. Burke, CSP, and Mexican Church-State Relations, 1927-1929*, an unpublished dissertation from St. Paul's College, Washington, D.C., written by Edward Whitley, CSP.

As Burke's life crisscrossed that of John A. Ryan, Francis L. Broderick's *Right Reverend New Dealer: John A. Ryan*, Macmillan, 1963, I found not only delightful reading but also a biography full of insights into the mood and mind of Ryan's and Burke's era. For the New Deal years, I discovered excellent background material in *The Coming of the New Deal* by Arthur Schlesinger, Jr., Sentry, 1958. A complete account of Catholic reaction to FDR and the New Deal can be found in George Q. Flynn's *American Catholics and the Roosevelt Presidency: 1932-1936*, Kentucky University Press, 1968.

Among Father Burke's more notable works are: *St. Teresa: an Autobiography*, edited by J. J. Burke, 1911 (a translation); *A Great and Humble Soul, Mother Therese Coudert* (a translation); *The Doctrine of the Mystical Body of Christ* (a translation); and many pamphlets including *Novena to the Holy Spirit* and *Christ in Us*.